Health Benefits at Work

Health Benefits at Work

An Economic and Political Analysis of Employment-Based Health Insurance

Mark V. Pauly, Ph.D.

Bendheim Professor
Health Care Systems, Insurance and Risk Management,
Public Policy and Management, and Economics
The Wharton School
The University of Pennsylvania

Ann Arbor

THE UNIVERSITY OF MICHIGAN PRESS

Copyright © by the University of Michigan 1997
All rights reserved
Published in the United States of America by
The University of Michigan Press
Manufactured in the United States of America
⊗ Printed on acid-free paper

2000   1999   1998   1997   4   3   2   1

*A CIP catalog record for this book is available
from the British Library.*

Library of Congress Cataloging-in-Publication Data

Pauly, Mark V., 1941–
     Health benefits at work : an economic and political analysis of
employment-based health insurance / Mark V. Pauly.
          p.   cm.
     Includes bibliographical references and index.
     ISBN 0-472-10857-3
     1. Insurance, Health—United States—Costs.   2. Employee fringe
benefits—United States—Costs.   I. Title.
HG9396.P38   1997
658.38'201—dc21   97-18341
                                                                  CIP

Acknowledgments

This book represents work I began during a sabbatical academic year in 1994–95. The sabbatical started just as the Clinton administration's health reform initiative was in its final days and ended as Republicans, after taking control of Congress, found themselves entangled with Medicare and Medicaid financing.

During that sabbatical year, I was able to pursue in more depth some questions I had begun to address in the 1970s and 1980s. One puzzle was how employers managed the health insurance they often provided as a benefit for their workers, an issue that Gerald Goldstein and I first approached in 1976 (Goldstein and Pauly 1976). The other question was that of the incidence of employer-paid health insurance premiums, the answer to the question of who ultimately paid when employers or unions channeled some part of compensation into insurance premiums rather than take-home pay. This was, I had argued (Pauly 1988), a question on which economists were out of step with everyone else, since the answer given from simple economic theory was at variance with what employers, policymakers, and intelligent noneconomists professed to believe.

This book presents further exploration (but not a complete resolution) of these two questions. If managers do not think like economists about who really pays for employee health insurance, and how that insurance should be managed, their views about key issues, from mandated universal coverage to mandated mental health benefits, will be affected. The Clinton proposal set the stage for the most thoroughgoing consideration of these issues to date. I had anticipated that I would find some circumstances in which the simple economic theory is not quite right and in which the divergent views could be reconciled. I did find some such cases, but their number and plausibility were smaller than I had anticipated. Along the way, however, I think I was able to gather and present a comprehensive view of the role of business in the health reform debate, a clear statement of many of the forms of the economic view, the implications of the economic view for the proper management of employment-based health insurance benefits, and some understanding of why managers and economists looked at the same phenomena in such different ways. In this book,

I present the results of these investigations into political economy, economic theory, and benefits management.

Most of my research and discussion of the beliefs and roles played by employers during the Clinton reform debate were undertaken during an extended stay at the American Enterprise Institute, to which I owe a substantial debt of gratitude, especially to its president, Christopher DeMuth, and its director of health policy studies, Robert Helms. I am grateful to many people who put up with my questions during this Washington sojourn, but most especially to John Hoff and Grace-Marie Arnett. I then was able to retire to the peace and quiet of the Institute for Advanced Studies in Princeton to reflect on this information, thanks to the efforts of Uwe Reinhardt and the institute's director, Philip Griffiths. I am indebted to my Wharton School colleague Jerry Rosenbloom for two things. First, he coauthored the paper on a total compensation approach to benefits management which, in slightly revised fashion, is chapter 5 of this book. Second, he was very helpful in instructing me on what benefits specialists really think and for helping me to interact with a group of benefits managers under the auspices of an International Society of Certified Employee Benefits Specialists program run at the Wharton School.

Needless to say, none of those who helped me should be blamed for the views I express here. They did often cause me to change my mind or think more clearly, but the final product is my own.

Contents

Chapter 1. Introduction and Purpose of This Book   1

Chapter 2. Who Pays When the Employer Pays for Health
            Insurance? How Employers and Economists Disagree   15

Chapter 3. The Economics of Employer-Paid Benefits   37

Chapter 4. Employer Payment Incidence and Health Policy   77

Chapter 5. Using a Total Compensation Approach for Wage
            and Benefits Planning   121

Chapter 6. The Macroeconomics of Medical Benefits   135

Chapter 7. How Business Looks at Health Benefits Incidence
            and Reform   149

Chapter 8. Conclusion: Toward Optimal Health Benefits
            Policy, Public and Private   169

References   179

Index   185

CHAPTER 1

Introduction and Purpose of This Book

Why Health Care Spending Matters to American Businesses

The great bulk of medical expenditures made by Americans who are neither elderly nor poor is paid for by insurance financed through the workplace. Payment by the employer of part of the worker's health insurance premiums or medical care costs is an important and growing item in most firms' total compensation costs and is the largest nonwage benefit in most workers' compensation packages.

The insurance the employer arranges for the employees is already regulated to some extent by governments. Incremental health reform is all that seems politically possible at present, and proposals for such reform usually envision adding more regulations and extending that larger set of rules to more employers. Many (though not all) large scale health reform proposals that were made during the debate over the Clinton health care plan would have further extended that regulation, coupled with a requirement that all employers either pay for or at least make available health insurance at the workplace. The recently passed Kassebaum-Kennedy bill extends less extensive but still important regulation to employer-arranged insurance.

Spending on medical goods and services consumes roughly one-seventh of the U.S. gross domestic product (GDP), an amount equal to the entire national output of Great Britain and Canada combined. From the viewpoint of many (though not all) U.S. firms, this spending on health care represents a cost. From the viewpoint of those firms that sell medical goods and services and from the viewpoint of the people who work in and for them, this spending represents their income.

So businesses pay for employees' health insurance, but why do they do so? Is such payment in the interest of the owners of businesses, and is it

Portions of the chapter originally published in Mark Pauly's "When Does Curbing Health Care Costs Help the Economy?" *Health Affairs* 14, no. 2 (summer 1995). Copyright © 1995, "The People-to-People Health Foundation, Inc., Project HOPE, http://www.projhope.org/HA/."

in the public interest? Would businesses gain or lose from increased regulation of this payment, imposition of it on more businesses, or reductions in its amount or rate of growth for those businesses who do pay it? Would society gain? It is clear that the policy questions associated with employer financing are many and important. It is clear that, regardless of public policy, how employers manage health benefits when they choose to offer or arrange them, and whether or not they choose to do so, is also important. It is also clear that there has been some erosion in employer payment as a way of paying for health insurance and some considerable skepticism of whether the employment-based system will or should continue to be the main way in which private health insurance is chosen and financed.

It is, however, quite unclear whether employer-paid insurance is a desirable social institution, what employers' interests are in financing, or how they would be affected by proposed changes in financing or regulation. Trying to clarify the confusion over what payment for health care and health insurance means to U.S. businesses, as both employers and sellers, is the purpose of this book.

At the heart of the confusion are two quite different conceptions of the impact on employers of health benefits costs. One view, commonly held by many business managers and their advocates and by some politicians, is that employer payments for employees' health insurance are part of the cost of doing business, no different from employer payments for rent, raw materials, electricity, or top executive salaries. Under this view, it seems obvious that higher levels of costs of health benefits represent a threat to firm profitability and viability, and lower levels of such costs provide advantages to any firm. The alternative view, held by almost all economists and policy analysts, some politicians, and some labor leaders, is that employer payments for health insurance premiums ultimately come out of what would otherwise have been money wages for workers. In this view, higher medical costs do not harm employers or owners but do reduce money wages for workers—and harm them if the additional costs are not associated with sufficiently high additional health or security benefits. Lower costs benefit workers, not employers; they add to take-home pay, not profits.

A related question is that of how businesses should think about the rising share of GDP Americans choose to spend on health care and health insurance rather than on other things. Some businesses and some politicians believe that high levels of and high rates of increase in this type of spending are harmful to the economy as a whole, with necessarily negative impacts on other businesses, on the government and its policies, and on citizens in general. Sometimes the view is that higher health spending is harmful even if the health services are useful, because the country just cannot afford to divert resources and spending away from more important outputs, like manufactured products and high technology, into less tangible services like health care. More frequently the view is that much of this spending represents waste and greed, which hurt everyone. The alternative view, held by most economists and some politicians, is that high spending on medical care per se is not necessarily harmful to anyone, that it will be harmful to consumers only if they do not receive value for money but that medical spending in itself does not harm other business, economic aggregates like GDP or its growth, or a properly run government. As (or if) some businesses seem to get their health insurance costs under control, is that helpful, and if so, to whom? This book will therefore also address the question of the "macroeconomics" of health spending and its impact on the economy and on other businesses in the economy.

This book will investigate the circumstances when these business beliefs (or beliefs about business) are in error, when they may be correct, and why many business managers and public policymakers often make mistakes about the burden and impact of employer-paid insurance costs. It will show how positions that managers and policymakers might take on questions of public policy can be quite contrary to the actual interests of all involved, and it will show as well that managerial decisions firms make may likewise be seriously in error when those decisions are based on an incorrect view of employer payments.

The most important recent policy choice for which these beliefs were important was during the debate over the Clinton administration's health reform in 1994. Based on the belief that they would be harmed by higher mandated benefits costs, many employers, especially small employers and their advocates, opposed various versions of health reform that relied on mandated employer payments. Other employers, adopting a more statesmanlike posture, expressed worry about the impact of high health spending on the economy as a whole and (at least initially) supported the plan and praised its cost-containment features. These businesses shared President Clinton's worry that health care was bankrupting the U.S. economy. Some advocates of reform, and some politicians, favored both mandated coverage and minimum mandated employer premium shares on the grounds that such "shared responsibility" was a fairer and better way of financing care than other alternatives—especially in view of the so-called cost shift from employers who did not pay for coverage to those who did. Most liberal groups (and the most liberal analysts) often preferred ability-to-pay–based tax financing of any type, while the most conservative politicians (but few conservative analysts) opposed all mandates and (almost) all taxes. But moderate liberals and moderate conservatives favored some type of employer mandates. By the time the administration was willing to compromise on mandates, it was too late.

While the dust has yet to settle from this titanic struggle, it does seem clear that the political positions taken by various groups were to some extent influenced by their perception of how employer payments were ultimately financed (as well as of their impact on the economy). In economic jargon, both political and (big) business advocates of health reform through employer mandates believed that the incidence of employer payment fell on employers (owners of capital), while opponents of reform had the same view about incidence but differed on judgments of its desirability. The analysts' view—that the incidence is on workers—appears not to have had much impact on the policy debate, although it was virtually unanimously accepted in quantitative analyses of reform prepared either by advocates or opponents of employer mandates.

My major purpose in writing this book is based on the view that, whatever one's position on objectives for health reform or what constitutes fair financing, the political debate then and the political debate now and in the future would be advanced if there is general agreement on what is a correct view of the incidence of employer payment, on who actually pays when the boss writes the check for the worker's insurance. There still will not be agreement, I suspect, on goals, but there can be agreement on the facts. An additional dividend of clarifying this issue is that voters, who largely stayed on the sidelines of the reform debate as skeptical spectators, might better understand what the different options really mean for their well-being—rather than, as sometimes happened, rejecting all proposals because they all were so unintelligibly risky. However, providing that information at present is not simply a matter of disseminating agreed-upon facts. Rather, since there is disagreement about incidence, the most one could honestly tell voters is that the choice is a big gamble. This is obviously unsatisfactory.

There is another dividend from a correct view, one that can be paid more immediately and more directly than the one associated with governmental activities. Owners of businesses themselves can gain from understanding the economic view if it turns out to be correct. At present, in all states but Hawaii, businesspeople pay for employees' health insurance voluntarily and complain about it instinctively. A reasonable question is why they continue to pay for something that they think makes management so difficult and so adversely affects the bottom line. A short term answer is that, if they were to stop paying for health insurance, employees would quit. Over the longer term, however, employers often say that they would like gradually to reduce this "burden" or convert it into a defined cash payment rather than engage in management of a health insurance business. Many employers have taken steps consistent with this view in changing their policies toward health benefits for retirees and in increasing the share of premiums paid directly by employees. But is this objective of graceful exit really the most profitable for the firm? Put more positively, is there a way to manage health benefits that can add to profits, that can create sustainable competitive advantage for the firm? In this book, I will outline an approach for placing health benefits in an overall total compensation strategy for firms that offers the potential to enhance owners' wealth *and* worker welfare.

What This Book Will Do

With these as the overall objectives, this book has several specific purposes. First, I want to summarize the role that business, and business views on incidence, played in the debate on health reform. It is most transparent to summarize what participants said, but I will also offer some analysis of how those views appear to have affected what happened (or did not happen) in the resolution of the reform effort and some suggestions on what differences there might have been had the economic view been accepted. I will not try to discover new strategies or inside stories, but I will try to develop an explanation of what actually happened. To my knowledge, there has been no serious in-depth discussion of the role incidence played in the politics of health reform.

I then provide an extended discussion and summary of the theoretical conclusions and the empirical analysis associated with the economic view of incidence. There are, as will be shown, some circumstances in which the burden of paying employees' health costs *does* fall on the employer—but these circumstances need to be distinguished from others in which the burden is shifted to wages. Regulation and reform almost always have impacts of the latter type, and so do many market level changes in health insurance premiums. The most fundamental skill that every participant—manager, analyst, and policymaker—should develop is an ability to tell one set of circumstances from another; showing how to make these distinctions will be the major purpose of this section.

Next I turn to the question of how a firm should manage its own health benefits, and how it should use benefits management as part of the firm's overall value maximization strategy, in order to develop sustainable competitive advantage. Doing so, I will argue, is easiest to understand and explain within a broader theory of compensation strategy called the "total compensation" approach.

I then deal with what I call the "macroeconomics" of medical care spending—the impact of different levels of spending, both public and private, on overall real income and real income growth. Here again, there is an important distinction between spending, which is what we measure, and true cost, which represents reduction in real income to all citizens. (This chapter summarizes and extends some work I have previously published in the journal *Health Affairs*.)

The next chapter deals with the question of coping with misconceptions about economics. I consider how public policy has proceeded and will proceed given this belief, and I develop an explanation of the amount of correction of misperceptions that might be expected from the political process. Then I discuss the results of a series of interviews and surveys intended both to find out what business managers think and to lead them through the economic approach—in order to see whether there are ways to reconcile that approach with what they think. The results here are cautiously optimistic.

While much of my discussion will focus on the large scale mandate that the Clinton administration advocated, this analysis is also relevant to the incremental mandates or rules currently being discussed. I do deal explicitly with a mandate for employment-based insurance portability; other possible mandate on or subsidies to employer-provided coverage will have effects similar to the ones I analyze here.

The conclusion addresses the longer term question of how understanding of this issue is likely to develop, what impacts it will have on both politics and management, and whether there are managerial and political changes that can improve that developmental process.

Defining the Issues

There are actually two economic propositions about incidence that are important and that clash with those of the common business manager or politician. They both refer to some long run period when wage contracts and employment in the market have readjusted to new levels. The first proposition, most frequently mentioned, is that the great bulk of employer payments for employee health insurance (and, therefore any mandated increase in payments) eventually will come out of worker wages. The most frequently accepted point estimate at the moment, based on an estimate by Lewin-VHI, is that 88 percent of premiums are offset by money wage reductions, with the only stated reason for deviation from 100 percent the payroll tax subsidy to additional employer premium payments (Lewin-VHI 1993). The other proposition, less frequently mentioned but with even firmer theoretical credentials than the first, is that (tax considerations aside) the employer share of mandated benefits does not matter (Pauly 1994). That is, whatever the incidence of the cost of a mandated benefit, the reduction in wages net of insurance costs is the same regardless of the employer share of the premium for a given insurance policy. Whether the employer is required to pay all, 80 percent, half, or none of the cost of mandated benefits, the worker's wage, net of the cost of any employee share of premium, remains the same. If affected employers should lose some profits from mandation, this striking proposition says that, in the long run, they will lose the same profits from an individual mandate as from a mandate for full employer payment. But they will in aggregate probably lose very little profit in any case.

The issue of incidence affects not only one's views on such big picture questions as whether employer mandates should be used but also one's view on smaller or incremental steps to insurance "reform." Proposals to require that employer-paid coverage in small groups be community rated, provide coverage for preexisting conditions, or be noncancelable might be viewed differently depending on whether one thinks it is the employer or the employees who will experience the impact of the premium changes necessarily caused by such new regulation. Even something so obviously "proworker" as removal of the Employee Retirement Income Security Act (ERISA) preemption takes on a different cast when (or if) one supposes that any adverse financial consequences of removing the preemption will be born by workers currently covered under ERISA plans in the form of lower money wages.

The issue of incidence goes beyond political regulation or mandation. Even if there are no substantial new laws for some time, how employers ought to feel about private sector efforts to limit the cost of health insurance plans might be affected by their views on incidence. Effective employer alliances might well raise worker wages, rather than employer profits, and employers may have different views of the desirability of alliances when they realize this. Incorrect views on incidence can lead business managers to make bad choices about how they will obtain benefits as well as about what lobbying position they will support.

I view this book as making two contributions. The first and most obvious one is that it may advance the rationality of the debate on health reform, not necessarily by leading to a particular position (since that depends on each individual's goals as well as on the objective facts) but by making sure that arguments are not about things that are not so.

The second contribution is toward an understanding of how or whether the economic and the political systems can function when people make mistakes in economics. Virtually all of modern microeconomics is built on the development of complex models of firm, employee, and consumer maximizing behavior and the equilibrium (if any) of interactions among maximizing agents. The agents are not assumed to be omniscient or fully informed—modern economics knows that information is costly and sometimes it pays to stop gathering or processing information—but they are usually assumed to be economically rational. That is, managers may be ignorant, but they should not be stupid. However, there is some research in economics that suggests that this is not a reasonable assumption. One of the classics in managerial studies was the discovery, decades ago, that owners or managers of profit-maximizing firms neither knew nor wanted to know their marginal costs and (where relevant) their marginal revenue—two pieces of information the economic theory of the profit-maximizing firm regards as crucial. Some theories of survival of managers who unknowingly did the right thing have been constructed. I think the analysis of the incidence of fringe benefits may provide another example of this sort of thing—but the difference here is that managers who are ignorant about economics not only make decisions that cost their owners profits, but they also support political lobbying that harms both the social welfare and their own firms' welfare.

There is one other potential subtext in political economy that I will explore. It is possible that some political advocates, analysts, and politicians do have an economically correct view but are unable or unwilling to admit it or use it explicitly in designing and analyzing policy. For example, if workers and managers incorrectly think that an employer mandate shifts the cost to the boss, those politicians who understand the economic view but who identify workers as their constituency may be reluctant to criticize proposals for mandates and may even support them as a way of deceiving workers into accepting a requirement to pay for their own coverage that they would not accept if made explicit. It may also be that politicians prefer mandates precisely because their incidence is confused. If it is hard for any voter, regardless, to know for sure how he or she is affected by such a confusing tax, it may help politicians to foster the fiscal illusion that benefits can be provided and no one pays for them. There may also be less blameworthy behavior by politicians: faced with workers who incorrectly believe that they do not pay an employer mandate but do pay an individual mandate, an economist-politician may be unwilling to advocate the latter because ignorant constituents (aided by unscrupulous opponents in the political process) will vote him or her out of office. It may be too difficult or too time consuming to educate the constituency, so the best thing may be to cave in to ignorance.

Prologue

In no state but Hawaii are employers obliged to pay any part of an employee's health insurance premium, and yet the great majority of jobs still does carry an employer-paid health insurance benefit. The only type of firm in which payment of health insurance premiums or benefits is not typical is the very small firm, of five employees or less.

What does it mean to say that the employer "pays" the health insurance premium for an employee? In such a case, part of the employee's compensation for work is received in the form of funds earmarked for health insurance premiums rather than in the form of cash that could be spent on anything. In effect, employer payment of employee health insurance premiums is equivalent to what economists call a "tie-in sale"; the employee who "buys" money income from the employer with labor is forced to buy health insurance from the same source. Of course, the employee could decline the job-related coverage, but if the employer paid all of the premiums, refusing coverage would not cause the employee's money wages to rise. In many ways, the arrangement is like local government: if you buy a house in Smallville, you are forced to pay for the local public schools; if you take a job at XYZ Corporation, you are forced to take the local insurance or insurance package. You can avoid either payment by living and working somewhere else, but then you must also sacrifice the benefit.

At first thought, such an arrangement (despite our familiarity with it) must seem puzzling. At best, this arrangement means that to get the health insurance policy one wants, one must choose the job that goes with it. At worst, it forces people to choose jobs or insurance policies that are not exactly what they want. Why do not employers just pay all cash and let employees then choose exactly the insurance they want as private purchasers in private markets?

The answer, of course, is that insurance is cheaper (or better) if you buy it at, and along with, your job. Having the employer send the check for your insurance premium before your take-home pay is calculated also saves on income and payroll taxes for the employees, and insurance is cheaper to administer if a large group at a firm takes the same policy, compared to each person seeking his or her own variant. While options and choices among different insurance policies offered at the workplace have been growing, it remains an inescapable fact that offering more choices increases costs—so most firms offer only a limited set of choices. (The main exception to this generalization is the Federal Employees Health Benefit Program, which does offer dozens of plans. Even here, however, not all plans are offered, and the federal government is not a profit-maximizing firm.) In addition, there may be improvements in quality possible if the benefits staff at your firm do the shopping for health insurance for you, even if they do not get exactly what you want. One may wonder why some employees of XYZ Corporation should have jobs as de facto insurance agents for other employees rather than being part of the team that helps to produce whatever XYZ makes.

What's Wrong with This Picture?

This simple story is the way economists, and some health benefits specialists, think about employer-paid health insurance. Employer payments in this view are really reallocation of compensation that belongs to employees, with employers taking on the job of helping employees decide how to spend their money because of some tax breaks and because employees may not be the most efficient shoppers in the world. Higher health insurance premiums hurt employees, and lower premiums help them, but the level of insurance premium does not affect what employers earn or what they should do about such things as employment, prices, or profits.

However, many employers, and many benefits specialists, do not look at things this way. Instead, they see health insurance premiums as moneys diverted from employer profit or net revenue. They see higher health insurance premiums as harmful to their competitive position in product markets and harmful to the bottom line. They see lower health insurance premiums as a boon, something that will bring smiles to stockholders or owners and terror to domestic and international competitors. For them, lower prices for health insurance the firm buys are like lower electric bills for the power it uses: they probably help, and they surely do not hurt. Higher prices for health insurance are reasons to cut back, hunker down, and complain to any politicians who care to listen. Lower prices are reasons to brag in the annual report.

The main purpose of this book is to try to sort out these two different sets of views. They cannot both be true. Moreover, if one is right, the other is wrong, and those who support the wrong view may be doing harm to themselves and to others.

Who Was Confused and Why Did It Matter?

What types of participants in the health reform debate had views on the incidence of employer premium payments that differed from those suggested by economics, and what difference did that make in the types of policies they supported?

It is generally not correct to view the development of proposed policies in Washington as the linear process described in the policy analysis textbook. The textbook says that, to come up with good policy, the policymaker should first specify goals (which may differ for different policymakers), specify alternative ways of reaching those goals, gather empirical evidence on which way works best, and then select a policy. Although the process occasionally works in this fashion, oftentimes it works in reverse: A policymaker, perhaps after some cursory and intuitive analysis, decides on a policy that sounds good and announces it. The policymaker then commissions his or her staff, and whoever works for them, to develop the theories and empirical evidence that support this policy. This means that, once a policy position is taken, evidence contrary to it must either be refuted or diverted. It is only in rare circumstances that the policymaker will confess that the original policy was in error and will need to be changed based on evidence. (In contrast, there is little disgrace in changing policy to fit "political realities" [views of other politically potent persons].)

In broad strokes, this is what happened in the debate over the role of an employer mandate in health reform. The Clinton team, well before the election, defined employer payment of a substantial share of the premium for employees and their families as a key element of their reform proposal. Republicans initially expressed skepticism and eventually, for the most part, hardened into opposition to a mandated employer payment. There was some fragmentation among Republicans in specifying alternatives: some proposed a mandate on individuals; others proposed requiring employers to offer but not pay for employee premiums; and still others hoped that some substantial insurance rating and underwriting reforms, combined with some modest subsidies, would achieve universal access (somehow defined) if not universal coverage.

The propositions, firmly founded in economic theory and empirical economic research—that employees paid for the great bulk of the employers' share and that the impact on business owners' returns of mandated coverage did not depend on the employer share—were awkward for both groups of politicians. For the Clinton team, the economic view implied that they were imposing substantial additional compulsory payments, taxes in all but name, on the constituency of working middle class Americans whose interests they claimed to represent. For Republicans, it meant that they could not logically oppose employer mandates as harmful to their small and medium-sized business constituency or to upper middle class or upwardly mobile workers, or even as something causing massive job loss for workers above minimum wage. (A mandate would cause unemployment among minimum wage workers estimated to be in the range of two hundred thousand to two million jobs.) The people who would be harmed by an employer mandate to pay for employee coverage would be the irresponsible (or otherwise preoccupied) lower middle income workers who choose a job that does not carry insurance and who make up the bulk of the uninsured. Technically, the Clinton plan would harm this group and Republican opposition would protect them from harm, but Republicans could hardly be apologists for this small minority of irresponsible and disorganized poor souls. The last gasp of the Clinton position, which did not really rise to the top until mid-1994, was that "employer-based health insurance that no one could take away (or give away)" was of value to the broader middle class, but the arguments never made clear exactly who was to pay for this coverage or whether it would be worth what it would cost.

Even the debate on job loss, which is a matter on which there can be differences of opinion, seems much less important once incidence is taken into account. After all, the smaller the job loss, the larger the wage offset. Either way, total incomes of workers fall, and the primary difference is whether those lower incomes are spread over "at risk" workers or concentrated on those who do lose their jobs. In some of the estimates of "job loss," moreover, the people who "lose" their jobs are people who voluntarily choose to withdraw from the labor force (when money wages fall and health insurance is provided in return).

If an employer mandate was like an individual mandate, this made it difficult for Republicans to oppose an employer mandate and difficult for Democrats to favor it. Consequently, the policy advocacy process made some strenuous efforts to ignore or somehow discount the economic view.

The most common basis for discounting the economic conclusion is to argue that it would prevail only in some "long run" distant enough in the future to be effectively ignored. An alternative version of the same argument is to say that money wages are "sticky" and so would not be reduced immediately to offset a mandated employer payment. It is true that money wages are often set in advance (though the kind of lower wage small firms that would be affected by a mandate are probably more likely to adjust quickly than a large firm bound by union contracts or bureaucracy). However, this kind of delay in response ought to apply primarily to an *unexpectedly* and *immediately* imposed employer mandate. Since the legislative mandate is usually due to take effect at some point two or three years in the future, there is plenty of time to plan raises and wages to accommodate the additional benefits cost.

Conclusion

We are left then with a strong set of economic propositions: for the great bulk of workers making more than the legal minimum wage, anticipated or expected changes in health benefits costs, whether caused by governmental regulation, employer coalitions, or competitive forces, have the same effect on wages and profits regardless of the employer share of payment for insured workers. The effect on profits is likely to be minimal but the effect on wages large. These propositions were either ignored or discounted as irrelevant in the real world by many business managers and politicians. Who had the greatest chance of being right, and what differences did (and does) it make? Exploring the understanding or agreement with the proposition by the actors in the market and political sides of benefits policy will be a primary goal of this book.

CHAPTER 2

Who Pays When the Employer Pays for Health Insurance? How Employers and Economists Disagree

Economists and employers often seem to think in different ways about health insurance furnished as part of job compensation. In this chapter I will provide an outline of the range of employer views, especially as expressed in public statements or survey responses in connection with the Clinton health reform proposal. There are also some differences in how different employers appear to look at their health insurance payments and policies, and I will describe those differences. The common characteristic of these views that is important for this book, however, is that they all differ from the economic view.

The Economic Model

In order to illustrate the contrast, and before summarizing the variety of employer views, I first provide a brief statement of the economic model. The most fundamental conclusion of the economic model is that actions that affect the cost or composition of employer-paid benefits, coming either from private market changes or government intervention, have the same effect on employees regardless of whether they initially impact the employee or the employer. That is, the payment for health benefits is viewed as if it were the employee's own money, regardless of whether the payment nominally comes from the employer or the employee. One direct implication of this model is that, if the decision to work is not sensitive to real compensation over the relevant range, a mandate on employers to pay part of employee health insurance premiums will not cause total employment to change or the firm's prices to rise but will cause money wages to fall by the amount of the mandated premium. (The only way firms will continue to be willing to hire as many workers after the mandate as before is if their total compensation cost does not change.) If labor supply is somewhat responsive to real compensation, and if workers do not value the benefit at what it costs, money wages will still fall but by less than the cost of the benefit, so that a fraction of the cost would then fall on profits. However, if supply is responsive, exactly the same decline in money wages and profits would appear if workers had been ordered to buy the benefit themselves but could avoid the obligation to buy by ceasing to work for wages. The share of the cost between employer and employee does not matter.

Why Offer Coverage?

Offering health insurance coverage as a benefit to workers requires an employer to expend resources to set up the program, to select insurance, to administer the program, to explain changes in benefits or in premiums the employee pays, and to send a check to the insurer for the share of premiums the employer pays. None of these activities contribute directly to the firm's sales or output. So why do employers do this? Why do they (in all states but Hawaii) voluntarily take actions that appear to cause them such misery?

The Employer Answer to These Questions

There are three answers to this question that employers provide. (Whether these answers are economically valid will be discussed later.) One answer, relatively rare but occasionally mentioned, is that employers pay for health insurance because health insurance coverage improves worker health (relative to what it would be if employers did not pay for health insurance), and improved worker health means higher productivity and reduced absenteeism. For example, Anthony Knettel, from the ERISA Industry Committee, said: "It essentially comes down to this reality. The cost of health care, as well as the cost of the lack of access to health care, is not measured exclusively in terms of the cost of health insurance. Its cost is measured in terms of increase in unnecessary absenteeism from work. It's measured in terms of decreases in productivity" (EBRI/ERF 1994). This argument is based on two assumptions: that the absence of employer-paid insurance will cause people to forgo other insurance and to forgo care that affects productivity or work loss days and that this decrease in productivity or increase in work loss days will for some reason not be offset by lower wage payments.

The second answer is that employers offer and pay for coverage because of a personal or morally interpreted obligation to treat their employees well. They provide insurance because they think employees ought to have insurance and might not choose to get it on their own. For instance, a small business owner's thinking was described this way: "Dropping health insurance as a benefit and raising salaries to compensate is something Bilderback has considered but so far resisted. He says that health insurance is too important" (Kimble 1990).

The third answer is that offering employer-paid health insurance, given the level of money wages, helps to attract and retain more and better qualified employees. In this version, no one would object to the argument. A more controversial but more economically relevant argument is that, for a given level of *total* compensation expense per worker, providing fringe benefits rather than cash may help the firm to attract more and better workers. One small business owner's version of this thinking goes as follows: "I've heard that talk—that the best way to hold down costs is to make workers pay part of the premium. I'm sure there's some truth to that, but it won't always work in the real world. We're in a highly competitive business and we can't expect to attract good, highly skilled workers if we're not offering a health plan that measures up to the competition" (Kimble 1990). Another story: "One thing holding this business owner back [from increasing the deductible from $100 to $300!] is a concern that diluting coverage will somehow harm his ability to attract good employees" (Zall 1990).

What causes firms to choose *not* to offer employer-paid health insurance? One might suppose that it would be the mirror image of reasons to offer it—a firm would not offer health insurance if it did not think that health-related absenteeism was a problem, if it did not feel a moral obligation to workers, or if it did not think that offering health insurance as a fringe benefit would be attractive to workers. In fact, however—and here we have good data—the most common reason employers give for not offering employer-paid health insurance is not any of these reasons. Rather, the overwhelming majority of employers who do not offer coverage give as the reason that they "cannot afford it" or (what I think is almost the same thing) that insurance costs too much. Small business owners especially tell stories of how they may at one time have offered health insurance but then chose to drop it when premiums rose too high to be affordable (CONSAD Research Corporation 1993).

This "affordability" explanation appears over and over in surveys of and interviews with employers (Morrisey, Jensen, and Morlock 1994). This simple version of the explanation of why employers do or do not "give" coverage—based on whether they can or cannot afford it—was accepted by both opponents and advocates of public programs to expand employment-based coverage. Small business lobbyists argued most strenuously that their clients would only offer benefits when they could afford them (though they would presumably not have argued that money wage levels were as high as they were because employers could "afford" to pay at that level). Advocates of mandates and similar devices tried to show that many employers not currently offering benefits really could afford to do so—pointing either to positive profit levels or employer ability to make payment of such benefits in other similar settings without causing financial distress to the firm.

Those who advised employers on this issue also did not point them in the direction suggested by economics. In an article on "Health Horrors: Coping with Soaring Costs," Daniel Kehrer summarizes: "Solutions [to rising benefits costs recommended to employers by consultants] include: sharing more costs with employees and involving them more in health buying decisions; availability of bare-bones policies unencumbered by frills" (Kehrer 1990, 29). There is no recognition that a bare-bones policy might cause disgruntled workers to demand higher wages to stay with the firm or that higher employee premium charges or higher deductibles are the equivalent of a wage reduction but without the tax benefits. And elsewhere, he reports the result of a 1989 poll in which "30 percent of independent business owners say they are able to pass along the costs to customers," but owners were not asked if they could pass the costs to workers. However, the implication of this answer is that business would react to higher premiums by raising prices if they could and that about a third of businesses think that they can. These price-increasing businesses, however, are not behaving in a consistent profit-maximizing fashion—if they could and would raise prices when health costs increase, they should raise prices whether those costs increase or not, since raising prices will always add to profits.

Even financially sophisticated businesspeople do not seem to think of the wage offset option. An owner of a CPA firm offered the following opinion about the Clinton proposal that employers be mandated to pay 80 percent of the premium. "Once they say [employer payment] is mandatory, the next step will be that we have to pay every cent of the premiums, and the way they've been going up, we couldn't afford that" (Goldwasser 1990, 40). The accountant further went on: "I know for a fact that many of my small business customers already can't afford health insurance, and there are others who are going to have to discontinue coverage if prices keep following their current trends" (Goldwasser 1990, 40). Leaders of the small business lobby also advanced the "unaffordability" argument. John Motley, vice president of the National Federation of Independent Businesses (NFIB), opposed employer mandates on the grounds that such mandates would be like "tying small businesses to a sled and pushing them down the mountain hoping they'll stay upright. Many of them will go bankrupt, threatening a national recession" (Johnson and Broder 1996, 159).

Nevertheless, even the most economically unsophisticated businessperson would generally not be completely comfortable with a simple zero-sum theory of affordability, in which every extra dollar of benefits costs reduces owner net income by a dollar, as a way of explaining a firm's willingness to pay some imposed cost. Instead, a somewhat more complex theory notes that the costs a firm bears must, if it is to survive, somehow be covered by the revenues it takes in; while revenues (and prices) might be increased, there is no guarantee that revenue can rise enough to cover all of a cost increase. So the affordability theory in its most elaborate version sought to analyze the impact of an increase in health benefits cost by analogizing it with other increases in input costs.

That is, for the most part, business thinking about rising health benefits costs seems to treat health benefits cost as any other cost. As Jack Lewin, former insurance commissioner for Hawaii, notes, because employer health insurance costs are just another business expense, like the cost of electricity or of environmental cleanup, that businesses either may choose to pay or may reasonably be asked to pay, in order to provide some social benefit, the result of Hawaii's employer mandate was a modest increase in prices. This "cost-like-any-other-cost" model also seems to be implicit in many of the predicted or recommended strategic responses for firms with rising benefits costs: if the cost of any input rises, firms should and will try to raise their prices; the extent to which the firm can raise its price depends on firm level demand elasticity (the "degree of competitiveness" of the market). If the cost of an input rises for all firms in a market, even if they are perfectly competitive, market level equilibrium price will indeed rise as firms reduce output. The extent to which output (and inputs) is reduced is larger the more elastic are firm and industry level demand curves. So firms facing a mandate were advised to plan to cut output and employment and to hope for (or assist with) increasing final product prices.

Concretely, the cost-like-any-other-cost approach seems to characterize the reaction of a local Philadelphia restaurateur (and prominent Democrat) to the Clinton mandate. She felt that an employer mandate would raise her costs and that she would have to cut back on employment, but then prices would rise. She added that a little extra added to the price of a restaurant meal would not discourage many customers from eating out but would represent their fair contribution toward the well-being of the people who serve them.

Not all reactions fit this story, however. If the cost of electricity rose, employers would not usually think of responding by asking employees to pay part of the firm's utility bill—and yet employers do think of asking employees to pay a larger share of rising insurance premiums. Tax considerations aside (these are important! see the following), there is no real difference at all as far as an employee is concerned between receiving $100 less in pay and being asked to pay $100 more of the premium for an insurance that is obligatory in that firm. Either way, the employee has $100 less to spend on everything else.

Who Thought What about the Employer Mandate and about Incidence?

This affordability or cost-like-any-cost attitude represented the typical business view of employer mandates and the incidence of employer premium payments. In this section I give more detail on what sorts of people held which views and how they expressed those views in the health reform debate. I have tried to summarize the literature on health reform and to extract representative views of identifiable groups or types of agents. I do not pretend, however, that this represents a completely exhaustive survey of who said what—but I do think it represents a good sample.

I will catalog views on mandates and incidence into three sets, after one exclusion. The exclusion refers to the effect of mandates or increasing health benefit costs for minimum wage workers. The conventional employers' view—that they will have to bear the costs—is generally (though not quite perfectly) correct in economic theory when money wages are fixed by the minimum wage—since then money wages cannot fall. I will, however, discuss implications of mandated benefits or benefit cost increases for minimum wage workers in the next analytical chapter.

The three categories of views among business and political leaders that I will treat are as follows: (1) persons who do not in any way accept the economic view of incidence but instead stick with the cost-like-any-cost view through thick and thin; (2) persons who accept the economic view in theory but argue that it is largely irrelevant to any of the internal management or public policy issues under discussion; and (3) persons who accept the economic view.

Who Thinks What about What and What Difference Does It Make?

I explore the views by examining statements on some key questions in health policy. I first discuss what answers would be consistent with either the economic view or the business view. I then analyze comments made on the questions by key actors to see which views they appear to support.

Should Health Care Be Financed with an Employer Mandate to Pay Part of the Premium?

This was one of the most fundamental issues for the health reform debate. President Clinton proposed that all employers be required to pay 80 percent of the cost of coverage for a standard benefit plan, with subsidies to help defray this cost to be directed at small businesses and with larger subsidies to businesses with lower average wages. Some liberal Democrats preferred instead a general tax-financed system, while Republicans either favored an individual mandate or no mandate at all.

If one took the business view, an employer mandate would represent an additional tax cost on those employers mandated to pay more for health insurance; it would add a governmentally imposed cost to the cost of doing business, one that would vary with the number of workers and the cost of health benefits. Employers would bear the major part of the responsibility for paying for insurance, obtaining the funds either from profits or by shifting the cost to buyers of their products. Higher labor costs would probably cause reduced employment, reduced output, and rising prices. Opponents of the Clinton plan felt that many businesses could not afford to pay so large a share of the premium. Supporters of the administration's bill felt that the employee could not afford to pay a larger share than 20 percent.

If, in contrast, one took the economic view, the policy question would not have been whether employers could or should pay for coverage. Instead, since the cost of the mandate would fall on wages, the question would have been whether the taxes on worker wages implied by the mandate were equitable and/or efficient and perhaps whether some small part of the tax might yet fall on some employers (Pauly 1994). In large firms, some of which did not offer coverage, mandates were equivalent to lump sum taxes on workers. In smaller firms, net premiums were to be proportional to wages but to be set at a lower rate, at a given income level, the smaller the firm.

The administration's problems with the business view came across most clearly when they argued for the employer mandate rather than for an individual mandate or a mandate with a large individual share. Walter Zelman (1994), one of the architects of the administration's bill, offered the following opinion: "It is no wonder that individual mandate proposals have limited political viability . . . These proposals suggest that coverage now offered by employers become the employees' own personal responsibility." The political opinion is consistent with the business view—that employer payments are paid by the employer out of profits and not out of employee wages—and are not consistent with the economic view, which would conclude that "coverage now offered by employers" is *already* "the employees' own personal responsibility," regardless of whether there is an individual or employer mandate, or any mandate at all.

Zelman went on: "under an individual mandate, employers would have incentives to drop coverage of lower wage workers, who might benefit from substantial government subsidies. These costs will be shifted from employers to government . . . unless, of course, subsidies were minimized and an unrealistic burden placed on low income families." In an economic view, the first sentence of this statement is correct—if the only way a low income worker can get a subsidy is to purchase insurance individually. But the second part is wrong. Such a step would shift costs from *employees* (not employers) to government; in the absence of subsidies, low wage employees are already bearing "an unrealistic burden." The Clinton team appeared to have trouble with incidence well into the process.

However, error was bipartisan. Haley Barbour, writing for the Republican National Committee, gave as reasons for opposition to mandates: "Employers will have to pay an additional $107 billion to health alliances, $107 billion that could have been used . . . to make capital investments" (Barbour 1994). Economists would say instead that the $107 billion came out of wages, not out of profits that might have been reinvested. Republican congresswoman Nancy Johnson, in responding to President Clinton's speech introducing his plan, said: "Many small employers are barely surviving. A new health care tax would certainly force layoffs and discourage hiring" (*USA Today* 1993). As a statement applicable to most small employers, who pay above the minimum wage, this assertion is economically incorrect. If it was intended to apply only to small employers with minimum wage employees, the statement would still be inconsistent with the economic view, because low wage workers would be laid off whether their employer was large or small, while other currently uninsured workers would not be fired if their wages were above the minimum wage even if their employer was small and barely surviving.

The administration's economists, in contrast, generally accepted the view that the incidence of an employer mandate is on wages. That was the primary reason why they concluded that job losses would be small; it was because wage losses would be large. One administration economist, Richard Kronick, did seem a little uncertain when he analyzed the precursor of the Clinton bill, the Massachusetts "pay or play" employer mandate (Kronick 1991). He said: "It seems likely that the primary competition for [small] firms [in Massachusetts] [is] other Massachusetts businesses, rather than businesses in other states. This will make price increases a more feasible response than would otherwise be the case." Strictly speaking, this statement is correct—except that price increases would never be an optimal response regardless of who Massachusetts small business competed with, since prices would need to increase only if wages did not fall.

There were some other economist analysts, arguing on behalf of small businesses, who first accepted but then heavily qualified the simple economic argument. The most common qualification, applied to the impact of mandates as well as to other things, was to note that the economic argument was only true "in the long run" but that the long run was not a practical political or managerial context. It is, of course, true that the economic model assumes that real wages are adjusted after a mandate, and it is obvious that such adjustments would not be expected to occur instantaneously, immediately after the unexpected implementation of an exogenous mandate. Of course, the long run in economics is not a calendar time period but instead is defined (tautologically) by the time it takes to change the relevant economic behavior—in this case, real wages.

The view then was that there will be no or little adverse effect from a mandate in the long run but that there will be important short run effects. For instance, O'Neill and O'Neill (1994) argue that "it is highly likely that the extent of shifting will be greater in the long run than in the short run, although the timing is difficult to predict" (7). Or, as a Service Employers International Union report puts it: "Employers are often less able, and less willing, to make dramatic changes in their compensation packages than economic theory suggests, at least in the short term" (Service Employers International Union 1994, 12). The report offers no evidence in support of this proposition.

A second qualification is that, even when reducing real wages would not strictly speaking violate the minimum wage laws, employers may be reluctant to limit money wages of low wage employees. The O'Neills trace this reluctance to "the need to maintain compensation differentials between groups of workers to reflect seniority and skill levels" (O'Neill and O'Neill 1994, 7). Other analyses, such as that done by CONSAD, appeal to a more diffuse notion of negative effects on morale and employee relationships, especially in a small firm (CONSAD Research Corporation 1993).

The third qualification is that a mandate imposes a fixed cost or cash flow problem on small businesses, which have a difficult time managing to pay bills because of low capitalization in any case. For example, Cong. Harris Tilwell, reflecting on his own experience in running a law office that did not pay for health insurance, observed: "I never got over the feeling, 'Am I going to make payroll this month?'" Businessman Dale Gillilland opposed a mandate on the grounds that it "would restrict ability to manage cash flow. We can't afford costs we can't control" (Connolly 1993, 3121). The administration seemed to share this view. Hillary Rodham Clinton, in response to a similar complaint from an owner of a small business, remarked to the House Small Business Committee: "I can't be expected to go out and save every undercapitalized business in America" (Johnson and Broder 1996, 227).

I could not find any example of a currently uninsured small business owner who responded to the prospect of a mandate by giving the economically correct answer: "The mandate won't hurt me, but it will take wages away from my workers, and those lost wages will be more valuable to them than the health benefits they receive. So the main reason for me to object is out of concern for my workers." However, some owners would have known what to do if a mandate had come. Dale Gillilland, mentioned previously, stopped providing coverage at one point, but, when he did so, he "gave everybody a salary increase" (Connolly 1993, 3121). Presumably the process would be reversed after mandate; paying for health insurance would displace many years' worth of salary increases.

Large Firm Responses to Mandated Benefits

While employees in the smallest firms (less than ten workers) are most likely to be uninsured, nearly one-quarter of the uninsured workers work for large firms, those with more than 1,000 employees (EBRI 1994). The argument that the owners (stockholders) of such firms could not "afford" to pay for the cost of mandated benefits is not generally credible. However, the economically correct response by managers of large firms should have also been the one in the previous paragraph. They might then have objected that their workers could not "afford" the pay cut or that such a tax was inequitable. This economically correct argument seems not to have occurred to managers of large businesses.

The most celebrated case concerning a large firm involved an activist attack on the management of Pizza Hut for not paying for health insurance for its U.S. workers while it did pay the payroll tax for health insurance required by law for its German employees. This showed, the activists argued, that Pizza Hut (and its parent company) could afford to pay for health insurance in the United States as well; the company was just choosing profits over people. Pizza Hut's CEO, Allan Huston, responded after being called to testify before Senator Kennedy's committee and presented an argument entirely based on the business view, without consideration of economics. He argued that "from what I have seen of mandates in Europe and elsewhere they contribute to the descending economic spiral of higher prices and unemployment" (Huston 1994). He went on to say that the "burdensome social costs" in Germany and Japan are responsible for operating losses for Pizza Hut franchisees in those countries and concluded that "our experience is that the high cost of mandates contributes to higher prices, lower profits, unemployment, and eventually stifles investment." (Note that lower wages are not mentioned at all.)

He then analyzed "how mandates might affect Pizza Hut in the United States." Because of high consumer demand elasticity, price increases would cut volume and profits, so price increases would not pay.

What about the "myth that we can magically absorb the cost increase"? He does note that Pizza Hut would respond by cutting minimum wage jobs but does not consider what might happen for employees making more than the minimum wage. Objecting to the mandate because it would wipe out raises for employees for the foreseeable future—the economically correct counterargument—was never mentioned.

When large employers opposed mandates, they did so because of possible strings attached. Michael R. Becker, vice president—benefits for the McDonnell Douglas Corporation, speaking for the Corporate Health Care Coalition (17 large corporations), said: "no business wants to see Congress mandate additional business responsibilities . . . The last thing any of us wants is to hitch a major element of our labor costs—health care benefits—to a cost escalator and turn over the operation of it to the federal government" (Becker 1994, 4). Here again, it should have been workers, not management, that objected to the escalator linkage, since rising benefits costs would necessarily put downward pressure on wages; but there should be no connection between benefits costs and total labor costs.

Impacts of Higher Health Benefit Costs on Business and the Economy

Another issue on which the economic and business views differ radically is on the possible effect of economy-wide increases in health benefits costs, caused by medical spending growth. The economic viewpoint is that such increases will be offset by lower real wages, which will make workers worse off if the higher costs are not offset by benefits of higher quality or greater value. However, the higher costs will not affect the profits of employers to any appreciable extent. The business view is quite different: even if all businesses provide the same insurance to their workers, the argument goes, rising medical care costs will raise labor costs, cut into profits, cause firms to raise prices where they can, and force them to lay off workers regardless of whether they can or cannot raise prices. As stated by Jerry Jasenowski of the National Association of Manufacturers, the problem with the Clinton plan from the viewpoint of his members was that "there is, to be frank, profound skepticism that your [Clinton] plan would successfully reduce the growth of health care costs" (Johnson and Broder 1996, 317).

Some employer lobbying groups supported government cost containment on these grounds. A typical viewpoint was that of the National Leadership Coalition on Health Reform, a nonpartisan group organized by policy advocate Henry Simmons that included big businesses, unions, consumer groups, and associations of health care providers, including about one hundred million people as employees or members. The group supported an employer mandate to achieve universal coverage because "it makes sense to build on that very large base—of coverage and of financial support for coverage" (Simmons 1993). It also supported health spending targets (at levels ideally equal to or less than the rate of growth in GDP) and government established payment rates and capital controls for health providers.

The reasons why such limits are needed is "the more money that businesses must spend on health care, the less money they have to invest in research and development, new plant and equipment, and training—which means not only that economic growth is hampered, but that American firms are at a competitive disadvantage with firms in other countries where health care costs are lower" (Simmons 1993).

A similar viewpoint was expressed by the Families USA Foundation in commenting on "the crushing burden of health insurance." The opening sentences in the report express no doubt about who pays for insurance: "American businesses are seeing a larger and larger share of their profits eaten up by health insurance costs. Total business spending for health care in 1993 was more than three and one-half (3.7) times business spending in 1980" (Families USA Foundation 1994, 1). Later in the report, second thoughts creep in: "Health insurance costs are a burden on American businesses. This burden is borne by companies of all sizes, but small businesses suffer the most . . . Without reform, thousands of businesses will continue to worry about the growing burden of health insurance costs and its impact on their businesses. Millions of workers in these businesses will continue to worry that they and their families could lose their health insurance or lose their jobs because of the burden of health costs. They are already losing salaries and other benefits due to these fast-rising costs" (Families USA Foundation 1994, 9). People worry about many things, but if workers are absorbing higher benefits costs in lower salaries and other benefits, they should not worry about losing their jobs, and business should not worry about losing profits. Imprecision about who really pays for health insurance seems to have resulted in a multiplier effect on worrying, with everyone thinking that they are bearing the burden of rising costs in all of the worst possible ways.

Even Republicans sometimes appeared to go along with this reasoning, if not with the implied policy. Haley Barbour: "Employer mandates dictate the need for price controls. Small businesses faced with this mandate will rightly expect, even demand, protection from huge cost increases" (Barbour 1994). Likewise business lobbyists who ended up opposing the Clinton bill still were concerned about the "burden on the economy." Ronald Bullock, testifying for the National Association of Manufacturers, said: "While difficult to quantify, there is a growing belief that as a result of increased spending on health care, less is being spent upgrading plants and facilities, research and development, training/retraining, and other critical business investment" (Bullock 1993, 9).

Finally, noneconomist policy analysts accepted the bad-for-business argument with even fewer qualifications than business leaders. Political scientist Cathie Jo Martin was puzzled: "Since businesses as a whole are getting badly stung by rising health costs, we might expect them to be major players in the reform battle . . . This historical antagonism [to government-led health reform] has been receding, driven back by the assault of health care costs on corporate profits" (Martin 1993, 368–69). This puzzlement is compounded, because, even if higher health benefits costs can be shifted entirely onto workers, in her view employers somehow still lose in the long run: "A final constraint against the political participation of business in the reform effort is the availability of short-term, self-interested alternatives. If firms are able to engage in cost shifting, passing their health care costs on to their employees, they will be less likely to pursue a collective political solution. Cost shifting may help individual firms for the short term but will do little to limit the aggregate costs of health over the long term" (Martin 1993, 371). (A similar type of puzzlement at businesses' lack of involvement—in a political science analysis that first cites but then wholly ignores the inconvenient economic argument—can be found in Brown [1993].)

Other interpretations by political scientists of the eventual failure of business to support the Clinton plan continue to express puzzlement at why the businesses that employed the most workers were not more supportive. In a recent, well-received study, Thea Skocpol of Harvard explains the U.S. Chamber of Commerce's apparent change of heart as the result of pressure within the chamber by businesses that would be hurt by the mandate and price controls and "reverse lobbying" by conservative Republican groups. She points to the lobbying of employers who did not usually offer insurance, such as the grocers, that (in her view) made the chamber take a position contrary to the interests of the 67 percent of its members who did insure their employees and were therefore suffering from cost shifting from those employers who did not (Skocpol 1996). Price reduction by providers would accompany universal coverage and, even if prices and premiums were reduced, the gain would go to workers, not employers.

There were a few business managers who did not accept this macroeconomic view and instead took the economic approach. The most outspoken was Paul O'Neill, CEO of Alcoa, who noted that "my view is that health insurance premiums that are paid by the employer are part of the employee cost structure . . . In my view, it is wrong to say that health costs are a principal cause of noncompetitiveness. One could just as easily point to the cash portion of compensation and say that's too high . . . The money [for insurance premiums] really belongs to employees and would be provided in cash compensation if it weren't being provided in health insurance coverage" (interview by Iglehart 1991, 90). The interviewer was incredulous, however, and unwilling to believe that higher benefits costs would not somehow "cause" some problems for Alcoa. O'Neill did make the small concession that "you are certainly correct in saying that rising health care costs exert pressure on company/union negotiations over compensation increases" (Iglehart 1991, 80–81).

Will Medical Costs Bankrupt the Country?
The Little Rock, Arkansas, Meeting

Employer misperception and misrepresentation of the incidence of benefits costs played an important role in the debate on health reform. In a conference of economists and business leaders in Little Rock, Arkansas, a month before Clinton's inauguration, both the president-elect of the United States and the head of Ford Motor Company (acting as the chief business spokesperson) adopted economically incorrect views. President-elect Clinton reportedly delivered a table-pounding lecture to the assembled economists; his theme was that the problem with the economy was not the absence of the macroeconomic fiscal stimulus that they thought important but rather was that "rising health care costs are bankrupting the country." Probably what he meant was that the costs of federal health entitlements were causing difficulties for the federal budgeting (making the slip of mistaking the central government for the country).

However, this outburst may well have seemed safe and sensible after a long complaint the previous day from "Red" Polling, the chairman of Ford Motor Company, which recounted the auto industry's problem. At the request of the president-elect's staff, Polling presented what were intended to be key facts: "health care costs give Japanese auto makers an advantage over Ford of $500 per car. Ford spends as much on health care as it does on steel. Health care providers are our biggest suppliers" (Reuters 1992). (The implied argument—that high health benefits costs affect ability to compete with the Japanese—resurfaced later as part of the Clinton administration's case for its eventual reform plan, with the cost increased to $1,000 per car.)

Many of the themes already mentioned were also part of the Ford presentation in Little Rock. The affordability explanation surfaced. Cost containment, for example, was supported by Ford because "neither large nor small companies can afford to continue their health care. Purchasers, providers, and government must cooperate to develop a plan to contain these growing costs." Cost shifting was also an article of faith. "Costs should be spread fairly among all participants and cost shifting must be eliminated" (Reuters 1992). It seems reasonable to conclude that, after this episode, administrative officials would have felt confident that many large firms would be strongly supportive of the governmental health cost containment policies eventually embodied in the eventual bill, even without its government bailout on their retiree benefit costs.

The Little Rock meeting probably was the high-water mark of business support for the Clinton approach. The "cost of health care and its enormous drag on the economy, as well as the marked disparity between health care costs in America and other nations," were interpreted to be one of the priority issues by observers (Yates 1993). Even respected macro-economist and Clinton advisor Alan Sinai asserted unqualifiedly that "high health care costs are weighting down the economy" (Sinai 1992, 11). Since Clinton proposed to do something about health care costs, John Ong, CEO of B. F. Goodrich and head of the Business Roundtable, concluded that the Little Rock meeting "was really music to our ears" (Johnson and Broder 1996, 318).

A reporter concluded that "all the CEOs and civic leaders now return to their respective boards, usually composed of still more movers and shakers, and spread the gospel about Clinton. All now have a stake in seeing that they or the interests they represent aren't the cause of continued gridlock in Washington" (Yates 1993).

There were, however, some other hints from the Little Rock meeting that the president-elect was to have a hard time with the economic question of incidence. One problem was conceptual. During a press conference held in connection with the meeting, President-elect Clinton turned to the question of payroll taxes, which, like health benefits costs, are thought by economists to fall on workers. After noting the regressivity of our tax system, he said: "I mean, the Social Security tax is very unfair. It is unfair to small businesses because you pay it whether you make any money or not, just based on your employees. It's unfair to people with incomes below $51,000 a year as compared with those with incomes above $100,000 per year because of what the cap is on the Social Security tax." It is obvious that the president-elect had the message garbled. He was first assuming that the incidence was on the profits of the owners of small businesses but then was distressed that workers making six-figure incomes paid no additional tax. The incidence cannot be on *both* owners and workers, however.

The other problem was political. The Arkansas liaison for the NFIB (Alan White, "one of the nation's prominent self-made entrepreneurs") concluded that "Bill Clinton knows more about the value of small business than any other president" (Kaslow 1992). While recent presidential knowledge of small business does not set a very high standard, White did conclude that Clinton was attuned to the needs of small businesses, the most important of which was "fending off costly mandates that many entrepreneurs say threaten to put small firms out of business." Errors in judgment were mutual.

The Cost Shift

Not all citizens have the same amount paid for their health care. Medicare and (especially) Medicaid pay less than typical private insurers or self-insured business plans, and the uninsured typically do not pay all of their bills. For many businesspeople and politicians, two propositions (as already suggested at Little Rock) are obvious. (1) This underpayment causes a cost shift from those who do not pay in full to those who do; and (2) the cost shift harms employers of those employees with employer-paid insurance who do pay in full.

The economic approach has difficulty with both of these propositions. It argues first that cost shifting, to any appreciable extent, may well not occur in medical markets. For our purposes here, however, it would also argue that, even if such shifting did occur, it would primarily operate to reduce the money wages of insured workers, not the profits of firms that employ them.

A related cost shifting argument notes that firms not paying for insurance may employ members of families that include workers whose employers do pay, and pay more, for family coverage—or the family member may choose not to take the additional coverage if it is less attractive or more costly. Family members who are self employed in the market or engaged in household work also do not receive premium contributions from any employer and so are covered by family plans from the insured employee family member. Consulting firm studies put the total amount "shifted" to large firms paying for generous benefits at about 30 percent of those firms' health benefits costs (Lewin-VHI 1993).

As Michael Morrisey has pointed out, however, in a simple economic model there will be no cost shifting of any type from firms that do not insure family members to firms that do (Morrisey 1994). All that will happen is that money wages of the person obtaining the family coverage will fall by the amount of employer payment for family coverage. If the other employer is required to pay, money wages of the first family member will rise to offset this, leaving the employer no better off than before.

President Clinton certainly took the big business view supporting the fairness of employer mandates: "[A mandate] is the easiest for ordinary Americans to understand . . . Every employer should provide coverage, just as three quarters do now. Those that pay are picking up the tab for those who don't today. I don't think that's right."

The cost shift from employers who do not pay for insurance to those who do is often cited by business as a reason for action. Michael Becker of McDonnell Douglas: "We really cannot afford to stay where we are—where we are is not working. With every passing day, the incentives grow for companies to drop health benefits . . . A continuation of this trend through the 1990s could result in a massive cost shift to employers who do cover their employees" (Becker 1994). Henry Simmons: "We recognize that firms that provide coverage now are disadvantaged in their competition with those that do not—first, because they have taken on this additional premium responsibility and cost, and, second, because the premiums they pay help to cover the costs of emergency care for employees of the firms who do not provide coverage" (Simmons 1993, 4). This is known as "leveling the playing field of competition." Even economists were not unanimous about this one. Uwe Reinhardt: "It's a somewhat silly debate; a lot of companies live on the margin freeloading off companies that do offer health insurance" (Connolly 1993).

The treatment of employed but uninsured dependents also causes some economists to depart from the simple economic model. Deborah Chollet, economist at the Alpha Center in Washington, DC, looked at it this way: "The export of health insurance to dependent workers represents in effect a self-imposed tax on firms that offer benefits, collected as a subsidy to workers and their employers in firms that do not offer benefits" (Chollet 1994, 323). An economic consulting firm, after arguing for incidence of benefits costs on workers, still concluded: "Less well publicized is the 'cost shifting' that occurs among employers when an employee of one firm obtains insurance coverage as a dependent under a health plan of another employer" (Cromwell 1993, 38).

Journalists agree: "On the face of it, large employers and the managed care industry stood to reap the biggest rewards from comprehensive health reforms. A requirement that all employers help finance their workers' coverage would have protected large companies—which usually provide coverage for their workers—from essentially subsidizing the care of the uninsured . . . Reform's demise creates problems for big employers. They will continue to pay an indirect subsidy for the care of the uninsured. If Congress follows through on its threat to cut Medicare payments, employers will feel the pinch because doctors and hospitals are likely to pass along some of that cost to their paying customers" (Kosterlitz 1994).

The Exact Employer Share

Why the employer share mattered was less frequently discussed. The Chamber of Commerce originally appeared to think that the share was important when they still considered the Clinton plan to be viable: "The U.S. Chamber of Commerce has staked out the middle ground, saying that the mandate is acceptable, just too high. [It] advocates charging business half the cost. There has to be a multiparty requirement, a shared responsibility among employers, employees, and government" (Connolly 1993, 3124).

The economic argument, in contrast, is that the employer share simply does not matter, since the amount that will eventually fall on employees is independent of the initial assignment of responsibility. Later in the reform debate, the question of which proportion employers should pay was rarely discussed.

Taxing High Cost Plans

For some Republicans and conservative Democrats who opposed binding federal spending controls, a fallback position was to impose taxes on the premiums of insurance plans with unusually high premiums, as an attempt to discourage the offering of such plans and (in some contradiction) as a way of raising money to subsidize the uninsured.

The economic approach would have favored imposing this tax by eliminating the exclusion of the value of employer-paid premiums from the worker's federal income and payroll taxes. While some bills would have done things that way, others proposed to deny the employer the ability to deduct as a business expense, for corporation or individual income taxes, expenses for high cost plans.

Some politicians took the view that such a tax would be paid by business, not workers. Representative Cooper, who included such a provision in his bill (as did Senator Mitchell), said: "Today, if you look at our nation's third largest health care program, what is it? . . . It is a system of tax breaks that really have no name but are extraordinarily expensive . . . The average citizen is not hurt with our tax changes . . . We take all or most of the money that we are taking away from corporations, and what do we do with it? We turn it over to individuals, average citizens, average employers" (Cooper 1994).

The opponents of curtailing this tax preference would have none of the argument that the corporation would pay. They fully accepted a Lewin-VHI report that accepted the economist view that "over time, employees will bear the cost" (Lewin-VHI 1993, 5). They also noted that restricting the tax advantage would cause some employers and employees, especially those in small firms, to move away from employment-based insurance. The implication of the Lewin study, however, is that a small number of workers would receive wage increases to offset the cost of insurance by approximately the amount of the employer contribution.

Other Impacts

The economic viewpoint argues that anything that affects the cost of health insurance impacts workers, not their employers. An implication is that anything that "reforms" health insurance markets and lowers or raises the cost of insurance for particular firms will affect their workers' wages. For instance, suppose insurers are forbidden from raising the premiums of small employer groups in which a worker or dependent contracts an expensive condition. In competitive insurance markets, enforcement of such "community rating" will cause premiums to rise for other groups. The net effect will initially be to raise money wages of people who work in the affected small firm and reduce money wages for all other workers. Likewise, proposals to prohibit charging more to cover middle aged workers will initially raise their wages and reduce wages of younger workers. Over time, if all workers are equally productive, these differences will be diminished, but they will still remain to some extent.

Consider also a requirement that employers pay all or part of premiums for part time workers. Nearly half of the uninsured who are in families with a worker are in families where that worker is a part time worker (or self employed). Some employers may not be affected by such a requirement. Starbucks Corporation currently pays benefits for its part time workers, because "these employee benefits underpin Starbucks' legendary service, which in turn has attracted a fiercely loyal customer base. By nurturing his most important resource—his work force—Mr. Schultz [head] has reduced his employee turnover to two thirds the average in his industry" (Bollier 1994, 11). Why Starbucks used more generous benefits rather than higher wages to attract its workforce is not investigated.

Conclusion

At an intellectual level, many employers are willing to agree that their employees eventually pay for health benefits. But even those who accept the abstract proposition that incidence is eventually on workers have a hard time with decisions that depend on an application of that proposition. Consider, for instance, the question of employer attitude toward state taxation of health providers. A participant in the EBRI forum from a telecommunications company reported that his firm was opposed to such laws. Would such laws harm employers? Presumably taxing providers will raise the price of medical goods and services produced in the state—although how much prices will rise will depend both on whether funds are used to pay for the uninsured and on the supply and demand for products. If we assume that insured demand is nearly perfectly inelastic, however, almost all of the tax will be shifted forward. This will also mean that health insurance premiums, and costs in self-insured plans, will rise. They will rise by roughly the same percentage for all employers that pay for benefits. If benefits costs rise for the manager's firm and for all other firms in the state in which his or her firm hires labor, shouldn't the manager find that he or she can take the additional cost out of wages, maintain employment where it is, keep the price of the product stable, and earn the same profits as in the absence of the law?

If the answer to this is yes, why should the manager waste a minute of sleep, or spend a dollar of the company's resources, opposing taxes on health providers? If the impact of such costs would be on wage rates in the state, not on total compensation costs, why is it important to oppose them? Of course, explaining to workers why raises aren't higher might be painful (if workers would reasonably have expected more than they got), and higher money wages would lead to better morale. So, if asked for an opinion, the firm might properly respond that it would slightly prefer that no tax be levied (although it is not obvious that it would prefer the state to tax something else to raise the same amount of money, since the "something else tax" might depress workers' wages or owners' net incomes).

The bottom line is that such positions would make sense if the firm were the only employer paying the tax but would make almost no sense if the tax were paid by all employers. If there are employers whose employees are uninsured, and who therefore will not pay the tax, there might be a modest competitive advantage in favoring a more general tax. It really ought to be workers who should oppose this tax if it does more harm than good. Changing tax and compensation policy so that "employer payments" are appreciated by employees to be part of their money might help to get the political pressures to emanate from the right sources.

Why Are Wage Offsets Overlooked?

Large firms typically maintain departments of specialists to set cash compensation for different jobs, and small employers agonize over the raises they can offer their employees. So why is it apparently so difficult to build in trade-offs between wages and benefits costs that are appropriate, smooth, and explicit?

One answer is related to organization. Often in large firms compensation policy (as applied to cash wages) is set separately from benefits policy. Increases in benefits costs that might be more than offset by reductions in cash wages then become hard to plan, because the benefits department is blamed for an increase in costs, and the wage/compensation department is not aware that a new benefit would permit lower wages or lower raises in wages. If the benefit were to be put in place, wages would eventually (and mysteriously) fall, but the benefit cost increase may get vetoed before this good fortune can occur, and, even if it does, the benefits department will usually not be credited with it. The fundamental problem is that organizational separation makes coordination difficult.

Organizational noise may account for some of the perception, but there is obviously more involved here than just a failure to communicate. The notion that rising costs sometimes are harmless (or even helpful) is so counterintuitive that managers reasonably have a hard time with it. If the economic argument is right, it contradicts common sense.

The remainder of this book will be directed at this dilemma. How can (or can) managers' intuition be reconciled with profit-maximizing policies for their firms and rational social policy for the country as a whole? Are managers sometimes right (so that it becomes harder to convince them when they are wrong)? Is it just a matter of tension between a complex strategic move or "gut feeling" for taking the shortest distance between two points? Are managers incapable of understanding sophisticated economic arguments and economists incapable of explaining them in an unsophisticated manner? We will see that most of the time the simple economic argument is right—but not all of the time. We will also see that, when the economic argument is valid, with enough effort it can be made convincing and acceptable to managers and policymakers.

CHAPTER 3

The Economics of
Employer-Paid Benefits

In the previous chapter I gave a simple version of the standard economic analysis of employer mandates and showed that this analysis concluded that workers will pay for health insurance in the form of wage offsets. The portion of the cost of a mandate that falls on employers' profits is likely to be zero or small and is surely independent of the distribution of mandated employer and employee shares. In this chapter I will explore the economic analysis of employer mandates in considerably more detail. I have two objectives. First, I will elaborate on the simple theory, showing when its conclusions hold and when they need to be altered. Second, I will consider a series of objections and qualifications to the economic view. Many of these arose during the health reform debate and were raised by persons who held the business view. Some were not discussed but may be of greater importance. Many of the objections will be shown to be inconsistent with the economic view, but some of them propose modifications of the economic view that are theoretically valid and might be empirically true; in the next chapter, I will examine the validity, the evidence, and the ways in which additional evidence might be obtained.

Two Slightly Rigorous Restatements of the Economics of Employer Mandates, Followed by Two Intuitions

I first need to offer a version of the economic textbook analysis of employer mandates, but I will try to do so in a somewhat different fashion than is conventional. There are a number of excellent expositions of the economic supply-demand model that are available (e.g., Reinhardt and Krueger 1994). An apology for reintroducing readers to undergraduate textbook economics usually precedes them. Here I will try a different approach; I will not begin with what economists teach. I want, instead, to begin with propositions I think every manager would agree with and to try to build to the economic conclusion based on logic any manager would accept. I will not even subject readers to the ordeal of contemplating the diagrams economists favor.

I want to analyze the consequences of introducing an employer mandate in a competitive labor market. We first need definitions (in reverse order) of "market," "employer mandate," and "consequences." The relevant "market" here is the labor market. If we think, for purposes of illustration, of some generic type of labor such as clerical or sales labor, we might imagine that the size of the market is usually a metropolitan area. Clerical workers would probably be willing to work at a number of different firms within the metropolitan area in which they live but probably would not be willing to leave town for a job with better wages and benefits over a realistic range. For some other types of laborers, such as engineers and some other kinds of professionals, the market might be nationwide. It is unlikely that any important labor market spans national boundaries, so we will be able to think of nationwide health reforms as impacting the entire current U.S. labor force. The market is competitive if there are many different employers seeking labor, and there is no dominant large employer whose wage offer can affect what other employers do. Although employers do have to decide what they will pay, they generally make that decision by seeing what other employers in town are paying and then paying the same.

By an "employer mandate" I mean an obligation on employers to pay some proportion of wageworkers' health insurance premium for a specified insurance benefit, in addition to the market-determined level of cash wages. An employer mandate means that a worker is not allowed to take a job that pays compensation entirely as cash wages rather than one that includes payment toward health insurance. That is, an employer mandate (or any other regulation of job-related insurance) constrains or limits workers as much as it does employers; it makes illegal certain compensation arrangements that the seller of labor (the worker) and the buyer of labor (the employer) might have preferred to any other. An employer mandate does not necessarily require all workers to buy insurance. It leaves out those who make products for sale but who are self employed or independent contractors and those who produce services within the household (such as housekeeping and baby-sitting).

The main "consequences" of a mandate that I will explore will be the level of money wages, the level of employment (in terms both of persons working and of hours of work), and final product prices. Initially I will assume that all workers work full time for a fixed number of hours—so that the "quantity of labor" can be defined in terms of the number of persons hired for work. I will ignore possible effects of mandates on the level of other employment-related benefits.

We first consider a situation in which there initially is no employer mandate and in which no employer in the labor market pays for health insurance. A key assumption is that the total number of workers who will be offered employment by all of the employers in the market depends on the money wage that prevails in that market. The lower that wage, the more workers each firm will want to hire and therefore the more jobs in total that will be made available. Businesspeople know that the less costly workers are, the more of them it pays to hire—both because they are less costly than buying expensive capital and because low wages allow more products to be sold profitably at low prices—and so more workers will be needed to produce those products. This "market demand curve for labor" is therefore drawn by economists as having a downward slope, to reflect business managers' views that they will hire more workers if market wages fall.

Assume that wages in this market have settled at some level, such as W_0, and at this wage L_0 jobs are offered and workers hired. Assume also (this will be important for some of the modifications) that this combination of (W_0, L_0) represents an "equilibrium," in the sense that employers are not looking for more workers to fill unfilled jobs, there are no workers who want to work at the going wage who cannot find jobs, and there is no evidence of upward or downward pressure on real wages. (In real markets, there will usually be some transitional "job-changing" unemployment, but that is ignored here.) The key idea is that in equilibrium employers have no reason to change the money wages they offer, since raising wages causes their profits to fall and cutting wages causes a labor shortage to develop.

Now we assume that a mandate to pay $P toward a new health insurance premium for every worker is unexpectedly passed. The initial impact of this requirement is that each employer will now seek to hire fewer workers at any money wage than before. After all, if $P must be added to any money wage rate W, the number of workers sought at that wage will fall to that smaller number that would have been demanded had the wage been higher at $W + P$. Another way to say the same thing is to say that the wage the employer will pay falls by $P at every quantity of labor—since the employer will only hire that quantity if money wages fall by as much as the mandate added to labor costs.

With a money wage staying at the initial level of W_0, it is obvious that, after a costly benefit is added, employers will no longer be willing to hire L_0 workers. Through firings or attrition, jobs offered in the market will then fall. With unemployment rising, however, each employer will find that he or she no longer has to pay W_0 to attract as many workers as before. So it is obvious that money wages will start to fall; that is, that there will be some shifting of the cost of the mandate back onto workers in the form of lower wages. But how far will wages fall? Let us take a benchmark case first. Suppose that all of the L_0 workers who initially worked for wages continue to offer to work even though the money wage falls. (I explore possible reasons for this behavior later.) Wages will stop falling only when all workers get jobs again. For this to happen, the money wage has to fall by exactly P. If it falls by less than this, employers will not want to hire as many workers as before, and there will still be pressure on wages from unemployment. If it falls by more than P, the total cost of a worker will fall below W_0, and employers will be eager to hire more workers than there are available, thus bidding up wages. So the wage per worker must fall by just P.

Here is the punch line: *if* the number of workers seeking to work is not much affected by the offering of a mandate or a fall in money wages over the range of P, money wages will fall by approximately the "cost" to the employer of complying with the mandate. That is, in this case, literally 100 percent of the cost of the mandate falls on workers in the form of lower cash wages. In addition, if the money wage falls just enough to offset the cost of the new benefit, total employment will not change either. Employers will offer just as many jobs as before, and just as many workers will be hired.

So far this is just a hypothetical case, but it shows that what happens to wages depends on the responsiveness of workers to changes in compensation. How will workers in a labor market respond if they get part of their insurance premium paid but are offered lower money wages? One simple answer, which does not seem too far off the mark, is that they will keep working. If their alternatives are self-employment, at a much lower annual income, or withdrawal from the labor force (and spending their time in leisure or household production) at almost no money income, working as an employee may still be the best job in town, even if it pays a little less than before. Of course, *which* job a worker will take depends on wage differences across firms; workers are not inert. But the choice of not working as an employee, for most people, even those who currently work for firms that do not pay for part of group insurance premiums, is not an attractive one.

We need to be concerned about the content of the mandate and how workers value it only if some significant portion of workers would stop working when the real value of compensation changed. If the supply of labor is approximately fixed, valuation does not matter; the cost of a mandate falls on wages no matter what value (even zero or negative) workers might attach to the required benefit.

Whether someone will even think of responding to a mandated premium payment by switching to self-employment or (voluntary) unemployment depends on three things: how much income the person earns or receives in the alternative, what insurance policy or medical care financing arrangement he or she gets in the alternative, and how much he or she has to pay for it. Let us take the purest case of an exclusive employer mandate. This type of policy tells a worker: If you work for wages you must take a job with employer-paid premiums, but if you are self employed or unemployed you cannot obtain group insurance coverage. (You may be able to get charity care if you are poor enough, and you may be able to obtain individual insurance only at a significantly higher premium than is represented by the wage reduction.) The only way to get group insurance is to take a job. For a person who values the mandated insurance at just what it costs, there will be no reason to stop working if wages fall by P. You will get P less in money wages, but you will get a benefit worth $P,$ so, on balance, you are no worse off than before if you keep working. In addition, the other options have not changed, so they are no more attractive. This case is what economist Jonathan Gruber calls "full valued benefits," and it too has the property that wages fall by just the cost of the mandate, even *if* the supply of labor is highly responsive (Gruber 1994). That is, the result that wages fall by the amount of premium can occur *even if* workers are responsive to wages in the special case in which the benefit is just worth what it costs. In this case, however (and even more strongly in the case in which the benefit is worth *more* than P), it is likely that the employer will already have been providing coverage. So those cases in which a mandate would require a "full valued benefit" to be provided to most wage-responsive workers who previously had not received such a benefit should be rare.

The much more likely case is that in which the mandated group insurance benefit is perceived to be worth *less* than P to most workers. (If it were worth more, rational and informed employers would probably already be offering it.) If a mandate is imposed, in effect, the return from working falls by the difference between P and the (subjective monetary) value of the benefit to the person. That reduction in the value of compensation *might* persuade the worker to stop working as an employee, especially if the other options had initially been close in value to working. Are there many employees like this? There are surely not many for whom almost equally lucrative self-employment is an option. The other alternative is to stop working at market work, sacrifice whatever money income would have been earned and the contribution toward health insurance, but receive more leisure in exchange. There probably will not be many workers for whom this will be an attractive option either, but there may be some on the margin.

If the number of workers willing to work does fall when benefits rise and money wages start to fall, the money wage decline will obviously stop before it hits P. If money wages do not fall by P, compensation cost per worker will be higher after the mandate than before. This means two things. It means that total employment will fall. Employers will hire fewer workers (since they can find workers only by paying more for each worker and since the number of workers they wish to hire at higher compensation cost per worker will be less than they hired initially). Some workers will decide not to work, since the nonwork alternatives are more attractive. However, although employment will fall, unemployment will not rise, since the lost jobs offered exactly match the number of people who withdraw from wage work.

This increase in compensation expense per worker also means that output will fall and that firms' profits will be lower (since costs have risen). Whether the fall in profits can be partially offset by an increase in price in any industry depends on whether its products are sold in markets so competitive that demand falls to zero if prices rise a little above the initial level. This high degree of demand responsiveness might characterize internationally traded goods, but it need not characterize either products sold competitively in the local market or other products for which area firms have some market power. Of course, some of the cost of the mandate will result in lower wages even if prices can be increased, since they will never be increased enough to cover the full cost of the mandate.

Interestingly, the more competitive the final product market, the more of the cost of the mandate that will be shifted to workers. The reason is that, if employers sell products in markets in which they must accept a single (world) price, the only way they can cope with rising labor costs is by substituting capital for labor; they cannot hope to see product prices rise. Compared to otherwise similar employers who sell products for which prices could increase when the quantity they make decreases, these more competitive employers must cut employment more if labor costs rise, thus putting more pressure on wages. However, the larger the decline in labor hired, the larger the fall in profits. So in more competitive markets both workers and employers generally lose more from a mandate than in less competitive product markets—again, *if* the supply of labor responds to compensation. If, in contrast, almost no workers withdraw voluntarily from the labor market, the degree of competition in the product market makes no difference. Since workers will bear the full cost of the mandate, employers will have no reason to raise prices, even when they could. Even employers with seller market power will make larger profits by keeping their prices down and paying lower wages, since increased prices can only partially offset the effect on profits of higher wages, because output demanded drops when prices rise.

To sum up: if the willingness of workers to work is largely unaffected by decreases in money wages accompanying the provision of employer payment for health insurance, the cost of a mandate will fall almost entirely on workers in the form of lower wages, and employer profits will be unaffected, regardless of anything else. If the willingness of workers to work does decline when wages fall, and increased benefits do not have equal value, there can be a decline in employment and profits. How large this decline is will depend on the relative responsiveness of the demand and supply of labor to changes in compensation. If employers want to cut back jobs when labor costs rise, most of the cost will still fall on workers. Conversely, if workers choose to stop taking jobs but employers still find it profitable to hire almost as many workers at higher labor costs as at lower ones, then much of the cost will fall on employers in the form of lower profits.

There is one special, but very important, version of this general story that we should also look at before moving on to more cases. Suppose the mandate to pay for insurance applied only to *one* employer in the town and not to any others; the others would be free to pay cash wages only if they wished. Since the labor market is competitive, that employer cannot significantly reduce the value of compensation much and still expect to attract any workers; workers do have good alternatives to working for this firm (even if they have few good alternatives to wage work in general). So if workers do not value the extra insurance at its cost, any attempt by this employer to reduce money wages will cause almost all workers to quit: this firm's supply of labor is *very* responsive to the wages it pays, much more so than its demand is likely to be. This single employer therefore cannot shift any of the cost of the mandate to its workers. Either it reduces employment and takes a reduction in its profits, or, if it cannot raise its prices or substitute capital for labor, it may just have to go out of business.

These conclusions apply, of course, to anything that affects one specific firm's benefits costs—a mandate, a tax, a change in health insurance premiums, or an increase in medical costs. If benefits costs rise for your firm and your firm alone, and if you hire your labor in competitive labor markets, these changes will affect your profits, and you will not be able to shift them to your workers. It is important to note, however, that government-imposed employer payment mandates are not like this "why me?" or one-employer case; they apply to all employers, especially those with whom you compete in the local labor markets. Thus they will have different impacts on the willingness of workers to work for your firm and therefore different impacts on who ends up paying the additional cost. I will return to this crucial distinction between changes in one firm's costs and changes in all (or many) firms' costs subsequently.

The fundamental story then is this: if we look at employers' decisions about how many workers to hire in the same way as employers do, and if we look at workers' decisions to work in a realistic way, we must conclude that the only possible outcome of a mandate on all employers is that (except for minimum wage workers) money wages will fall by nearly the cost of the mandate. This conclusion does not come from a set of assumptions about facts or behavior that is peculiar to academic economists: instead, it is based on exactly the kinds of behavior managers rationally say they would engage in.

A Universal Mandate instead of an Employer Mandate

The preceding section analyzed the case of a true and unique employer mandate: only employees were required to obtain insurance; the self-employed and the nonemployed were not. Does it matter if the requirement to obtain and pay for insurance is extended to the self-employed and the nonemployed? A simple answer is that, if the number of people willing to work for wages is approximately constant, such a change would not matter much—since these other alternatives must not be attractive options to workers. If, however, wageworkers might be willing to stop wage work if money wages fall, that would imply that the two other alternatives—and they do exhaust the possibilities—are relevant for them. Then we can say that the degree of responsiveness of employees to a decrease in money wage combined with mandated purchase of insurance is smaller the more similar is the obligation to pay and obtain insurance that they would bear if they switched to one of these two other options.

For instance, suppose government mandated that all citizens obtain insurance and pay for it themselves, regardless of whether they were employees, self employed, or not employed. That is, if all citizens were required to sacrifice P and get insurance in return, regardless of their employment status, there would be no reason for workers to stop working for wages when their wages fell by P and they received employer-paid insurance instead; they would experience the same cost of P and get the same insurance if they stopped working or went into business for themselves.

What about the other extreme, in which insurance for those who do not work or who are self employed is free, or heavily subsidized, possibly in a way that is related to income? Creating such an option would make the leisure (or household work) option more attractive, cause more people to switch to self-employment, and cause larger impacts on firm employment and profits. What is important to note in this case, in contrast to the universal mandate just mentioned, is that *all* of the impact on work effort and profit comes from the structure of subsidies that rises as wage incomes fall. The impact of such a program on employers is virtually identical to one that explicitly proposed subsidies and taxes of a similar pattern, without a health insurance mandate. That is, the impact on behavior in this case comes from the work disincentive effect of uneven subsidies, not from the type of benefit being subsidized.

Extension to Other Impacts on Benefits Costs

Now we come to an important point. *These observations about impacts of mandates for employer payment on wages and profits hold for all external changes in employer benefits costs, whether imposed by government or by the market, that affect all firms.* Suppose, for example, that health care costs suddenly and miraculously fell by an equal amount for all insureds, and suppose that insurance premiums employers were charged followed suit. The initial impact of such a change would be to cause employers to want to expand hiring, since the compensation cost per employee would have fallen. But if all employers try to hire more workers, and if the number of people willing to work is given, the effect of this seller's market will be to force up money wages. If indeed the supply of labor does not change much when wages rise, the increase in wages will only stop when wages have risen just enough to offset the fall in benefits costs. Any successful market-wide cost-containment effort will therefore not be good for business, but it will be good for workers because it will set the stage for them to get larger raises than would otherwise be the case.

The converse is also true: increases in health care costs that are roughly equal across the board do not affect profits or employment, but do depress worker wages, as long as the number of persons willing to work for wages is roughly fixed. If the supply of labor does respond more strongly to changes in real compensation, there will be some sharing of costs and benefits with employers. Whether health care costs rise, fall, or stay the same, employers and stockholders should be equally happy; of all the things they have to worry about, market-wide changes in health benefits costs should, according to economics, be at the bottom of the list.

Acceptability of the Economic Model

Part of the purpose of this book is to describe in more detail how employers respond to various versions of this economic argument about employment benefit costs. Economists have, however, already offered some explanations of why their messages are misunderstood.

The most common explanation for employer misunderstanding is based on what Reinhardt and Krueger call a *fallacy of composition* (Reinhardt and Krueger 1994). I have already noted that, if either a mandate of less than full value or an increase in quality-constant costs were to be experienced by just one employer, those external forces could affect both labor costs and profits at that firm. The employer could not cut money wages to offset the high benefits costs, because then all employees would quit. Instead, he or she rationally maintains wages and fires some workers. The employer raises prices if possible and goes out of business if this is not possible. The fallacy of composition is that this behavior, rational for a single employer, is not rational when all employers are equally affected by a mandate or by a market-wide change in the costs of health benefits. When all employers are affected by the same influences, the strategy of cutting money wages should not cause any employees to quit in order to obtain better wages, since all other employers will also be reducing wages. In contrast to the single firm case, employment, profits, and prices can be maintained at the prechange level.

The decline (relative to the no-intervention level) in the money wages employers must offer will, for employers without foresight or analytical capability, eventually seem like fortuitous good fortune. They might even say, after the fact: "Had I known wages were going to fall, I wouldn't have fired people and raised my prices." The mistake of the myopic employer is to react passively to changes that ought to have been predictable, either with economic analysis or common sense, and that would have called for more than a passive reaction. Being myopic has a cost, since profits are lost during the period when employment and output are reduced.

One reason (though not an excuse) for such behavior is that employers, especially small ones, have many more pressing business decisions than predicting the course of health benefits costs. This reasoning does imply, however, that those employers who put some resources into foresight, or into hiring benefits consultants or brokers with foresight, will avoid self-harmful behavior. The problem for the employer or consultant is that of distinguishing between those changes in benefits costs that are market wide and those that only apply to this business. Likewise employees faced with a wage cut might foolishly quit, not recognizing that all the good job offers elsewhere will dry up if all employers are subject to the same mandates. This kind of economic illusion is similar to the money wage illusion that macroeconomists use to explain why wages are sticky downward in the absence of inflation, and it may likewise account for a sluggishness or damage in labor market response to misperceived benefit cost changes.

The paradox here, as in the macroeconomic case, is that if these harmful behaviors keep happening time after time, why does the competitive market not induce employers and employees to make the effort to develop foresight, and why do not middlemen emerge who can successfully sell foresight? One answer is that public policy may be much less predictable than more "natural" market changes (like growth in the real cost of medical care, whose annual rate actually has been fairly stable over time after adjusting for overall inflation). This implies that providing some warning of what is going to happen, some time to adjust, and some information on how to cope might be good public policy strategies.

For purposes of the discussion here, however, the sources of and solutions to myopic or fallacious behavior on the parts of employers and employees will be one of the key questions we will wish to explore.

Some Hypotheses

Suppose health benefit costs for all the employers in a labor market change. When are employers more likely to recognize this trend and respond in the economically optimal fashion, by cutting wages, rather than by the individually rational but economically nonoptimal strategies of raising prices and/or reducing employment?

One obvious answer is as follows: in those circumstances in which it is more difficult to recognize that the change is market wide. This suggests, among other things, that wage adjustments to a consistent, long term trend should be more likely to occur than wage adjustments to unexpected changes in trend. Concretely, a politically imposed change, such as a mandate, will have a smaller potential impact on profit, and therefore should be less strongly opposed, if it is announced well in advance of its effective date than if it is imposed unexpectedly to be effective immediately. Market-determined changes in benefits costs that are consistent or predictable likewise should be fully incorporated into wages, whereas unexpected shifts (either increases or decreases) should not.

In both cases, employers would be expected to do two things. First, they would be expected to expend resources to try to identify or forecast economic and political changes. This effect is symmetrical, whether those changes represent cost increases or cost decreases. Second, they will adjust to unexpected benefit cost increases by trying to delay, resist, or modify the increase and its impact on them. For unexpected decreases in cost or the rate of cost growth, however, the results will obviously not be symmetrical. Employers will accept whatever benefit cost savings they are given but will try to delay, resist, or modify the money wage increase that would eventually be anticipated to occur.

In addition, some market-wide changes may be easier to predict or to detect once they have occurred. Contrast, for example, adjustment to the imposition of a clear mandate with adjustment to the increase in insurance costs associated with gradual diffusion of unexpected technical change. Some firms will be more efficient at anticipating such changes. Other things equal, larger firms probably experience economics of scale in forecasting and so may be more likely to adjust wages than smaller firms   and be less likely to resist or complain about increases. That is, part of the objection of small business to a mandate may relate to its comparatively greater difficulty in anticipating charges in benefits costs, relative to larger firms. Even an unexpected benefit cost decrease can hurt a small firm if it does not raise its money wages and so loses skilled workers to those (larger) firms better able to forecast or detect market-wide changes. Rather than having to keep an eye on yet another potential disaster, owners of small business might prefer to forgo offering health benefits.

Summing up and Going Deeper:
Why Changing Employer Health Insurance Costs
Do Not Affect Firm Profits or Sales

The economic story of the preceding sections has a strong logic to it, but is it really right? How much does it depend on assumptions of rationality and foresight, which sometimes themselves seem to be in fixed and limited supply? Does it require busy employers to become little economists?

Suppose that health insurance costs for all employers providing health insurance as a fringe benefit in a given labor market fall. Suppose also that the labor market is competitive, with many similar employers seeking to hire many similar workers; all workers attach similar positive values to fringe benefits, and all firms have similar costs of health insurance. Will this fall in the cost of health insurance help employers, in the sense that their profits will be increased or their sales volume will rise, or will its benefits really fall to workers, as economics says?

Each firm obviously must determine in some fashion the total compensation costs (wages plus fringes) that it offers workers. Since all workers are similar, initially both wages and benefits are also similar. That level of total labor cost permits (or encourages) the hiring of the current number of workers.

The story in the previous discussion was simple: suppose that each employer raises the money wage by just enough to offset the drop in fringe benefits costs. Total labor cost remains the same, no workers seek to change jobs, and profits and prices remain the same. This change results in a new and stable labor market equilibrium, which can be sustained. No firm will want to raise or lower money wages or to hire or fire workers.

Suppose, in contrast, all firms had maintained their initial (lower) money wage. Then total labor costs per worker would fall, and all firms would seek to hire more workers. Thus the lower compensation cost associated with lower benefits costs and old money wages cannot be an equilibrium. Instead, the attempts of each firm to hire more workers will bid up money wages until the increase in money wages just equals the decline in the cost of benefits.

What if employers do not automatically take such a farsighted "total compensation" approach? What if, instead, they decide what level of money wages to set based simply on what they have to offer in the labor market to attract the number of workers they wish, and they decide how many workers to hire by comparing the total cost (wages plus benefits) of a new worker with the additional revenue associated with hiring that worker. No foresight and, indeed, little rationality are assumed here—nothing beyond the fundamentally good idea of not paying more than you have to.

The decline in total labor costs will prompt the firm to seek to hire more workers. If the supply of labor is not perfectly elastic, this decision will eventually cause wages to be bid up. How high wages will rise depends on the responsiveness of both labor supply and worker demand to price. If the supply of labor is not very responsive to money wages, those wages will rise until the total labor cost returns to its initial level. The key point is that this process of groping toward the equilibrium described earlier will occur even if firms do not think about total labor costs or what other firms are doing.

Contrast these stories with what would happen if a single firm experienced a reduction in its health benefits costs. If it changed nothing, its profits would rise. But it would want to hire more workers and cut its product price if it needed to do so in order to sell more output and make even higher profits.

Now here is the puzzle. Why is there a difference between these two scenarios? Why, really, is the single firm story so different from the market-wide story? An analogy may help. Suppose a new nonpatentable technology is discovered and publicized that permits every firm producing some product to improve the quality of its product without increasing its cost. Will this increase firm profits? The answer is negative, since competition will induce (or compel) all firms to offer the higher quality product at the same price as was charged initially. In contrast, if only one firm knew about the technology, and could keep it secret (or patent it), that firm could increase its profits and its sales.

This example makes the important point: the reason lower health benefits costs do not add to employer profits is because of competition among employers in the labor market. In the case of improved product quality, all of the benefit ends up going to customers. In the case of lower health benefits costs, all of the benefit ends up being captured by workers.

Possible Exceptions to the General Argument: Introduction

Now I want to modify this simple example to deal with nine possible bases for exceptions to the general conclusion that the incidence of benefits cost is not on profits.

1. How long does it take for money wages to adjust to benefit cost changes?
2. What if increased benefits and increased costs are required for some but not all employers because some employers were already doing what the mandate requires?
3. If the firm has market power in the product market, does that matter? When (if ever) can there be forward shifting of fringe benefits costs?
4. Within-firm incidence
5. Uninsured employed by large firms versus uninsured employed by small firms
6. Two-worker families and multiple employers
7. Cost shifting and mismatching
8. Risk variation
9. Incidence with a tax subsidy

Time to Adjust

The empirical question of the precise speed of adjustment of money wages to higher fringe benefits costs is unknown. What firms typically do if they cannot adjust money wages, or do not think of doing so, is also unknown. Here we consider in more detail how a firm might react to an unexpected mandate to pay more for health insurance for its workers.

One possible response is to change nothing except to pay more for benefits and let profits suffer. That would not be the action that would preserve profits, but it would be least harmful to workers. A second possible action, apparently the one most natural to business managers, is to react to the additional labor cost by leaving money wages untouched but then discharging (or failing to hire) workers who are now too expensive relative to the revenue or output they generate. If the manager was entirely unfamiliar with the economics of compensation as outlined in the preceding discussion, this would be the course of action that would cushion the negative impact of an increase in compensation cost on profits. In addition, if all employers reacted this way, and if demand for those employers' products (the market demand, not the firm level demand) was not perfectly elastic, the equilibrium price would rise as output was cut, further cushioning (but not eliminating) the profit impact. (We know that prices can never rise enough to make it profitable to hire as many workers as before, since if such a large number of workers was hired output would return to its previous level and then could only be sold at a lower price.) As Herbert Stein has noted, there would be a further step: "The process of shifting would involve enough squeeze on profits to force enough layoffs to make workers accept a reduction of their cash wages" (Stein 1994). Once this reduction did occur, some (and possibly almost all) of the discharged workers would be hired back, since the money wage would fall by enough to return total compensation cost per worker to where it started.

Is reacting in this myopic and atomistic fashion, waiting for the labor market to work to force real wages down or cut raises, the best strategy for any employer? The answer is negative. Suppose you as an employer thought that all other employers with which you compete in the labor market were going to follow the myopic strategy. You contemplate trying something different: at the next pay period, you tell workers that you will now be offering them health insurance, but, as a result, you will have to cut their money wages or reduce their raises by enough to pay for it. Will your workers quit? They will not (rationally) quit to go to work for another employer, since all other employers will be firing, not hiring. If they do not value health insurance, they may quit to exit the labor force, but this response should be small and, in any case, could be prevented if you cut money wages less than the full amount of the extra cost. On balance, then, the best thing for you to do would be to cut money wages as gracefully but as quickly as you could.

Is there any reason not to follow this strategy? One reason sometimes suggested is that there may be negative effects on morale. If you have to fire 10 percent of your workforce, you only anger the 10 percent who are fired—and they are gone. If you cut money wages, you potentially anger all workers. "Anger" has no obvious place in the theory of labor economics, and it is difficult to know how to analyze it. If you told your workers that you could respond to the governmental mandated benefit either by randomly selecting some of them to fire or by cutting everyone's wages, risk averse workers would presumably prefer the latter strategy. If you had identified beforehand the workers most likely to be fired if times get tough, you might not have this problem. Either way, to avoid worker anger you would be paying a price in terms of lost profits. Could the anger have enough of a negative effect on morale to cause problems? If a firm had high labor turnover anyway, for other causes, the "cut wages" strategy would make the most sense, since angry workers could be replaced.

Internal Labor Markets and the Speed of Money Wage Adjustment to a Mandated Benefit

In this section I provide a more detailed discussion of how an employer should adjust wages in the case of a mandated employer contribution. Consider a firm not currently offering health insurance to workers whose total compensation is substantially above the minimum wage. Let a mandate be imposed. Why might employers not make immediate downward adjustment in money wages in response to a mandated fringe benefit? And if they make no adjustment in money wages, do they adjust by reducing employment?

One obvious reason why money wages may be slow to adjust is the presence of administrative or contractual rigidities. Most obviously, if employees have multiyear contracts that specify the rate of growth in cash compensation, these rates need not be affected by mandates—unless the employer can use the mandate as an excuse to reopen negotiations. Even if there is no binding contract, it may prove difficult to change wages quickly, because of compensation and personnel policies. (However, this is usually not a problem in a less bureaucratic small firm.)

A less obvious reason for failure to cut immediately is the possibility that an internal labor market in the firm may result in spreading compensation changes over time. Assume that the mandate is unforeseen, and assume that a firm's current workers have some firm-specific human capital, some skills that they developed over time and that are of special value in their current job. Assume that they expect to stay in this job at this firm for many years. We know that the present discounted value of the mandated employer payment must be subtracted from the present discounted value of future money wages from this firm, but we do not know what the optimal timing will be. It is, however, unlikely that the optimal timing will involve a year-by-year pay-as-you-go reduction, for two reasons. First, the uncertain nature of the mandate means that employees will probably want to spread the "shock" of a reduction in their take-home pay over more than one year. Second, workers may wish to distribute the cost over their working life. All of this is tempered, however, by the possibility that an employee may leave a particular firm—then earlier overpayments in anticipation of future offsets may be wasted.

One implication is that the incidence should be more likely to equal the imposed cost when the type of job is one in which switching costs are low; conversely, in jobs with more of a career aspect the employer may be willing to shift the cost of the mandated benefits to the future. It also implies that the incidence should be stronger on workers near their lifetime earnings peak. The other implication is that, for a given level of incidence, fewer workers should be fired in firms with high turnover costs. So we have a trade-off. In firms with low turnover costs, wages should fall by less, but layoffs are more likely if wages do not fall.

Slightly more formally, both the extent of overall wage adjustments and their distribution over time must be a function of the general policy each firm has adopted toward unexpected changes in the cost of compensation relative to productivity. A health insurance mandate is just one of a number of things that could happen unexpectedly to change the firm's total compensation cost, and there are even more things that could happen to affect the money value of the output the firm produces. Different firms have adopted different policies about the extent to which they share such risks with workers and, if they do, how those risks are shared—whether by changes in wages, employment, hours, or working conditions. The policy of absorbing or spreading some of the risk must be known to workers in advance.

If the employer does absorb the risk, that benefit is itself presumably offset by a lower overall level of cash wages. After wages are fixed, however, events like a costly mandate do adversely affect profits (just as a favorable event would positively affect profits). So in this sense one can say two slightly contradictory things: an unexpected mandate will adversely affect profits in some firms. But in those firms it will not adversely affect expected profits.

Things are quite different if the mandate was anticipated. If it literally comes as no surprise, past and present levels of money wages will already have been adjusted to take it into account. The more interesting case is one in which the announcement or discovery of the possibility of a mandate is unexpected, but the effective date is far enough in the future that it will not be a surprise when it occurs. Such a situation approximately describes the Clinton plan, which was not due to become fully effective for several years after it passed, and which was discussed for nearly two years before Congress voted on anything. (It never did vote on the Clinton plan as such.)

Some firms with very risk averse, very long term employees may still choose to absorb some of the cost of the mandate. But it is likely that most firms will adjust wages so that profits absorb little or none of the cost of the mandate, although there may be some smoothing of the process over time.

The general conclusion with regard either to an anticipated mandatory payment or an expected change in insurance premiums is that workers will bear the cost in terms of lower wages. Far from being irrelevant, the long run actually is the period in which changes that are permanent will occur. Temporary unexpected fluctuations (for instance, the current slowdown in employer premium cost growth) may give firms positive or negative windfalls. But once the changes become stable enough to be noticed, they will be manifested in wages (and not in profits or employment).

Cross-Industry and Cross-Firm Effects from an Employer Mandate for Universal Coverage

The preceding stories have all been based on the simplifying assumption that the market can be described by considering the situation of a typical firm and a typical set of workers (who value insurance at less than its cost). In this case, mandates and benefits costs increases affect all firms and workers in the same fashion. It is quite obvious, however, that both workers and firms are different; after all, even in the absence of any mandate whatsoever and (to judge from the experiences of other countries that do not offer tax breaks) without any tax subsidy whatsoever, some employers would still find it desirable to offer employer-paid group health insurance. The two major differences I will discuss are differences across workers and families in the value they attach to insurance and differences across firms in the pure administrative cost of insurance. Either one of these kinds of variations could lead to the result that some persons get insurance and others do not, but they are probably both operative in reality.

Variation in the values families attach to insurance can come from a number of sources. Families may differ in their attitudes toward taking risk, taking the chance of incurring high bills that will have to be paid without insurance coverage; this kind of variation in risk aversion is the usual explanation of why some people buy all kinds of insurance and others do not. We also suspect, for reasons to be discussed in the following, that the availability of less attractive but free care to low income uninsured people—in the form of Medicaid, public hospitals, or charity care by private providers—causes some to prefer money wages to insurance. Put more bluntly, lower income people will rationally be more likely to choose to save their money for important things they need more than health insurance and to seek charity care should they get sick. Coverage available through a spouse will also affect the value of insurance at a given job. Finally, people value insurance at a given premium more if they are more likely to make claims against it, if they are higher risks. What is less obvious is whether people at higher risk who are actually charged the higher premiums associated with that level of risk are more or less likely to buy insurance than people at lower risk facing lower premiums. This question is also one I will discuss in more detail later. All of these reasons can lead to different insurance decisions by employees or employee groups facing the same price for insurance, but I will concentrate on the effect of pure variation in taste in this section.

Variation in the *cost* of insurance to groups of identical risk within any market primarily arises because the administrative cost of insurance varies with group size and with the employer's search and bargaining effort. Some costs of administering and (especially) of selling and billing for insurance are largely fixed and so are lower per insured unit in larger groups. We know that small groups can combine together to get some reductions in costs and premiums, but, for present purposes, we need only assume that the loading rises to some extent as group size falls. Across local markets, the degree of competition among insurers also varies, leading to different profit rates and therefore different prices for the same insurance. This variation in prices is thought (without a great deal of supporting evidence) to be larger for managed care–type insurance than for indemnity insurance; it is thought to be small for conventional indemnity insurance because the market for that insurance is national, highly competitive, and constrained by the availability of self-insurance as an alternative.

Now let us consider some simple cases to see what happens when health care costs increase or a mandate is imposed in different situations. Suppose that all workers are of equal productivity and attach equal values to health insurance, but firms of varying sizes face different premiums for the same insurance policy, because either the administrative cost or profit margin on insurance differs by firm size. The value of insurance to workers is assumed to be less than the premium for insurance in groups smaller than some critical size G^*. In the absence of any government intervention, we would then expect workers in groups of size larger than G^* to get insurance and workers in groups smaller than G^* to go without. (We also assume that individual insurance is more expensive than group insurance, so that workers who do not get group insurance also do not buy it individually.) In order to attract and retain workers, firms that do not offer insurance would need to offer higher money wages in an amount equal to the value to workers of the insurance. Firms of size G^* are indifferent between paying those higher wages or paying for the insurance.

With the model so far, one possible (though ridiculous) outcome would be for all production of all goods and services to occur in one giant group—since the largest possible group minimizes the cost of insurance and would always be able to undercut any smaller group. We therefore need to assume that, beyond some optimal size, average production costs rise as group size increases, so that these "diseconomies of scale" in producing products offset the economies of scale every group would experience in its insurance purchasing. To yield the result that there are groups of different sizes coexisting, we assume that this optimal size is different for firms in different industries—for instance, that it is larger for machine tool firms than for beauty shops. Such variation in optimal firm size across different industries will be important in predicting the effect of insurance mandates on relative prices of different products.

Assume that the insurance policy offered and the employer contribution are the same among all firms that do offer insurance. In the absence of a mandate, all firms larger than G^* will offer insurance and will have to pay the same wage rate. Firms smaller than G^* will have to offer uniformly higher wages. The difference in wages between firms that do not offer insurance and those that do will equal the value of insurance. Firms larger than G^* will therefore have lower marginal compensation costs per worker than firms of size G^* or smaller, with the cost being lower in larger firms within the set of firms offering insurance. In contrast, firms smaller than G^* will all pay the same wage (and therefore have the same value of marginal product produced by workers).

Now suppose a mandate to offer and pay for the initial insurance package is imposed on *all* firms. In the first round, firms smaller than G^* will see their compensation cost increase by the difference between the firm's cost of coverage and the value of coverage. For example, suppose initially that the firms that offered coverage paid $10,000 in wages and firms that did not offer coverage paid $11,000—implying that the value of coverage was $1,000. A (small) firm whose cost of coverage was $1,200 would find its net compensation cost would increase by $200, while an even smaller firm with a $1,800 cost of coverage would find that its net compensation cost would rise by $800.

These smaller firms would start to lay off workers, and there would then be downward pressure on money wages at *all* firms—those affected by the mandate and those unaffected by the mandate. Employment levels would be rearranged across firms, rising at the larger firms that had originally offered insurance and falling at the smaller firms affected by the mandate. How far would wages have to fall at such firms to restore equilibrium?

The answer to this question (regrettably) turns out to be complicated, since it depends on the elasticity of demand for labor in each of the firms in each of the industries, which depends in turn on the possibilities for substituting labor for capital and the demand elasticity of the final product. What we can say in this case is that the final wage levels in the larger firms initially providing insurance—who will have to absorb some of the discharged labor—will be reduced, and that wages in the mandated firms will also be reduced, but by an amount that is generally greater than the initial differential (i.e., more than $1,000 in the previous example) but which could be greater or less than the additional premium cost the particular firm bears. All smaller firms affected by the mandate will find that their compensation costs will rise, however, so that employment in such smaller firms will decline, profits will fall, and (to the extent that final product markets permit) prices of products in industries where small firms are common will rise. In contrast, larger firms and industries unaffected by the mandate will find rising employment, rising profits, and falling prices. In aggregate or on average, we cannot say how this type of mandate will affect total profits or overall prices, but we can say that there will be relative price or "excise tax" effects.

In this case—in contrast to the uniform mandate discussed earlier—*some owners do lose profits* (and therefore lose wealth if their capital is not perfectly mobile) *from an anticipated mandate,* while others gain. Workers as a whole are made worse off; the workers subject to a mandate get insurance that is worth less to them than the wages they will have had to sacrifice, while workers in the firms initially offering coverage will just get paid less. The reason, of course, is that workers bear much of the cost of the tax or wedge between the value of coverage and the cost of coverage that is imposed by the mandate.

Things are somewhat different (and a little less complex) when we consider an alternative story based on the assumption that workers have different tastes for health insurance but all firms have (or could have) the same cost for a given policy. In this scenario, workers with weak tastes for insurance will work in firms that do not offer coverage. If the per worker cost of coverage is C, those workers who value the insurance as worth less to them than C will work in firms that do not provide coverage but that pay wages that are $$C$ greater than wages in firms that do offer coverage. Suppose there were some workers who attach no value at all to insurance. One might wonder why they would be paid more (than workers who value and therefore get insurance). Wouldn't they be willing to work for almost the same money wage as those workers who do get insurance? The answer is that the level of money wages in the uninsured sector is determined by the values of the *marginal* worker, who (in this case) is the one just indifferent between a job that pays W and offers insurance worth (almost, but not quite) $$C$ to him or her and one that pays a wage of $(W + C)$ but offers no insurance. Let a mandate be imposed. All firms will now have to pay for coverage, so wages in the newly mandated firms will fall by the cost of coverage if the supply of workers is perfectly inelastic.

As in the previous case, however, the requirement to take a job with coverage imposes a tax on workers who value insurance at less than C. If some of these workers do respond by withdrawing from work for wages (supply not perfectly inelastic), then there will be fewer workers seeking work, and money wages *for all firms* will settle at a value that is less than $C below the initial wages in the firms affected by the mandate. As Danzon (1989) notes, in this case the workers with initial coverage may benefit from a mandate because their money wages will increase. They would benefit, at the expense of those affected by the mandate, even if there was no cost shifting across insurance plans as such. Conversely, their employers who were ostensibly unaffected by the mandate (originally offering insurance) in this case may actually lose profits, since they experience a rising cost of labor, as do employers affected by the mandate. These changes are the consequence of a tax that imposes costs greater than its benefit.

The two cases analyzed therefore lead to different patterns of effects. Workers in firms who already had obtained coverage lose in the first case but may gain in the second. Employers affected by the mandate always lose or are at best no better off, but employers unaffected by the mandate (whose competition is, nevertheless, affected by the mandate) may gain (because the mandate imposes higher costs [a tax] on their competitors in the labor market). One of the issues I will address subsequently is which of these cases (if either one) employers seemed to have in mind when they took positions on the desirability or effects of mandated employer coverage. Of course, the Clinton plan tried mightily (through the device of mandatory health alliances and subsidies to small firms) to eliminate differences in the cost of coverage—but did allow large firms to continue to self-insure.

Interestingly, if the Clinton proposal had been successful in eliminating all cost differences, and if most of the variation across firms in offering of coverage had been caused by these cost differences in group insurance, small business should not rationally have objected to the mandate. However, it was rational for those small businesses if they felt that they would still be at a cost disadvantage and the subsidy (intended, in any event, to be temporary) was less than this cost disadvantage. The general conclusion, however, is that the cost of a mandate to a small business was not, as owners of those businesses and their lobbyists appeared to believe, the full employer contribution. Instead, at most it equaled the *difference* between the premium they would pay for a basic policy and what that policy would have cost a larger employer.

Market Power in the Product Market

If the supply of labor is perfectly inelastic, and if the demand for a firm's or industry's product is not, then the implication is perfectly clear: all of the cost of fringe benefits, whether mandated or not, whether valued or not, will fall on worker wages. It will not matter how competitive the final product market is for some or all firms; the only thing that matters is the willingness of workers to remain in the local labor market as benefits costs rise and wages fall. However, if labor supply is somewhat responsive to the real wage—if some persons do choose to stop seeking work—then the extent of forward shifting to consumers for any industry varies inversely with the industry demand elasticity. At the most extreme, if demand for an industry's product is perfectly elastic (say, because it is a small part of a highly competitive world market), then there can be no forward shifting, regardless of supply responsiveness. If the industry is highly competitive, so that *firm* demand curves are perfectly elastic, but the industry demand curve is not, then the comparison of supply and demand elasticities discussed in the preceding will apply. But what if the industry is not perfectly competitive but firm level demand curves are somewhat elastic? What happens then?

The key question here is what percentage of an input price increase a monopolist will pass on. The answer is that, since price for a monopolist equals some multiple greater than one of marginal cost, and since an increase in wage rates increases marginal cost, it is possible that prices will increase by more than the increase in labor cost per unit and possibly (if the firm level demand elasticity is close to unity) by more than the increase in fringe benefits cost. This would require rather highly elastic labor supply and rather less elastic firm demand—but it could happen that prices would rise by more than the increase in premiums. Of course, the firm's profit would still fall, but some of that fall would be cushioned.

The message then is that the extent of forward shifting depends on labor supply elasticity, industry demand elasticity, and firm demand elasticity. For several combinations of extreme values of these, there can be no forward shifting. But some excise tax shifting is possible and will generally be greater the more market power (bigger markup) the firm has. This of course requires benefits cost to be part of the *marginal* cost to the firm.

Within-Firm Incidence

Different workers will have different costs for their health benefits. Expected annual benefits under a given health insurance policy differ by age, family size, gender, family composition, and health risk. At least the first four of these can easily be known to the firm. Do high health cost workers bear higher wage offsets than low health cost workers?

To the extent that firms administer wages through wage schedules that do not take account of an employee's specific fringe benefit costs, the answer must be negative in the short run; a worker will not be paid less just because his or her benefits cost more. Classes of workers may, however, bear the incidence. For instance, if foremen are mostly middle aged males, their money wages will be reduced by the larger cost of their insurance coverage, compared to the wages of predominantly younger stock clerks.

There is some evidence in support of the proposition that there is variation in incidence across workers within a firm. Gruber (1994) found that mandated maternity benefits reduced the wages of female employees and males buying family coverage more than those of males buying worker-only coverage. Sheiner (1995) found that older workers' wages were more affected by higher health insurance costs than younger workers' wages.

On the other hand, it is hard to believe that, in general, within-firm incidence is perfectly worker specific. Such variation would appear to vary with firm size, with smaller firms more likely to make such adjustments in money wages. If administrative convenience or law requires firms to pay uniform money wages, they can offset such regulations by choosing which workers to hire. Older, sicker workers with large families will be less likely to be hired. This can lead to segregation of workers of different risk levels across firms and, in the limit, a full offset of the worker-specific health benefit cost.

However, firms often do pay the same money wages to workers with obviously different health benefits costs. Age, family size, the costliness of hospitals and doctors used, and the presence of chronic conditions all lead to different benefits costs but not obviously or necessarily to different wages. This behavior upsets some benefits specialists, since they feel that total compensation should be based on a worker's merit or value to the employer, not "on the basis of employees' wages or whether they or their covered dependents get sick" (Bowen and Wadley 1989).

Why does this behavior happen? One answer obviously is the presence of laws that forbid discrimination based on disability, age, or gender of the worker. Administrative difficulties both in calculating the true benefits value to different workers and in adjusting each worker's wages for it are probably also part of the reason. A more subtle argument, however, is that by making compensation independent of variation in risk, the employer is providing further insurance to risk averse employees, which can lead to further wage offsets. The "glue" that keeps the employer from moving away from such commitments is the firm's reputation in the labor market.

Why Don't All Large Firms Provide Health Insurance to All Their Employees?

About 21 percent of uninsured workers work for firms with more than 1,000 employees, and only 35 percent of all uninsured workers are employed in small firms with fewer than 25 workers. More than half of the uninsured workers work for firms that are not small. These larger firms are much more likely to insure a given worker than are the small firms, but they employ a large enough share of the total labor force that they account for most of the uninsured workers even though they insure a larger proportion of their workers than do smaller firms.

Some of the reasons offered by small firms to explain why they pay for no insurance at all do not seem to apply to these larger firms. The small firms claim that they cannot bargain well with insurers; big firms can. The small firms claim that they cannot "afford" to pay for health insurance, in the sense that the owner would be deprived of almost all income; big firms do not have that problem. So why do such larger firms sometimes fail to pay for health insurance?

There are three answers such firms offer that are consistent with the economic approach. One explanation is that they do not need to divert part of total compensation into health insurance, because their employees do not seek it; workers prefer cash to benefits. A senior official at the Bank of America told a *New York Times* reporter: "If there were a tighter labor market with fewer people looking for work, we might have to offer health insurance. But no one has run into that problem in California, with so many college students who are potential part time employees." In itself, this statement does not fit economic logic, since it does not explain why Bank of America pays high enough cash wages that it has an excess of college student applicants looking for work. Moreover, the official opined that insuring the low wage part time workers would "add substantially to the bank's costs and that profits would suffer, hurting shareholders." This assumes, however, that more generous benefits would not come at the expense of wages. The real issue is whether the potential employees would prefer wages to benefits, something that might be traced to potential workers being "healthy young people seeking to earn some extra money by working for a while, but . . . uninterested in health insurance" (Uchitelle 1994).

The second reason has already been suggested: many of the uninsured workers are part time workers. If the employer pays the same amount toward premiums for all workers, regardless of hours worked per time period, fringe benefits cost per hour would be higher for part time workers than for full time workers. The firm could pay a smaller amount toward premiums or could pay lower hourly wages for part time workers. In any case, one would have to explain why part time workers would not so value health insurance that they would be willing to sacrifice the same dollar amount out of their total wages as would others, even if this dollar amount were a larger proportion of their wages, so that they ended up taking home less cash per hour. Thus the "part time" explanation is really a subcase of the "unwilling to sacrifice money wages" explanation.

A third explanation is that these workers work for hourly wage levels so near the minimum wage that employers could not reduce money wages enough even if they wanted to, *and* these workers are not attracted by insurance.

Small Firms and Adjustment to a Mandate

Advocates for small firms were strongest in opposition to an employer mandate in the Clinton plan. The opposition came both from those firms that did pay for coverage and from those that did not. In both cases, as noted previously, the primary reason for opposing a requirement that the employer pay part of the premium is that the employer could not then, or might not in the future, "afford" to pay this amount.

As already noted, this type of reason for opposing mandates is at odds with the economic models of the long run determination of labor compensation levels. I have also discussed the general problem of adjustment of money compensation to an expected increase in fringe benefit costs and have argued that an employer would be seriously harmed by such a requirement only to the extent that it requires him or her to provide a benefit that is more costly to the firm than to other firms. Small employers offered other explanations for their opposition to mandates in addition to the difficulty of anticipating increases in a component of total compensation cost. Here I will deal with three of them: (1) the notion that adjusting to a mandate will affect employee "morale" and, subsequently, productivity; (2) the notion that a mandate saddles small firms with a fixed cost that they cannot handle; and (3) the notion that a small employer's decision to offer insurance depends on his or her own valuation of insurance.

Consider a firm with ten employees and suppose that it is subject to a mandate to make health insurance payments that amount to 10 percent of payroll. Suppose that if it added the 10 percent on top of current money wages, it would maximize its profits by reducing employment by one worker. The latter strategy would be the second best response if money wages cannot be touched. If the firm had previously projected zero raises, the trade-off is as follows: harm one employee and take a hit to profits or disappoint all ten employees and take no reduction in profits. However, if the disappointed employees retaliate by working less energetically, the final impact on profits could be greater. And then, even while taking the best (layoff) option, the firm is still harmed by a mandate.

To the extent that there is turnover among employees, this argument loses force. But to the extent that employees of small firms are "family" (and misbehave as family members sometimes do), the employer may be harmed. What he or she should try to do is to convince employees that the wage reduction is caused by the mandate, and the mandate in turn is the fault of the government, not of the employer. There is, however, little evidence in support of this morale argument.

The second argument is the "fixed cost" or "meeting payroll" argument. The notion here is that, from revenues received, the employer's first obligation is to pay wages—and the requirement to pay a health insurance premium means that the first obligation may not always be met. However, this argument is only true if there is no wage offset. If there is a complete wage offset, the employer's compensation obligation is the same after a mandate as before, and so the chances of not being able to make payroll are no higher than before. Of course, once money wages have fallen it will look like the obligation to pay for health insurance interferes with the ability to meet that smaller payroll, so it is important to keep clear—to employers and employees alike—the essential connection between premium payments and lower money wages.

The third reason is suggested by the fact that, if the small employer and his or her family is uninsured, it is much more likely that no insurance will be offered to the firm's employees. We should not overemphasize this fact: an owner of a small business whose major source of income comes from that business will often choose insurance for him- or herself only if the insurance can be obtained at the lower group rate.

Disequilibrium in Large Firm Employment

The economic argument is that large firms that already pay for worker health insurance are not harmed by increases in health insurance premiums, because those increases should be offset by reductions in money wages—either in competitive labor markets or in collective bargaining. There is however another possibility that may characterize some large firms: they may not be in equilibrium with regard to the number of workers hired. Specifically, because of declining demand and restructuring, they may be employing too many employees at the current compensation cost. Either unions may prevent them from laying off workers or their own bureaucratic process may make it difficult to discharge workers rapidly enough. How would an increase in health benefits costs affect such a firm? Would it reduce profits?

The most obvious thing to note is that if there are redundant employees, it may be that no future raises in pay are anticipated regardless of what happens to the cost of benefits. Then the only way to adjust to rising benefits costs is by actually reducing nominal wage rates, something the firm may be reluctant to do, largely for the type of morale reasons discussed in the preceding. The response of laying off workers is then more reasonable, although it is not obvious why the firm had to wait for a benefits costs excuse before terminating excessive employment. A rise in benefits costs obviously makes it more costly to carry that employment, and again it may be better for the firm to concentrate the pain on a few discharged workers rather than cut wages for the whole workforce.

The response of large firms in disequilibrium (excess supply) may help to explain why their money wage rates did not rise in 1994–95 to offset declines in the growth of their health benefits costs in those years. These firms may still, in an era of desired downsizing, regard their employees as overcompensated. Wages will only begin to rise when employment falls to an equilibrium level, something that appeared to be happening in 1996.

Two-Worker Families

One of the major sources of confusion in the way businesspeople and policymakers think about employer-paid coverage concerns the payment for insurance for two-worker families. If a husband and wife both work, it is common for one of them (which I will assume to be the husband in the following examples) to elect family coverage that covers wife and children. The wife then either makes no claim on the policy offered in connection with her job, or declines coverage if there is some type of cafeteria or flexible benefit plan, or chooses a job with (typically) a small firm that does not offer coverage. As the *New York Times* analyzes it: "The small company may get a free ride, paying little or nothing" (Uchitelle 1994). Even when a small business provides coverage to its workers, it often pays little or nothing toward the coverage of children and spouses.

So owners of business large and small, policymakers, President Clinton, and the *New York Times* reporter all appear to believe that the current system offers a subsidy or free ride to small business. Economic analysis says something quite the contrary, however; indeed, it says that the primary recipients of subsidies under this system—if there are any beneficiaries at all—are employees without working spouses who obtain coverage in firms that employ many spouses insured elsewhere. In general, it will be employees, not employers, who will bear the burden of shifted costs.

Consider the following example. The economy in a local market consists of two types of firms. Firms in one industry employ only married men; half of these men have wives who do not work in the market, and half have working wives. Firms in a different industry employ these working wives in a different type of job and, in addition, they employ other persons who are single. Half of these small firms' employees are spouses of workers in the first industry, and half are not. All jobs in both industries are identical within the firm, but are different across the two industries in terms of needed skill and experience. The supply of labor of each type is fixed. All persons in any firm are given the same take-home pay, regardless of their insurance cost. Employers in the first firm pay the full premium for all workers; employers in the second firm pay all but $10 per month of the premium for workers who elect coverage. The employer insurance premium for family coverage is assumed to be $4,000 per year, and the employer premium for individual coverage is $2,000 in the second industry.

In this situation, all workers in the first industry will choose family coverage; their money wages will therefore be reduced by $4,000. In the second industry, wages per worker will fall by $1,000 (since half the workers use coverage that costs $2,000 per person). In effect, families with two working adults pay $5,000 for $4,000 worth of coverage, families with one working adult (and a stay-at-home spouse) pay $4,000 for $4,000 worth of coverage, while single workers pay $1,120 for $2,120 worth of coverage. Obviously, if the money wages of each worker in the second industry could be adjusted according to whether or not he or she uses the health benefit, the cost of coverage for single workers would rise to $2,120. The main point so far is that nearly half of the cost of coverage in the second industry is borne by families who work in both industries, while the single workers benefit. The transfer is from worker type, not from employer to employer.

To show this conclusion more strongly, we now modify the example. We suppose that a law requires employers in the second industry to contribute the same $2,000 they pay for single workers toward the family insurance premiums of the working spouses of workers in the first industry—much along the lines of proposals to average employer contributions in the Clinton plan. This will cause wages in the first industry to rise by $1,000, and wages in the second industry to fall by $1,000. The net effect will be to reverse the redistribution across workers that was just pointed out, but to leave the per employee cost of compensation the same in both industries as it was in the previous example. The main point is, as long as there are wage offsets, it is employees, not employers, who are affected by "cost shifting."

This example shows that employers who do not pay for coverage for all workers do not necessarily gain, and those who do pay do not necessarily lose. Could cost shifting to employers ever happen? The answer is negative because variation in family situation or anything else that might lead some workers to decline coverage that others would accept is unlikely to be related to the identity of any specific firm. Since, in competitive labor markets, any firm can hire any worker or set of workers, no firm can be stuck with a set of workers who are above average in terms of total compensation cost—since it will replace them with lower cost workers. It is true, of course, that getting to this equilibrium may disrupt workforces and upset workers; the offering of coverage tied rigidly to work requires workers to move when desired coverage changes. Eventually an equilibrium will be realized, and it will be one in which owner profits are unaffected.

All of these problems would be avoided if employees are given a flexible spending account or budget, in all firms. Then they pay for whatever insurance they get. For instance, the single women in the small firm would pay the full $2,120 premium for their insurance, and the married women covered by husbands' plans would pay nothing.

The "problems" that arise from two-worker families are primarily related to wage averaging among workers of equal productivity who have different health benefits costs. The current system does *not* subsidize the profits of small businesses, but it does subsidize (largely single) workers who use the coverage at small businesses that do provide coverage. It does not subsidize small businesses that do not provide coverage, because the spouses who obtain family coverage pay for their entire family, and the uncovered single workers do not obtain health insurance. If the small business is forced to pay for coverage, it will further reduce the net money wages of the two-worker family.

Who Bears the Cost of Cost Shifting?

One of the arguments for universal coverage, most recently made by Rep. Richard Gephardt (1994), is that the 70 percent of small businesses that do provide health insurance for their employees "would like all the other businesses, large and small, that are their competitors to exercise the same responsibility." He also alleged that the House Democratic bill "would free the vast majority of our population from paying for the cost of people who decide not to have health insurance." Adam Clymer (1994), a *New York Times* reporter writing on the editorial page, alleged that universal coverage was necessary to get cost growth under control because the cost shifting from the uninsured to private sector insured care was causing the cost of that insurance to rise more much rapidly than it otherwise would. Representative Gephardt also argues against allowing people to choose catastrophic insurance policies. He alleges that people who choose high deductible policies "would not go to the doctor when [they] get sick because [they] do not want to pay out of pocket" but then eventually get sicker and sicker and wind up "[in the emergency room] with no money, [and their] cost just gets added to everyone else's bill." He also alleged that cost shifting from the uninsured and the partially insured adds "a 30 percent tax to most of the other people in the country who are struggling to pay for their own health care."

There are two questions here that I want to address.

1. What is the net subsidy (difference between payments and cost) received by the uninsured and the incompletely insured?
2. Who pays that subsidy?

To answer these questions, it will be helpful to use a numerical example. Let 100 represent the total amount paid on average by insurance for a person; 80 of this is covered by employer-paid insurance. Since the absence of insurance coverage discourages the use of care, an uninsured person uses care that would be billed at 70, reflecting the approximately 30 percent lower rate of use of care by the uninsured. (The use of more expensive care, after skimping on care in the case of moderate illness, raises the use of the uninsured somewhat but not to the level of use of the insured. If the uninsured person is low income, less use does seem to be associated with poorer health by some measures.) Since an uninsured person does not obtain employer-paid health insurance, he or she pays more taxes out of a given amount of total compensation. Assume that the extra amount in taxes is approximately 25 percent (income plus payroll tax) of the 70, or 17. In addition, the uninsured do pay for about a quarter of their care, or 17. So the total amount the uninsured pay is 34, about half of the charges they generate.

The uninsured are about 20 percent of the under-65, non-Medicaid population, so the net cost they impose on the rest of us is $(.2)(70 - 34) = 7.2$. This means that the 100 I pay as an insured person includes about 7 percent to pay for the uninsured. Representative Gephardt's 30 percent figure looks much too high.

But wait! How is the "tax" levied on the insured? It allegedly happens as hospitals and doctors raise their charges for the rest of us to cover the cost of the care furnished to the uninsured. This implies that covering the uninsured will remove this tax if and only if being able to collect for care from the previously uninsured causes hospitals and doctors to *cut* their charges by the excess amount. Will they do this? Almost surely not. If they no longer have to use the money to pay for the uninsured, there are certainly other good uses they can make of that excess of payments over costs earned from the rest of us. They can pay for research, medical education, or (in the case of doctors and owners of for-profit hospitals) additional dividends or income. The evidence suggests that some of the surplus may be cut by nonprofit hospitals but not all. I will deal with this issue in more detail in the following.

Any cost shifting will therefore have to wait for long run equilibrium in the medical services market. Eventually a city with more uninsured who cannot be refused treatment by providers will have higher long run equilibrium levels of provider prices than one with few uninsured, since the total costs of care have to be covered by revenues in long run equilibrium.

What of Clymer's (1994) claim that cost shifting is significantly responsible for *rising* medical spending? This is surely wrong. There is no way that the modest increase in the number of uninsured over the past decade, even with cost shifting, can account for more than a minimal percentage of the increase in total private premiums. The uninsured may make private premiums a little higher than they would otherwise be (say, 7 percent), but their presence does not make them grow any faster.

When the price of employer-paid insurance is increased because providers raise charges to cover bad debts, who currently pays? Representative Gephardt (1994) talked about "families coming to realize that they are picking up the tab not only for their own insurance, but for colleagues and friends who decided they did not need insurance." This implies that he accepts the view that the cost of employer-paid insurance falls on worker wages. But then the absence of cost shifting under universal coverage will benefit, not employers, but employees. That is, it is not a matter of employers "accepting responsibility," but of employees doing so—of refusing to (or being forbidden to) take a job that does not carry health insurance. However, this means that firms that now do offer coverage are not currently disadvantaged. This is so for two reasons: to some extent, their competitors must pay higher money wages in lieu of health insurance and whatever costs are shifted to them go straight through to their workers' wages, not to their profits.

But let us assume there is eventually some cost shifting of the conventional type. How will this affect the profits of the firms that are providing insurance. That is, if all firms were mandated to provide insurance to their employees, what effect (compared to the current level) would that have on the profits of firms that currently provide?

The answer depends in part on the reason why firms were not providing coverage. Suppose that all firms have the same potential cost of insurance, but some employees place lower values on it. They will then work for firms that do not provide insurance, but they will receive higher cash wages (if all workers are identical and interchangeable) by the amount of the premium cost. All workers who value insurance more than its premium will work for firms that do offer it, and all workers who value it less will work for firms that do not. Suppose also that all workers will choose to work for someone, even if wages fall substantially.

The key question is what the premium will be if a universal mandate is imposed. If there was cost shifting, the new premium will be less than the old premium by the average amount of cost shifting. This is the cost that will be imposed on all firms. In this story wages in the formerly uninsured firms will fall by the amount of the new premium, and wages in the insured firms will rise by the amount of cost shifting. Total compensation costs will not change for either type of firm. In effect, the originally insured firms will not gain any profits; their workers will gain take-home pay as they no longer have to pay the cost shifting "tax." Workers who were formerly uninsured will lose pay but gain insurance—which will still leave them worse off on average. The key point is that the employer gains zero additional profit; the employer does not gain from eliminating the cost shift.

Can we change the assumptions to change this conclusion? One possibility is to assume that there are two different kinds of workers (based on skill or training) and also assume that the demand for insurance is correlated with this worker characteristic. Workers of one type are at best an imperfect substitute for workers of another type. If carpenters value health insurance and truck drivers do not, building contractors will initially provide insurance and trucking firms will not. Now impose a mandate; it will only fall on trucking firms. If truckers have to work at something, money wages in trucking will still fall by the cost of the fringe benefit.

The only thing that can make a difference is something we already know: if the cost of insurance is higher for the formerly uninsured firms, and if workers are equally skilled in any job, then costs will rise in formerly uninsured firms. The difference in utility from being uninsured compared to being insured is larger when cost shifting occurs than when it does not.

When there is cost shifting, more workers therefore work in uninsured firms than when there is no cost shifting and all workers are required to pay for their care. If cost shifting is then removed, there will be a larger advantage to firms that insured than if there were no cost shifting—but there will be fewer such firms. Insured firms will therefore gain more short run profits.

The key question then is how much of the difference in insurance purchases is explained by differences in administrative costs. As discussed previously, this may not be large. If different areas differ in the extent of cost shifted, this implies that the main differences will be in worker wages, not in firm profits.

Mismatching and Local Public Goods Effects

Suppose a class of workers demands zero insurance coverage, but suppose they are most productive in firms in which most workers do demand insurance coverage. That is, they are most productive in firms with heterogeneous workers. Complementarities in production among different worker types would produce such a result. If the difference in utility from not having insurance is larger than the difference in productivity between heterogeneous and homogeneous firms, these low taste workers will congregate in firms that do not offer health insurance.

Mandated insurance benefits remove this possibility. Then the employees might as well work where they are most productive. This will lead labor to shift to heterogeneous firms; their relative prices will fall.

The key issues then are (1) the correlation in insurance demand with labor type or productivity and (2) the optimal mix of labor by type. If segregated firms are possible, then there are no excise tax effects. If firms in some industries optimally should use a mix of worker types, the presence of a uniform group good like health insurance increases their relative cost; mandates remove this cost disadvantage.

Risk Variation

The average level of risk varies across employment groups. Compared to other firms, a particular employer may have employees who are older, consumers of care in higher priced settings, or unusually likely to have costly chronic conditions. These influences are tempered somewhat by firm size: other things equal, the frequency of groups with above-average risk will be greater among smaller groups than among larger ones. On the other hand, larger groups are more likely to be self insured, so that a dollar of expected expense translates directly into a dollar of expected costs for the firm, whereas small employers often buy outside insurance at premiums only partially based on their own group's experience. There is some pooling among groups covered by the insurance firm as a substitute for the greater within-group pooling possible in larger groups.

Whatever the mechanism to determine the cost to the group, there is a certainty that some groups will have higher than average costs. What is the incidence of these variations? Here I only consider a "short run" version of this question in which employers adjust wages and premiums based on current period benefits costs. I will consider the possibility of longer term implicit contracts in the next chapter.

The answer to the question of incidence obviously depends on a simple issue: can the employer in some fashion charge more to the high risk workers than to the low risk workers? There are some common explicit variations in premiums with risk or expected expense. Families with multiple members frequently pay more for given nominal coverage, and worker premiums often vary with the costliness of medical care in one geographic area compared to another. There is also some empirical evidence, to be reviewed in the discussion of community rating in the next chapter, that money wages *are* adjusted for some risk characteristics, such as age and gender.

But would the insured individual employee at high risk because of the presence of a chronic condition pay a higher premium or receive a lower wage? Both the presence of laws forbidding discrimination against the disabled and the administrative complexities of making such adjustments suggest that the answer is "probably not." In such a case, employers lucky enough to have a low risk workforce will pocket profits, whereas those with high risk workers or dependents, to the extent that they cannot deny benefits, will suffer losses in profits.

There is an important implication of this discussion. It means that the impact of high risk on the welfare of workers who remain insured is independent of firm size, employer market power, or other characteristics. While workers probably bear all or nearly all of the cost of *predictable* and *permanent* influences on risk, the impact of unpredictable and temporary changes in risk—such as the development of a high risk condition by an employee of a small firm—will fall on the employer, not on the worker. As long as the employer continues to provide insurance coverage, the employee is shielded from long term risk. Only if the employer drops coverage or goes out of business will the employee be at risk.

The Tax Subsidy and the Incidence of Employer Payments for Employee Health Insurance

When the employer provides compensation to the employee in the form of payment for all or part of the employee's health insurance policy, that payment is not counted as part of the employee's taxable income. In contrast, payments the employee receives in the form of money wages are taxed. (I ignore the employer's share of the payroll tax in what follows.) In competitive labor markets, what impact will making such payments be expected to have on worker cash wages?

Assume first that the supply of labor is perfectly inelastic. Also assume that the marginal tax rate is 40 percent. We know that employees will want their money wages to be reduced in return for spending the money on insurance as long as their valuation of a dollar's worth of additional insurance spending exceeds 60 cents. Suppose the cost of such a policy is $2,000 per worker. Suppose that, in the absence of a tax subsidy, each worker would have chosen a policy that costs $1,800. When the tax subsidy is present, money wages will fall by $2,000 compared to the no-insurance equilibrium. When the tax subsidy is absent, they will fall by $1,800. In either case, when the number of workers who wish to work is fixed, exactly 100 percent of the cost of employer payments will fall on worker wages; the only difference the tax subsidy makes is that the size of the wage reduction will be greater if there is a tax subsidy than if there is not because a more costly policy will be chosen.

Even if the size of the policy were fixed by a mandate, the decline in wages would still be dollar for dollar. Workers affected by the mandate might all value the coverage at less than its cost (less the tax subsidy). But if their decision to work does not depend at all on the real wage, the money wage will in equilibrium fall by the amount of the cost of insurance— *whether there is a tax subsidy or not.* The only difference is that, if there were a tax subsidy, there would be fewer persons whose behavior would be affected by a mandate, since more of them would voluntarily choose to buy coverage. However, although the worker's money wage falls by the same amount, tax subsidy or not, the worker's disposable income is obviously greater when the tax subsidy is present since, in this case, the decline in money income leads to a drop in taxes. Employers are no better or worse off, but employees are affected.

Now assume that the willingness of workers to work depends on the real value of the compensation they receive, and assume that the demand for labor is not perfectly inelastic. By how much will worker wages fall in the two cases? In the case of voluntary purchases, offering the health insurance presumably increases the quantity of labor supplied at each money wage. How much it increases depends on the value attached to health insurance by those potential workers who would not be willing to work at lower money wages. It is possible that the supply curve might shift out so much that money wages would fall, relative to the level before group health insurance was "invented," by more than the cost of the coverage. It might do so in the non–tax subsidy case because it is cheaper to administer insurance through an employment group than to obtain it individually. (This would need to be traded off against the chance that the group would not choose to offer each person's most preferred policy.) It might do so in the tax subsidy case because workers attach value to gaining the tax subsidy. It does not appear that there are any easily interpretable conditions to tell when this will happen—other than to say that if labor supply is relatively unresponsive to money wages, it is probably unresponsive to subsidies or the offering of better benefits, so that the difference from dollar-for-dollar shifting will in such cases be small.

All we can say is that, for potential workers who attach a high value to health insurance, tax subsidized group insurance should have the same effect as an increase in cash wages equal to the sum of the tax subsidy and the net cost advantage of group over individual insurance. For persons with low values, the question is how many have values less than the cost of individual insurance but greater than the cost of group insurance less the tax subsidy. Neither of these pieces of information can be read off the money wage labor supply curve.

However, there is relatively little interest in understanding the effect on money wages of voluntarily offered group health insurance. Instead, most of the policy interest and most of the research have been concerned with the impact of a mandated benefit. Obviously a mandated benefit has no effect on those workers who have already been buying health insurance; it can only affect those with values below the cost of insurance (net of a tax subsidy if one exists). Consider the no–tax subsidy case first. If money wages fall by the cost of insurance, we know that the shift in the labor supply curve, though positive, cannot be enough to make up the reduction in supply due to lower wages. So the wage will fall by no more than the cost of insurance or (more probably) less. What if there is a tax subsidy? The employer's wage offer at any quantity demanded will fall by the gross cost of the mandated insurance, but the affected workers will be those affected by the decline in the net (of tax subsidy) cost of insurance. That is, if the policy costs $4,000 and the tax rate is 40 percent, the net reduction in what a worker will take home is $2,400. If uninsured workers attach zero value to health insurance, the decline in labor supplied is that predicted by a decline in money wages of $2,400. If they do attach some value, that value must be less than $2,400, so again the supply curve cannot shift out enough to make up the difference.

The imposition of a mandate lowers the demand for labor curve by $4,000. If the supply curve were somewhat responsive, wages would fall to some level representing a smaller decline than dollar-for-dollar shifting. However, if there is a tax subsidy, the supply curve would shift out even if insurance was no value—since a $4,000 lower gross money wage translates into a $2,400 lower net money wage when the tax subsidy is taken into account. If health insurance is of value, the supply curve moves further to the right. There would be somewhat less of an impact on employer profits.

The conclusion then is that the presence of a tax subsidy probably has little effect on analysis of the consequences of an employer payment mandate. If there is an effect of a mandate on employer profits, that effect is smaller with a tax subsidy than without. With or without a tax subsidy, the great bulk of the cost of the mandate falls on worker wages. The nominal value of these wages falls by the amount of the premium. The difference is that, with a tax subsidy, some of this decline is offset by lower taxes workers will owe.

APPENDIX

This appendix provides the diagrammatic "supply and demand curve" analysis of mandates of which economists are so fond. Its purpose is to reinforce (or clarify) the simple story told at the beginning of the chapter. I also use it to discuss some theoretical debates in the economics literature that are relevant to the question of incidence.

Will the imposition of a mandate that employers pay for their employees' health insurance cause total employment to rise, fall, or stay the same? Perhaps surprisingly, the theoretical answer is "it depends," with the result depending both on worker preferences and on the precise form of the mandate. It is surely possible in theory, and cannot be ruled out in practice, that a mandate will cause total employment or work to rise rather than fall. However, such an increase will not occur because jobs were created—whatever that means—but rather because formerly nonemployed individuals were willing to work for less, and so employers were willing to hire them.

A diagrammatic analysis shows the possibilities. Assume first that the number of hours of work per worker is fixed. This means that the quantity of labor input supplied depends only on the number of persons who work for wages. An initial equilibrium, before a mandate, might be represented by the quantity L_0 and the wage W_0 in figure 1. Now suppose the employer is mandated to buy an insurance with a premium of $\$P$. This law reduces the money wage employers are willing to offer for any quantity of labor by the amount of the mandated premium, and so the money wage demand curve for labor falls from D_0 to D_1. What happens to employment obviously depends on what happens to the supply curve of labor (or workers). If the supply curve is unaffected by the provision of insurance, so that it stays at S_0, total employment will fall as long as the curve is not vertical (perfectly inelastic). On the other hand, if the supply curve shifts out exactly to S_1, the level of employment will be unaffected, as will the total compensation cost per worker faced by the firm. If the curve shifts by less than S_1, employment will fall, whereas if it shifts by more than S_1, employment will rise.

When will the supply curve remain unaffected? One answer is when workers attach no value at all to the insurance. Then the mandate is like a lump sum tax of $\$P$ per worker, and the standard discussion of incidence of a payroll tax follows. Given a demand curve, the size of the reduction in employment, and the size of the increase in employer total compensation cost, varies directly with the elasticity of labor supply.

The other case in which this result will occur is the situation in which the person will be entitled to be insured (or be required to be insured) whether he or she is employed or not but in which the person does not have to pay for the insurance obtained if he or she is not employed. Ignoring the effects of taxes needed to fund subsidies to pay for insurance for nonworkers, the effect of such universal provision of insurance is to cause the payment by employers to be equivalent to a tax on employment.

The version of this problem analyzed by Summers (1989) does not assume that the value of insurance V is necessarily zero. Summers con-

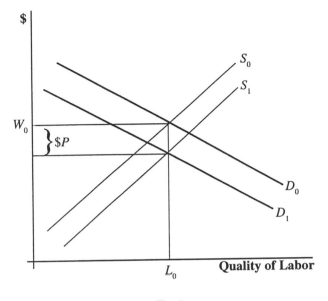

Fig. 1

cludes that an employer mandate is equivalent to a per worker tax of ($P - V$). The policy he has in mind is one in which people are required to take insurance if they work, but if they do not work they are neither required to pay for insurance nor entitled to get it. Only workers, in Summers's model, are covered.

Suppose, in this model, that V equals P—insurance is worth to each worker just what it costs the employer. Then the supply curve will shift out to S_1 exactly. The reason is simple: if each worker is indifferent between money wages and insurance, imposition of a mandate does not change the amount of labor supplied at a given level of total compensation cost per worker. However, it might be plausible to assume that V is less than P since, otherwise, it would have paid for employers to pay for coverage. Then employment falls somewhat, and total compensation cost rises somewhat. The size of the decline in employment now depends on two things: the elasticity of labor supply (which depends on how people value money wages relative to leisure and also on the distribution of those evaluations) and the deviation between V and P.

In Summers's model, when might labor supply shift by more than $(S_1 - S_0)$? One situation would be the case in which employers were ignorant and failed to provide health insurance even though it was worth more to workers than it cost. Viscusi and Moore (1989) have made such an argument for workers' compensation insurance. The other possibility is the situation in which the mandate is accompanied by actions that lower the cost of insurance, so that the value of insurance, that was formerly less than its cost, now becomes greater than its cost. If we believe some of the advocates of insurance reform as reducing administrative cost (or even the argument that mandates themselves will lower administrative costs), this becomes a possible case.

Are there other things that might shift the supply of labor? The answer is yes if there are income effects. One type of income effect will arise if people are required to get coverage, and pay for it entirely themselves, if they are not employed—that is, if (as in the original Clinton bill) there is an individual head-tax–type mandate as well as an employer mandate. Then if the person does not work, the family must sacrifice the cost of the insurance. If V is less than P, this amounts to a reduction in real income, making the family demand less leisure if leisure is a normal good. If the family has to pay for insurance to which they attach little value, teenagers may have to get a job to make ends meet because of a budget depleted by insurance premiums. In this case, the only effect on labor supply is an income effect—there is no substitution effect of the mandate, since the reduction in money wage per worker of $P just equals the extra cost imposed on the family if persons do not work.

The other, perhaps more plausible, case of income effects has been suggested by Roger Feldman (1993). He considers a case in which the number of hours of work supplied is variable and notes that the premium the employer must pay per worker will not, over a wide range, vary with the number of hours worked. There is thus no effect of the mandate on the wage for a marginal hour of work, but there is a reduction in total real income. Even a single individual who stays in the workforce will want to work more hours to make up for the premium bite on other consumption. Thus, *if* a person continues to work at all, he or she wishes to work more hours—although there still may be persons who react to a mandate by deciding to cease market work altogether. In Feldman's model, there may be fewer persons willing to work at a given wage *per hour,* but those who are willing to work will wish to work more hours. Since the quantity of labor hours supplied is the product of workers and hours, it is possible that the quantity (at any money wage) might increase. The answer depends on the elasticity of supply of *workers* (not work) and the size of the income effect on hours for persons who do work.

CHAPTER 4

Employer Payment Incidence and Health Policy

As indicated in the previous chapter, there are strong logical arguments for the proposition that labor market–wide health benefit costs changes fall almost entirely on workers' wages and not on firms' profits. There can be exceptions when the cost of health benefits for individual firms changes at rates that differ from those prevailing in their labor market, and there can be some "cross firm" effects, but these exceptions are unimportant for many policy issues. In this chapter I want to show that looking at benefits costs in an economically correct way affects some important issues of health policy and health benefits regulation.

I will also consider whether the participants in the debates over these issues have generally based their own positions on a correct view of their own interests. The differences in views over benefit cost incidence matter to individuals and firms in two ways: they matter for how they think (as participants in the political process) about what the outcome of public policy will be and in their decisions about whether they should support or oppose a given policy. Once the political process institutes a policy, the differences in views then imply different optimal managerial strategies for dealing with a new policy.

I will discuss a series of policy issues that are or are likely to be important questions for government and will show, for each of them, that incidence matters. For the most part, consistent with the theme of this book, I will address how these policies affect or ought to affect employers—but, given the importance of employees in the economic theory of fringe benefits, I will necessarily be concerned about them as well.

In most of what follows I will generally characterize the economic view of fringe benefits as one in which the cost falls on workers. As will be shown in more detail in chapter 5, the employer's objective therefore should be to make those choices that workers would make if they were spending their own money; the employer or union group becomes the proxy buyer for workers. There will be one major exception to this simple but usually correct view: when policy changes will affect which persons will work for a firm, I will need to take effects of changing workforce composition into account. This extension will be most important for considering policy changes that affect benefit portability and therefore employee turnover. I will characterize the alternative view ("cost like any other cost") as one in which employer impacts and employer decisions are made as if changes in the cost of benefits operate like any other cost change the firm might experience. This view has little to say about how benefits of a given cost should be structured, so there will be some ambiguity in representing the alternative view in such matters.

Erosion of Employer-Paid Insurance Coverage

There has been moderate growth in the number of uninsured persons since the mid-1970s (when, based on the fragmentary data we have, the proportion reached a low of 12–14 percent of the under-65 population). About 18 percent of the nonelderly population is currently uninsured at any point in time. It is well known that a majority of the uninsured are in families where at least one person is employed. It is natural to think that public policy directed at inducing more employers to offer coverage might help to reduce (although it can never eliminate) the problem of the uninsured.

Current information on this issue paints a somewhat inconsistent picture. Relative to the mid-1980s, studies indicate that the proportion of workers who take insurance related to their job has been dropping (Shactman and Altman 1995), but most recent analysis (Sheils and Alexcih 1996) indicates that the percentage of workers covered has been fairly flat since 1989, actually rising slightly from 58.7 percent in recession plagued 1989 to 59.0 percent in more prosperous 1995. Surveys of benefits offerings of medium-sized and large firms indicate that, averaged across firms, 81 percent of their workers are eligible for coverage (KPMG 1995). The trend in the mid-1990s has been toward larger proportions eligible for coverage (up from 74 percent in 1993); analysts attribute this growth to employers' "growing awareness of the importance of health care coverage as a tool in recruiting and retaining high quality employees" and "a trend among workers to seek health coverage through their employer instead of purchasing private [individual] insurance" (KPMG 1995, 18).

There is also a somewhat inconsistent picture in the pattern of growth among the employed uninsured. The growth in the uninsured in the mid- to late 1980s appeared to concentrate on relatively low wage workers, often in smaller firms (Kronick 1991; Acs 1995). The conventional explanation was that, as this group faced declining real income and rising premiums for a given level of coverage, they could no longer "afford" such coverage. (Why they dropped coverage entirely, rather than just reduced it, is less well explained.)

The period of the early 1990s appears to display a somewhat different pattern (Holahan, Winterbottom, and Rajan 1995). For the poor and the near poor, the proportion uninsured stopped rising (and in the case of the poor, actually fell). The proportion of such persons with employment-based coverage continued to decline (although the absolute number of low income jobs with coverage actually held constant), but growth in Medicaid coverage more than offset this. In contrast, high income workers began to take jobs without coverage at a much higher rate. Among workers with incomes in excess of 200 percent of the poverty line (about two-thirds of all workers), the proportion uninsured rose by 28 percent (from 8.7 percent to 11.2 percent).

One way to reconcile the earlier difference between the overall trend and the trend for workers in higher wage and medium-sized and larger firms is to hypothesize that patterns of coverage differ by firm size, with coverage falling among low wage, small, unstable firms, even while it actually grew during the past periods of low employment among the higher wage workers who work for the large firms. The reasons for the more recent changes, which have, to some extent, reversed this pattern, are more obscure but probably include the growth of Medicaid coverage.

However, the most striking recent change in the composition of the uninsured has been a pronounced decline in the percent of workers' dependents covered by employment-based insurance, which fell from 83.0 percent in 1989 to 78.9 percent in 1995 (despite the improvement in macroeconomic conditions) (Sheils and Alexcih 1996). We can identify some of the probable reasons for this decline: an increase in the proportion of children over the age of 19, who often lose eligibility for their parent's insurance, and an increase in the proportion of the premium paid by the employee for family coverage. It is also likely that the number of dependents per insured worker fell, while the number of dependents per uninsured worker rose, as the number of low wage single-parent households grew.

We therefore have had the unusual pattern in the 1990s of relatively greater erosion of coverage among dependents (at all income levels) and among higher wage workers. The problem now is less one of deteriorating opportunities for vulnerable workers and is more suggestive of either voluntary changes or shifts in family composition.

The desire to stem the perceived erosion of job-related coverage was certainly behind the employer mandate in the Clinton plan and in mandates and programs in a number of state plans (enacted but not implemented). It is also behind a number of state and (potentially) federal efforts to encourage or subsidize employers to offer coverage, and it provides some of the support for the current tax-free status of employer-paid premiums. I will deal with the question of the tax subsidy per se subsequently, but, even in the absence of the tax subsidy, it would seem important to understand why employers do or do not choose to offer insurance to employees or their dependents.

The noneconomic view, shared by businesses and activists alike, as already noted, views offering employer-paid insurance as a matter of employer generosity and affordability: employers offer insurance when they can afford it and do not offer it when they cannot. The economic view would be different: it would say that employers offer insurance when their employees (actual or potential) demand it and are willing to pay for it with wage offsets and do not offer it when employees do not demand it by accepting sufficiently large offsets. Which view can better explain what has been happening to employment-based coverage and what will happen in the future? How should employers respond to policy actions intended to slow or reverse the erosion in employment-based coverage under either theory?

Surveys of employers who do not offer insurance do not find the most important reason to be "employees do not want it or need it." The most common and highest priority reason is "I [the employer] cannot afford it." The no-demand reason is usually third or fourth on the list. So the simple survey evidence is mixed and not especially helpful.

To get much further we need to formulate a model of demand for insurance by employees. If insurance protects risk averse people against risks, and if the alternative to insuring a loss is sustaining the loss as an out of pocket payment, the only reason not to buy insurance is that the premium is too high *relative to* the expected loss. Of course, if the loss is high, the premium will be high, but the response from someone that he or she cannot afford the high premium and therefore will not seek insurance is not rational; if the person cannot afford the insurance, he or she can even less well afford the loss—so it is sensible to buy the insurance. That is, the alternative to insurance is not "no loss"; it is "uninsured loss." So the only rational basis for rejecting insurance is if insurance costs more than the expected loss.

Some of the reasons why employees might fail to seek insurance are also obvious reasons why an employer who takes the cost-like-any-other cost view also might refuse to buy. Increases in the administrative loading make insurance more expensive, and purchases should decline. Smaller groups have higher administrative costs, and so one popular explanation for the decline in employment-based coverage, consistent with either theory, is the shift in average firm size to smaller firms, especially in the service sector. However, if this explanation were all there was to the decline in coverage, one would expect to find that the likelihood of offering coverage, conditional on (small) firm size, should not have changed. Instead, we find that the likelihood of offering coverage has declined over time, for small firms.

The other influence on the net cost of employment-based insurance to workers is the tax subsidy. Falling marginal tax rates, given some positive level of administrative cost, should discourage the purchase of insurance, since insuring one's medical expenses would no longer reduce one's taxes by as large an amount. The income tax rate reductions of the Reagan years may been responsible for some of the drop in employment-based insurance coverage. But increases in payroll tax rates during those years meant that, for many, the tax rate did not fall. Moreover, the increase in the proportion uninsured has not been concentrated in those higher income levels at which a fall in the tax subsidy would matter.

The conclusion is that the most obvious "demand curve" explanation for the decline in insurance coverage seems unable to explain all of what has happened, although it might explain part of it. Are there other reasons possible?

There are two alternative explanations, and they do in principle lead to different predictions about what ought to be happening. The theory of "affordability" would seem to imply that those firms that earn low profits or whose profits are declining would be the ones who would stop offering coverage. This is not exactly the prediction of the cost-like-any-other-cost theory—no manager would argue that he stopped buying raw materials because he could not afford them. But it is consistent with a generosity or moral obligation view. The key variable here at the firm level would be the level of premiums relative to profits.

The alternative and more subtle economic view notes that, for the employee, there *is* an alternative to facing the same loss without insurance—the alternative is to face a smaller loss. The loss can be reduced in one of two ways. First, the uninsured person or family can simply purchase less medical care than they would have purchased had they been insured. If moral hazard is present, this is what we would expect to happen. Second, people may expect to obtain some care without paying for it—in which case their expected out-of-pocket loss will be zero. Anyone would prefer the kind of care you can get if you have insurance, but even the inferior care rendered to persons who receive charity care or bad debt or are on Medicaid may be more attractive when it is free than paying for insurance to get higher quality care.

We do have documentation supporting the argument that Medicaid expansions in the last decade caused some reduction in private coverage (Cutler and Gruber 1995). About 17 percent of the 9.9 million person decline in private coverage is attributed to federally mandated expansions in Medicaid eligibility. Interestingly, however, Cutler and Gruber found no evidence that Medicaid expansion caused employers to stop offering an *opportunity* for coverage. Instead, employees frequently failed to take coverage that was offered (either for themselves or, often, for family members), either because the employee share was increased or because they would drop coverage for dependents who became eligible for Medicaid. Cutler and Gruber came to these conclusions through examination of cross-section data and do not explore the possibility that rising costs for private coverage may also have increased the attractiveness of going on Medicaid.

A similar view explains why people who would not be eligible for Medicaid may stop buying insurance, or stop seeking employers who offer insurance, when insurance premiums increase, even if the premium increases perfectly match increases in expected expenses: inflation increases the cost of insurance, but the cost of free care remains at zero. That is, as long as the uninsured can expect to receive a moderate amount of care as charity care, bad debt, or emergency patients, they do have an alternative to the lower wage job with an insurance benefit. Thus the *relative price* of "going bare" declines as insurance premiums increase. This is not the end of the story, however, since part of the reason why premiums rise is because the quality of medical care is rising, and higher quality costs more. If all of that higher quality could only be obtained by being insured, then there would be less erosion in coverage. Thus the other determinant of the decision to become insured is the *relative quality* of the care one would receive when insured compared to being uninsured.

So one explanation of a decline in demand for insurance by some employees is that the relative price of being uninsured has declined more than has the relative quality. Since the probability that one will receive free care falls as income rises, this explanation also implies (in contrast to the tax subsidy explanation) that the increase in persons not obtaining employer-paid insurance should be concentrated among lower wage workers.

The combination of the increased cost of private coverage (relative to the free care option) and larger numbers of people with low real incomes is the most frequently cited explanation for the decline in coverage (Kronick 1991; Acs 1995).

Although economic theory implies that the insurance offered to a group depends on the demand for insurance by members of that group, the traditional methods for providing group insurance required that a single policy be chosen for all employees. This meant that firms with workforces at different wage levels still ended up providing insurance to low wage workers, even if those workers might have preferred a package with no insurance, higher cash wages, and reliance on charity care. Low wage workers were trapped into buying insurance that they may not have wanted.

Several changes in the labor and insurance market have probably reduced the number of such trapped purchasers. The increase in the proportion of employment in small firms, in part through large firms contracting out functions they formerly performed themselves, means that firms can become more homogeneous with respect to worker wages. The janitor at General Motors had to have the same insurance as the high paid assembly line workers, but the employee of the janitorial service contractor can be uninsured. Second, the spread of cafeteria plans means that employees can opt out of a firm's health insurance plan, get back some of the premium contribution (how much is up to the firm), and take the money in cash or day care. Third, increasing heterogeneity of family units, as family sizes shrink, female-headed households grow, and two-earner families proliferate, means that firm payment of the higher premiums for family coverage becomes quite inequitable across employees; the spread of coverage for ambulatory visits (the primary type of care received by children) has also caused a greater divergence in premiums between employee-only and family coverage.

The increase in the share of the premium paid by the employee, quite pronounced between 1994 and 1995 (Sheils and Alexcih 1996), may have several explanations. Employers often give the economically incorrect explanation that they can no longer afford to pay the full premium. More rationally, the spread of managed care options in the form of a fixed dollar employer contribution across all plans will lead to an increase in the average employee share. Moreover, increasing use of employee contributions may deal with increased worker heterogeneity.

The evidence strongly suggests that the reduction in employer-paid contributions to health insurance has not substantially increased employer profits, nor was it motivated by shrinking profits. Instead, the changes are largely the result of changes in worker demands for employment-based insurance and would be expected to continue as long as the determinants of insurance demand by workers or dependents continue their downward trend. Increases in workers productivity could slow the erosion of coverage. So would (although one hates to say it) actions that reduce the quality of charity or bad debt care furnished to low (but not poverty-level) wage earners and their family members. The changes in both family and labor force composition appear likely to continue, although greater education and training for workers that enhance productivity may help to slow them.

These changes may also help to explain why, in the 1990s, higher income workers have joined the ranks of the uninsured. Employment (even some higher wage workers) has shifted toward smaller firms, so that the average loading may have risen somewhat; and perhaps being a patient with bad debt carries less social disapprobation than before. However, the most plausible explanation for the increase would trace it to the increase in the share of employee-paid premium. Even when those premiums are tax shielded, it is still true that the employee who owes a larger share of the premium saves more by dropping coverage. Since the employee premium is usually (though not always) community rated, such arrangements may encourage workers who are lower risk or only mildly risk averse to drop coverage.

How would acceptance of the economic view change one's attitudes toward the erosion of coverage? The most obvious conclusion is a negative one—the erosion of coverage is not attributable to an increase in social irresponsibility among business owners, and, indeed, imposition of a requirement to provide coverage, without additional subsidies, will make worse off—in their own estimation—exactly those uninsured workers one presumably wishes to help. The reason is that the workers preferred the cash compensation that employers will have to sacrifice if they are to pay for insurance.

Would some workers gain, or would some employers gain, because of the fall in bad debt and charity care that might be associated with a mandate? The earlier discussion of cost shifting suggests that, while such gains are possible, they are not especially likely and certainly will fall short of the reduction in wages for those mandated to obtain coverage. Instead, such coverage will cause an increase in the use of medical services and an increase, at least for a while, in the net incomes of health care providers.

Are there policy actions short of mandation to stem the erosion of employment-based coverage? One major and desirable action, to be discussed in the next section, is reform of the system of tax subsidies, so that subsidies to purchase insurance flow to those who need them to make their insurance purchases possible.

The main message for employers is that imposed obligations to pay for employees' insurance, or a positive response to subsidies for such purchases, will have little effect on employers' bottom lines. Workers may be a little healthier and a little happier (the latter greatly depending on the degree of coercion and the pattern of subsidies), and that will presumably benefit employers a little. But the main consequences, positive or negative, of increasing workers' insurance coverage will fall on the workers themselves.

Which theory, the economic theory of wage incidence or the managerial theory of affordability, better explains the secular erosion of insurance coverage and its pattern? At the aggregate level, the economic theory comes out ahead. Although net business income fluctuates over time, there is no evidence of a long term decline in profits or net income that would cause employers to be increasingly unable to afford coverage. It is true that because of the rise in health benefits costs, the ratio of those costs to profits has risen. However, employers could have continued to pay the same dollar amount toward insurance premiums (letting employee contributions rise), rather than dropping coverage altogether. Moreover, there is no evidence that profits have been negatively affected in industries or firms that have retained coverage.

Of greater interest is the pattern of change in the uninsured. The most remarkable change—the shift of the composition of the uninsured to dependents—is hard to square with the affordability theory. There is no obvious reason why dependent costs are less affordable than workers' costs or why firms under pressure should increase the premium share for dependents relatively more than that for workers. In contrast, the economic theory of incidence coupled with the presence of the tax subsidy offers an easy explanation of what has happened. As workforces have become more heterogeneous, with more workers having fewer dependents or having their dependents covered by a spouse's plan, it has become increasingly inefficient for employers to provide large tax-free contributions to workers seeking family coverage. Instead, the employer contribution was cut back to an amount closer to the premium for individual coverage, with the result that the explicit employee premium share for family coverage rose, reducing the demand for such coverage. In addition, the minority of workers who decline coverage for themselves or their dependents cannot find an alternative source of group insurance; the tax subsidy to employment-based groups displaced other groups that might have displayed less heterogeneity.

The most direct comparative test of the economic theory has, as far as I am aware, not been performed. It would ask whether a given dollar payment toward the premium is less likely to be offered to the worker, employee productivity and compensation held constant, as firm profits fell—as firms were unable to "afford" coverage. While there is some correlation between profitability and wages that confuses the issue, we do not find low wage profitable firms eager to offer benefits, nor do we find firms that employ high wage workers, such as law firms and management consultants, dropping coverage when profits fall. Finally, what we do know about the determinants of coverage a firm offers its workers strongly suggests that the coverage is tailored to what the workers demand (given their incomes), not to what the employer might be able to afford to pay.

Risk Variation and Community Rating

Workers will vary, at any point in time, in their expected medical expenses for the upcoming period of insurance coverage. In one sense, virtually all of this variation in risk must be attributable to the presence of "chronic conditions," if a chronic condition means a physiological state in which illness is more likely over an extended period of time. Even the presence of a genetic predisposition or a positive test for some latent disease could be thought of as a chronic condition. However, the presence of a chronic condition does not necessarily mean that medical care will have to be used in any particular current period or that functioning is impeded.

Someone has to know about an employee's or a dependent's chronic condition for it to matter. Usually the employee will know first, but the employer and/or the insurer may know as well. Often, however, what an employer knows about a population of employees is not the exact identity of persons with chronic conditions but rather information about characteristics usually correlated (but not perfectly so) with such conditions, such as age or gender. Knowing these characteristics will not allow perfect prediction of future medical expenses, and knowing exactly which chronic conditions a person has will add predictive power above and beyond knowing the person's age or gender. The other important fact is that (definitionally) chronic conditions develop and persist over time, often in an unpredictable fashion. Thus, beginning with a population of persons with no such conditions, at some point in the future some of those persons will have higher expected expenses than the others, but which persons will experience elevated expected expenses is itself a random variable, viewed from the beginning of the period.

Given these facts how do group insurance markets deal with risk? Do they deal with it in a way consistent with the economic theory of incidence (given the tax subsidy), and do they deal with it well?

Insurance markets have a difficult time dealing with the problem of variations in medical risk. It is not the variability in risk per se that is the problem—if an insurer can distinguish perfectly among different risks, it is a simple matter to propose different insurance premiums. The complications here arise from imperfect information about risks, and from the possible desire, by the employer, employee, or society, to spread the risk of having premiums fluctuate, to insure against the "risk of becoming a high risk."

Risk Spreading, Redistribution, and Social Objectives

Discussions of appropriate social policy in situations in which risk levels vary are very confused. Some people simply assume—without any explicit justification—that a desirable social situation is one in which all persons pay the same premium for a given nominal insurance policy, regardless of their risk level. Sometimes this type of insurance pricing is called "spreading the risk" and even identified as the primary social function of insurance markets, but it is not. The reason is that voluntary insurance markets (the only kind that deserve the name "market") will only spread the risk of things *that are uncertain and have yet to happen.* Things that have already happened cannot be insured after the fact. More precisely, such "insurance" (or "reinsurance") is really a euphemism for a transfer—possibly socially desirable but not insurance and not a market transaction. And there is no point in buying insurance to cover the consequences of things that are certain to happen, such as growing a year older.

Regardless of the problems of definition, the procedure of charging everyone the same premium for a nominal policy regardless of known risk has a name, "community rating," and a constituency, persons who think that insurance should serve social rather than individual purposes. Community rating is also part of the regulation of some kinds of health insurances, in some states. Few would advocate community rating of other insurances such as term life insurance—advocate that the young should pay the same premium for one million dollars in coverage as the middle aged—but they do advocate it for individually purchased and small group health insurance. How would adopting the economic theory view on the incidence of premiums matter?

Some Facts

Although people, as individuals and as employee groups, may vary in risk at any point in time, not all risk variation known to those individuals is either measured or used by insurers and employers in setting premiums. When the employee pays some part of the premium for employment-based health insurance (not usually the full premium), that premium will usually vary only with a few of the risk indicators known by the employer or insurer—it will be higher if the person buys family (or, in some cases, employee and spouse only) coverage, but it will not vary with the employee's or dependents' age or gender or the known presence of chronic conditions. Of course, older employees do not all have higher expenses than younger ones, but then neither do all families have higher expenses than all single employees. In the past, this type of community rating *within the firm* was not required by government regulation but rather was chosen by (or accepted by) the employer, outside insurer, or HMO.

The variation of premiums for the entire *group* of employees at any firm is not consistent with community rating. For groups of any size that fully self-insure, it is obvious that there is no community rating whatsoever; what is eventually paid for the insurance is whatever claims turn out to be, plus administrative costs. Many smaller firms that self-insure also buy coverage in case outlays exceed some prespecified level.

For groups that do purchase insurance from outside firms, premium determination practices vary by firm size, by type of insurance, and by state. Conventional or indemnity insurance is usually sold to large firms on a full experience rating basis, beyond the first period, but with no individual employee underwriting (gathering of information on risk indicators). That is, the total premium a firm pays this year is roughly based on what its claims were last year, sometimes with some upper bounds on the maximum premium. Except for possible state regulation of benefit packages and state premium taxation, experience-rated outside insurance for large employee groups is indistinguishable from self-insurance. Smaller groups may receive insurance that is only partially experience rated—in the sense that a group's premium depends only partially on its experience but may also depend on some characteristics of the group as a whole (age distribution, family size distribution) or on the average premium estimated for all firms similar to the firm that is offering coverage. There will generally be no inquiry into individual employee risk levels or past claims experience.

Very small groups, in contrast, are usually not experience rated as a group but may be individually underwritten, with at least some past histories and medical information gathered on individual employees. High risk for a particular employee, or just high claims in the past, may cause the very small group's premiums to jump drastically, unless the employee or dependent is dropped from the group of those who are covered. This is roughly the same practice that insurers follow in selling insurance to individuals. The extent to which premiums can be varied based on the development of a high risk condition or past high claims is usually specified in advance by the insurer; for a higher premium, the individual or small group can, when permitted by state regulation, obtain a guarantee of renewability at average premiums. Most states regulate the extent to which premiums for individual and small group coverage can be varied with experience or with underwriting information.

One issue on which there is a great deal of opinion but little fact is the question of the impact of small group underwriting practices on the number and type of people who get insurance coverage. A common fear is that outside insurers will only write coverage for one year, with no assurance, explicit or implicit, of protection against premium increases or exclusions from coverage when a chronic illness strikes a group member or dependent. When premiums rise, the high risk or unlucky group may, according to this theory, reduce coverage.

Such rating practices surely do occur, and reports of such practices, coupled with the belief that they have become much more frequent over time, have fueled proposals for insurance regulation that have been adopted by many states. Why small group insurers did not discover such practices until recently is usually not explained well; the most common explanation is a decline of market power for community rating Blue Cross/Blue Shield plans. This explanation is not convincing overall, however, both because many states never had a dominant Blue Cross/Blue Shield plan and because such plans typically engaged in their own underwriting and exclusion (though not risk rating).

If such rating practices were increasing, we would expect to see an increase in the proportion of the uninsured population represented by persons with chronic conditions, along with a high current level of that proportion. However, most of the uninsured are young and healthy, and, more to the point, I know of no evidence that, as the uninsured population grew, it became less healthy on average.

A final point that is important both for public policy and employer choices is that the chances of having a group's risk jump significantly, even for a small group, must by mathematical logic be relatively low. The reason is simple: premiums increase from the average only when some group member becomes a significantly above-average risk. But, by the definition of averages (and by the nature of the risk generating process for health insurance), such above-average cases must be a small part of the population—otherwise the average would be higher than average! This proposition does not mean that such changes in premiums or coverage are of no concern—it is precisely the rare but serious event against which risk averse people most seek protection. But it does mean that the gain from such protection is limited and must be (and presumably is) balanced against the administrative and preferred risk selection costs associated with community rating.

The most serious difficulty with the argument that such rating practices would cause groups to drop coverage is that, in general, it is not consistent with the economic theory of incidence. There are actually two different possible outcomes, depending on the *reason* why a group is a higher than average risk.

Consider first a simple situation in which all employee groups are self insured and have the same mix of risks, but risks differ across workers. For the moment, assume the only indicator of higher expected expense is older employee age, and that this fact is known to the employee, employer, and insurer. The employer knows that, on average, an employee who is older will be associated with a higher total compensation outlay than one who is younger, if they both receive the same money wage. The insurer knows that, on average, older workers will generate higher claims cost. And employees know that the net benefit from buying insurance at a given premium increases with age.

Paying the same money wage and having employees of varying ages all paying the same community rated premium cannot be an equilibrium in this situation. The reason is that some other firm can hire only the younger workers, provide them with the same insurance as in the "community rated" firm, pay them higher money wages, and still break even. The only possible equilibria in firms with mixed risks are either (1) charge higher premiums for the employee's share for older workers or (2) pay lower wages to older than to younger workers. Administratively, if older workers tend to occupy certain job categories, the second version may dominate. Indeed, this seems to be what happens; Sheiner (1995) has shown that the additional cost of insurance does fall entirely on older worker wages.

One implication is that attempts to provide community rating that ignore observable, nonrandom risk indicators such as age or gender will be inconsistent with profit maximization and/or equilibrium in the labor market. Regulatory rules that attempt to engineer transfers from younger to older workers will be undone either by adjustment of money wages (which will be very difficult to monitor) or by incentives to segregate employment by age. Another implication is that despite the higher premium or lower wages, older workers will still prefer to retain coverage, since the alternative of being uninsured involves larger expected losses for them than for younger workers.

What about the random or unexpected emergence of chronic conditions? This is a very different case from that of age or gender. Age and gender are, after all, not risks; they are certain. In contrast, desire to protect against the risk associated with a chronic condition should lead to an insurance structure that smooths out premiums. At any point in time, some workers will be healthy and others will have chronic conditions, but the former set of workers may still be attracted to firms who (adjusted) community rate because they realize that they could contract a chronic condition and want protection against that risk. We should not assume (as do Bandian and Lewin [1995]) that employers necessarily *want* to engage in community rating, but we do want to show that such practices may reduce labor costs by offering a valuable benefit to workers.

Analyzing this case is complex, however, since the employer's strategy must take into account not only the desires of current workers but also those of other workers who might be hired. Indeed, the extent of community rating that will maximize employer profit requires considering the preferences, not of all workers, but of the marginal worker—the one just ready to take or leave a job at this firm. But the marginal worker's identity will be affected by firm employment policies. For instance, if the firm adopts the strategy of avoiding workers who are already high risks or who have high risk dependents, the marginal worker will be one initially in good health and will generally have a risk level lower than that of existing workers. What combination of policies toward insurance premiums and money wages proves attractive to this worker?

A key assumption here is that for benefit policies to be credible, they have to be maintained continuously over time. A promise to a new worker not to raise premiums or cut wages, should that worker become higher risk, would not be credible if the firm is engaging in such behavior for current workers—even though the new worker would prefer not to make transfers to current high risk workers. If offering implicit guaranteed renewability (through community rating of any employee-paid premium and constant wages regardless of risk) did not affect the risk level of new workers, such a strategy might well be the profit-maximizing one. Indeed, it will be less administratively costly to ignore risk level variation than to try to take it into account.

There is some evidence in favor of this view. Cutler (1994) shows that the extent to which a group's total premium varies over time itself varies across groups but that this variation can be explained in part by demand variables.

Contrast these views with the alternative cost-like-any-other-cost view. Under that strategy, employers should not engage in community rating but rather should try to get their benefits costs down by raising premiums, cutting coverage, or cutting wages for high risk workers. In this model, higher claims or premiums paid for high risk workers only eat into the bottom line. For benefits managers, the message is clear: if workers are risk averse, and if turnover is moderate, according to the economic model community rating within the employment-related group may well be the strategy that maximizes firm profits. No regulation or tax subsidy is needed to get this to happen.

Community Rating for Small Groups

Now I turn to the question of risk rating of insurance provided to a group as a whole by an outside insurer and the properties of regulations that forbid or limit such risk rating. The most obvious point is that any firm can avoid any state regulation on insurance by moving to self-insurance, which is protected by ERISA from state interference. Even small firms can self-insure the bulk of their medical spending and still protect profits by buying stop loss insurance (which often is not subject to community rating rules in any case).

Suppose, however, that there is a set of firms that would never consider self-insurance. For them, community rating is a vehicle for protection against jumps in premiums, but it sets up undesirable incentives for insurers. In particular under community rating, insurers will be eager to sell insurance to small firms identifiable as having better risks and reluctant to sell to high risk firms that will cause losses. If the amount of coverage is variable at a community rate, high risk firms will be eager to buy as much as possible, while low risk firms will seek minimum coverage. In contrast, under risk rating, insurers would be willing to insure anyone—since the premiums could always be adjusted upward to make high risks financially appealing.

The predictable result is that insurers will invest in high selling costs to good risks and will do what they can to avoid or deter bad risks. In both cases, these actions are an inefficient but unavoidable side effect of forcing a uniform premium on a situation in which costs are different.

Should owners of high risk firms favor community rating of market insurance, and should owners of low risk firms oppose it? Under the conventional managerial view of incidence, the answer is obviously affirmative: community rating will shift costs from high risk to low risk firms, relative to risk rating. Under the economic view, the answer is less obvious. Firms with employees who are high risks for reasons for which there appear to be wage offsets, such as age or gender, will be paying lower money wages, other things equal, while risk rating prevails. If the switch to community rating does not change the composition of firm workforces, the effect of community rating will be to raise the money wages of high risk workers and lower those of low risk workers; employer profit will not be directly affected. However, it may be that some other causes of high risk, such as chronic illness, may not lead to wage offsets—in which case owners of firms that are high risk for these reasons would gain from community rating. Moreover, risk averse workers may see community rating as a way of smoothing premiums, if risk at the group level is a random variable. It seems unlikely that the desired level of smoothing would produce literally uniform premiums regardless of risk, and there is no particular reason to believe that regulators will come up with the right bands or limits. On the other hand, there are voluntary market devices available to produce level premiums that do not distort insurer incentives.

Community rating may also set up incentives to alter insurance offerings so that low risk workers may avoid making transfers they may not be eager to make. Given a community rated premium calculated as an average of some mix of high and low risks, the desired level of insurance will be smaller for the low risks than for the high risks—for the simple reason that community rating subsidizes premiums for high risks by taxing premiums for low risks. One would expect low risk groups to opt for policies with less coverage—either in terms of high deductibles or in terms of managed care that is less generous than average in what it provides for serious illness. Not only is giving up some expensive but little-used coverage advantageous to low risks, they will find in equilibrium that the people who buy the policies they like are also predominantly low risks—so that the "community rate" for such policies will primarily reflect the experience of lower risks. This artificial adverse selection, caused by the regulatory requirement that premiums ignore risk, will cause the alleged social objective of community rating to be frustrated, some have alleged. Low risks will pull out of the policies high risks buy, and the premiums for those policies will have to rise as cross subsidies evaporate.

In order to prevent such adverse selection, the new leak will have to be plugged by a new regulation, this time one that forbids policies designed to appeal to (or pick off) low risks. This sort of regulation represents a serious issue, since it will end up forbidding policies that people might have chosen even in the absence of adverse selection, in order to prevent their use by those trying to shirk their obligation to make transfers. From the viewpoint of employers, such regulations seriously limit their ability to use variations in insurance coverage to obtain sustainable competitive advantage and, in the limit, push toward Clinton-like mandatory purchasing groups. In order to stop yet another leak, the regulatory body will have to grow another tentacle and may end up as a monster.

The potential tragedy is that such regulation may not even be necessary to prevent risk segmentation by plan type, if one has patience. It is true (according to the economic theory on this subject) that any pooled risk equilibrium calls forth a profitable policy that will be selected by low risks and that premiums will then rise in the "old" policy. But this need not be the end of the story. As premiums rise for the kind of policy favored by high risks, they may find that policy less attractive than the stricter policy chosen by the low risks—and so the high risks may join the low risks in their new policy. There may not be risk segmentation after all, only an incentive to select more cost-containing insurance policies. Of course, once everyone has moved to the catastrophic policy or to the strict HMO, some of the rationale for that policy may be lost, and more generous policies may be feasible. So the main consequence of adverse selection (in economic theory, at least) can be a kind of churning or cycle that is, in itself, of little social consequence as long as the low risks still choose a decent insurance policy.

Conclusion

Regulation to require community rating tries to achieve some laudable objectives. It seeks to smooth insurance premiums for the average person who experiences bouts of high risk, and it seeks to help those unfortunate enough to become permanent high risks (even if they are rich). But it is an inefficient, inequitable, and illogical way to achieve those goals, since it creates distortions in insurance markets that probably are worse than the problem it tries to solve, and it cannot stop short of virtually complete regulatory control over insurance offerings and premiums. Far better to handle risk variation with more subtle devices, such as requirements for renewability and high risk pools for the few really high risks. Employers in general definitely do not obtain any long run benefit from community rating (not even those with older workers), and it can require them to jump through some quite complex and narrow regulatory hoops. While competitive labor markets and the ability to vary money wages can offset any negative effects of community rating on employers of low risk workers, planning and coping with the artificially caused side effects of a solution to a minor problem impose managerial costs of their own.

Tax Subsidies and Employer Interests

As already noted at several points, that portion of compensation paid as health insurance premiums receives special tax treatment. Such payments are permitted as a deduction ("cost") from gross revenues for purposes of calculating an employer's taxable net income; they are also excluded from the base of the employer's share of the payroll tax for Medicare and Social Security. For employees, such payments do not increase either income or payroll taxes; they are excluded from taxable income and wages. In contrast to pensions for which premiums can also be excluded from taxable income but benefits are taxed, for health insurance, no tax is paid on the value of medical benefits received.

If the firm sets up a cafeteria (Section 125) plan, employees can shield from federal income taxation both their share of the group insurance premium and deposits in a flexible spending account to cover out of pocket payments. Most states follow federal procedures in dealing with the exclusion, but some tax income shielded from federal taxes in a cafeteria plan.

The regulations dealing with the exclusion are fairly permissive. They require that employer payments be "nondiscriminatory" for classes of workers (e.g., the same for low paid and high paid workers). This rule can easily be satisfied by a uniform employer contribution, with any variation in premium to be paid by workers. Even those worker contributions can be tax shielded if there is a cafeteria plan.

Ending or limiting these "tax subsidies" has been a prime target for economists trying to identify a stimulus to health care spending that government action could remove. The argument is as follows: since medical expenses can be shielded from taxation by having them insured, it is rational for taxpayers to do so. But insurance is known to stimulate medical care spending. In addition, spending more on tax shielded medical care can reduce the employee's total taxes, so that the net cost of medical insurance (or of medical care, if made via a flexible spending account) is reduced by the amount of saved taxes. That both the tax advantages and the stimulus to spending are larger for higher income workers who save more taxes per dollar of excluded medical spending has buttressed the case for removing the tax exclusion.

Putting some limits on this tax loophole was part of the health reform debate, but, as noted previously, some bills (most especially the Cooper bill) seem to have been based on the assumption that insurance premium payments represented inappropriate costs for the employer, because they limited the *employer's* tax deduction. Political interest in doing something about the open-ended exclusion remains high.

There is another potential adverse consequence of the tax subsidy to employer-paid health benefits: it can lead to excessive employer interference in the choice of the form and amount of health benefits. This interference takes two forms, one certain and one a little more speculative. The form of interference that is certain is the stimulus the tax subsidy gives to imposing employer or group choices on all workers, regardless of their preferences. Group purchase of insurance necessarily implies some uniformity, relative to what people would choose. People may rationally choose to limit their choices. Those groups that are large (so the cost advantage is great) and homogeneous would be expected to obtain insurance through the workplace, even under neutral incentives. The difficulty arises because the tax subsidy offers small and heterogeneous groups an incentive to provide group health insurance in a setting in which the individual market would have worked reasonably well.

The more speculative question is whether the tax treatment of employer-paid health benefits offers an incentive to incorrect choice, even of the uniform benefit. There are some informal reasons why this might happen. Because the portion of compensation paid in the form of health benefits is not taxed, employees do not realize, it is often alleged, that they are receiving benefits of high value. While a few firms do go to the effort of issuing statements to employees that document the dollar cost of the benefits they receive, these statements do not have the uniformity or the force of the W-2 withholding statements required by tax law—and the W-2 statement itself cannot legally be modified to reflect the cost of benefits.

With employees ignorant of the full cost of the benefit they receive, their reactions appear to run to two polar cases—either they ignore the details of their "free" insurance or they discover to their alleged surprise that the benefits are not as good as they thought. This pattern, one may speculate, led many employers to move aggressively into managed care and then caused many employees to react in horror at finding that this coverage was, in some dimensions, not as permissive or accommodating as the more costly conventional insurance coverage they were used to receiving.

Slightly more formally, the exclusion of employer payments from employee taxable income probably contributes itself to employer misperception on incidence. Roughly speaking, an employer or group must do one of two things to keep the "employer payment" from becoming taxable income: either it must provide opportunity for the same insurance benefit to all employees (uniform benefit) or it must provide the same dollar payment toward the insurance of each employee (uniform contribution).

The simplest version of the first approach is when an employer provides a fully paid insurance to all workers or, alternatively, allows a choice among a number of alternative plans at no additional cost. The simplest version of the second approach is a Section 125 plan in which the employer gives each worker a given amount of tax-free "flex dollars." The key issue is that in both cases the worker is unable to convert the "contribution" to cash (taxable or not). Instead, it remains in the form of an earmarked and employer-managed benefit—rather than the proxy payment for the employee that it truly represents.

If such employer payments were both reported as income and taxed as income, it seems plausible that there would be some substantial changes. To begin with, in the first case of full employer payment for self-insured benefits, employers would be required to allocate this spending to different workers. They might do by simply dividing the total payment on an equal per-worker basis, but they might also choose other bases for allocation. For example, they might allocate more to older workers, more highly paid workers, or workers who smoke or fail to maintain their health. The outcome should be greater employee awareness of both the value of the benefit and of the value of the employer payment as a way of avoiding a higher tax share. Likewise a reduction in the overall costliness of the benefit in itself will reduce taxable income—and lead to better choices.

The federal law requiring continuation of group coverage for employees who leave a group provides a model of how premiums might be determined. Those rules permit a simple per-employee calculation, but they also permit a more complex actuarially based set of calculations. The only constraint really required is one that prevents allocating the cost of coverage disproportionately to low tax workers.

More generally, the current tax law treats employer payments for health insurance—from the employer's point of view—as a cost like any other cost, fully deductible for purposes of computing the employer's net taxable income. But, in contrast to any other employer expense, which can in part become taxable income for the supplier of the input, the cost represented by insurance premiums is not part of taxable income for the employee or anyone else. This inconsistent and asymmetric treatment seems almost purposefully designed to foster the illusion that health benefits are a gift from the employer, not earned compensation by the employee. With this illusion operating it is no wonder that the employer feels free to tamper with, modify, or curtail his or her gift and also no wonder that employees are in a continual state of dissatisfaction. In effect, the worst consequence of the tax treatment of health insurance may not be the impact of the subsidy to excessive health benefits; rather, it may be the subsidy to the illusion about whose money this is and whose interests are at stake that has distorted and continues to distort the way Americans evaluate their private health insurance.

Limiting the Tax Exclusion

In the face of these outcomes, proposals to limit or remove the tax subsidy by taxing employees on the value of the benefit or the contribution to the benefit have been made. Employers appear to be resistant to such proposals. Would taxing benefits reduce profits?

Consider first the economists' favorite solution: requiring any employer premium contribution (as well as any money run through a cafeteria plan) to be treated as taxable income for the employee for purposes of calculating the employee's income and payroll tax liability. The simple device of including the value of these contributions in taxable wages would permit such a change in tax treatment, although the self-insuring group would need to determine how to divide the total cost of its benefits among different workers. Who would bear the consequences of such a tax increase, and would it adversely affect employers who pay for employee health insurance?

We need to consider two different labor market situations. In one, all employers provide the same premium contribution. In the other, some provide more than others, and some provide none at all.

In the first situation, both models would yield the same conclusion about the impact of the tax: raising taxes on employees should not affect the employer. This would amount to an increase across the board in taxes on wages. Its only economy-wide impact would be to discourage working for wage income, in the same way as any payroll tax would. If the supply of labor was somewhat responsive to net wage economy, the economic model would predict an increase in wage rates as some workers withdraw from the labor market.

However, there is a striking difference in views in terms of the choice of insurance benefit. The economic view would indicate strongly that, after the tax increase, employees would desire (and employers would gain by) a reduction in the generosity of the insurance plan offered. The reason, of course, is that removing the tax subsidy in effect raises the net price of insurance, or of paying for medical service via insurance, and so employees should want less of it. Going along with this change in employee demand, by raising wages and cutting both contributions to insurance and the overall level of the insurance plan, would make working at a firm more attractive. In contrast, the managerial view would not see any connection between higher employee taxes and the insurance the employer chooses to "give" the employee.

A further difference between the two models would emerge in the second situation. Those who believe that benefits costs are paid by the employer would presumably view an increase in taxes on the wages of workers at firms that pay benefits as, again, like an income tax on workers, of no concern to the employer since the tax was not levied on the employer. In contrast, under the economic view, such a tax would reduce the relative attractiveness of working at firms that pay for health insurance premiums and would have the kind of firm- or industry-specific excise tax effects of mandated benefits discussed in chapter 3, but this time labor costs would increase and profits would fall, at least until firm-specific capital adjusted, at firms that initially did offer premium payment as a benefit.

The most important difference between the two views would emerge if the tax were initially imposed on the employer, by limiting or eliminating the tax deductibility of compensation payments in the form of health insurance premiums. (Some versions of the flat tax have a similar property.) If the benefits were viewed as the employer's cost, removal of their tax deductibility would raise employer taxes. Either the employer would stop paying compensation in this fashion, or else profits would fall. Whether ceasing to pay for insurance would be helpful to the employer is unclear in this view, but presumably any reduction in premium payments would have to be offset by higher money wage payments.

In the economic view, there would be no difference in effects on employers and workers from removing deductibility and increasing the employer's tax payments and an identical increase in taxes on workers— but with the tax levied at the tax rate applicable to the employer (i.e., the employer's personal income tax rate or the corporate income tax rate) rather than at the employee's income and payroll tax combined. The incidence of this tax would fall on the employer only if the supply of labor were responsive to net wages, as discussed earlier. However, employers would gain by shifting from premium payments to employees only if the employees' tax rate was less than the employer's tax rate. In some circumstances (e.g., corporations that employ high wage workers), the economic view would suggest that it would be better for the employer to pay the tax than to stop paying for insurance premiums and increase employee wages by an equal amount.

Conclusion

The two views of incidence differ most in terms of the impact of the tax treatment of employer-paid insurance on the employer's choice of insurance plan—how generous would the benefits be? The economic view draws a much stronger connection between taxes employees may have to pay on employer-provided benefits and the desired generosity of those benefits. In contrast, the managerial view pays much more attention to the distinction between reducing or eliminating the employee tax exclusion rather than the employer tax deductibility. The economic view looks only at the size of the net tax paid, regardless of on whom it is initially levied.

The Employment Effects of Mandates and the Incidence of Employer-Paid Insurance Premiums

One of the more contentious issues in the debate on health reform, and one which may resurface in the future in various ways, was the question of possible employment effects of mandates for employer premium payment. One's conclusion on this subject ought to be strongly affected by one's views on the incidence of mandated payments. If such payments cause wages to fall, with little or no impact on the compensation cost per worker, there is no reason for employers to seek to change their hiring and employment plans. In contrast, if mandated payments are a dollar-for-dollar add-on to the cost of hiring workers, this increase in price should affect the number of workers demanded and may also affect the hours demanded from a given stock of workers. To the extent that exact incidence on wages reflects a worker value of mandated health insurance payments just equal to the value of money compensation, worker supply will be unchanged. But to the extent that the additional payments differ in value from wages forgone, the supply of workers at a given total compensation cost per worker may change as well.

In what follows I review the controversy over employment effects of mandated benefits. Most of the participants in this controversy were economists, and so it may be especially useful to see whether their views on employment effects depended on assumptions about incidence. The less elaborate view of policymakers and lobbyists may also hint at their more fundamental beliefs on incidence, as well as at the presence or absence of logical consistency in their thinking.

The Simplest Theory

If all labor markets were competitive and there were no restrictions on money wages, full incidence of employer premium payments would imply no change in the quantity of labor demanded. In effect, if benefits cut wages, they have no need to cut employment demanded. The only possible cause of reduced employment would then be decisions of persons not to seek work, because the premium payment was not as valuable as the wages it replaced. Thus the only kind of unemployment that could be caused would be *voluntary,* and, since it would represent withdrawal from the labor force, it would not even be counted as part of the unemployment rate. That is, the number of jobs available would not fall, although the number of jobs accepted might fall.

Analysts who concluded that a mandate would affect employment and unemployment were then required to find some reason why wages would not fall by enough to offset the benefits cost. No one argued that the supply of labor would be affected, perhaps because supply of labor to a market is thought to be unresponsive to compensation offered over a wide range or perhaps because voluntary decisions to withdraw from the labor market would not necessarily be regarded as a policy problem. Recall that, in the economic model, compensation cost per worker would only increase (and profits fall) if the supply of labor were somewhat responsive to real compensation. But this case would *not* be one in which there would be an increase in involuntary unemployment.

Why Wages Might Not Fall

There were three broad categories of reasons offered as to why money wages might not fall by enough to offset premium cost increases. One, occasionally mentioned in the policy literature but not taken into account in the analytic literature, is that there might be lags in the adjustment of money wages. Since, as noted previously, no one knows how long the lag is if it occurs, and since mandated coverage was due to be phased in gradually, this was not a very strong argument.

The most common argument was that minimum wage laws would prevent money wages from falling for some part of the labor force. Wages could not fall for those who began at or near the minimum wage.

A third argument, as already noted, is that wage equity within the firm would require that money wages of low wage employees not be cut in response to a mandate. The notion is that the minimum wage cannot be cut, and reducing wages close to the minimum would compress the firm's wage structure. Rather than cut wages by the full amount of the cost of the mandate, the firm would reduce wages by less and fire workers (O'Neill and O'Neill 1994). Firms were assumed to leave money wages untouched for employees earning less than $25,000 and to reduce wages by only half of the cost for all others. Not surprisingly, these assumptions led to higher estimates of "job loss" than those that focused on minimum wage workers alone. Similar assumptions about limits in wage reduction caused similarly larger estimates from CONSAD Research Corporation (1993).

Some Ignored Issues

As already noted, none of the estimates paid any attention to the question of labor *supply* responsiveness or elasticity. As Klerman and Goldman (1994) noted, they turned primarily on the question of whether one supposed that a mandate would cause some increase in average labor cost per worker (by assuming something less than full backward shifting) and then used a labor demand elasticity, or whether one assumed full backward shifting for all but those constrained by the minimum wage and then used estimates of the elasticity of employment with respect to the minimum wage. In part supply responsiveness was left out because reductions in employment caused by workers withdrawing from wage work could not be labeled "job loss." The jobs would still (potentially) be there; it's just that, given that they pay low wages and high benefits, no one would want them.

The other issue is the reliability and applicability of estimates of the effects of minimum wage changes on employment. While estimates of the size of this effect vary, the ones that had recently become available at the time of the debate on health reform suggested that the impacts of increases in the 1990s have been small or zero. These estimates were based primarily on case studies; estimates using larger samples were generally from older studies and did show impacts for teenagers and young adults, with elasticity estimates ranging from nearly zero to 0.3. Other estimates are as high as 0.5 (Neumark and Wascher 1992).

Quantitative Estimates

Using these estimates, and taking account of the subsidies built into the Clinton proposal for low wage firms, estimates of job loss are generally in the range of 0.1 percent to 0.2 percent of employment (Klerman and Goldman 1994) but could be as high as 0.65 percent. More recent studies of the effects of minimum wages have been inconsistent with the small or zero impact result and more consistent with the larger estimate of job loss.

One important source of imprecision in these estimates is an estimate of the number of minimum wage workers who would receive (temporary) subsidies under the Clinton plan. According to Klerman and Goldman, approximately 10 percent of all workers, or about 10 million workers, earn low enough wages that they might be "vulnerable" to minimum wage–related wage increases under an employer mandate. O'Neill and O'Neill estimated a larger number, at about 15,000,000, or a little less than 15 percent of the workforce. Minimum wage workers in large firms with high average wages would receive zero subsidies, but those in smaller firms with low average wages would receive subsidies at first. Klerman and Goldman estimate that about a quarter of uninsured employees are in firms with wages large enough that they would probably receive little or no subsidy. They estimated that, after the effect of the subsidy is considered, the average currently uninsured worker's employer will pay a premium equal to 10.4 percent of payroll expense.

However, they were unable to estimate what this would mean for minimum wage workers. If we assume that the average wage in firms employing the average uninsured minimum wage worker is $20,000 per year, an additional 10.4 percent of payroll expense is indeed equivalent to an increase in labor cost of approximately $1.00 per hour. Assume that half the vulnerable workers earn just the minimum wage and that the remaining wages are uniformly distributed. Then the average percentage change in wages for the vulnerable group is 18 percent. Using the elasticity of 0.3 and applying it to the ten million to fifteen million vulnerable workers, I conclude that about 600,000 to 900,000 workers would lose their jobs.

However, there are some important differences between the analysis of a standard increase in the minimum wage and this analysis. One difference is that the wage subsidies in the Clinton plan were not guaranteed. Without them, the job losses would be much greater. The O'Neills set this "no subsidy" number at more than three million.

The other difference is more relevant. If providing 80 percent of a health insurance policy for a worker costs about $2,000, the effect of mandated payment of that premium is approximately equivalent to raising the minimum wage by $1 per hour. If employers are making profit-maximizing decisions about employment, they will have to discharge enough minimum wage workers to raise the productivity of those who remain by $1 per hour. Taken literally, the minimum wage elasticity estimates imply that cutting only 7 percent of workers will be enough to accomplish this. This seems implausible, although we have no external evidence to check it.

One explanation for why minimum wage effects are so small is that employers do not base hiring and retaining decisions entirely on a comparison of a worker's productivity today with his or her wage today. Instead, they anticipate that, over time, a worker's productivity within the firm will rise. So they pay wages higher than those based on productivity to start and then take this excess payment out of wages, setting wages a little lower than productivity, when workers become more experienced. If the increase in worker productivity is associated with firm-specific increase in experience, the lower subsequent wages will not cause workers to switch firms. Inflation may also erode minimum wage limits, and more productive workers do not leave for other firms because their skills are to some extent firm specific.

A mandated health benefit is not the same as an increase in wages, however, for two reasons. First, the cost of paying 80 percent of premiums is sure to increase over time; a mandated benefit is like a built-in cost-of-living escalator in the minimum wage. Second, the cost of benefits is likely to rise as workers get older and have families with higher medical expenses. These considerations led me to conclude that the elasticity of employment with respect to a mandated benefit was likely to be much higher than the elasticity with respect to the minimum wage. Using the O'Neills' estimate of 15 percent of the population as vulnerable, the elasticity could be as high as 0.6, so that the job loss would be approximately twice the figure given in the preceding, or as many as 1.6 million workers, even with subsidies.

I do not wish to defend any of these estimates; my point is that they are necessarily imprecise. What one can say is that, to the extent that job losses are small, one of two things must happen: either there must be more of an impact on wages, or there must be more of an impact on profits. Part of the O'Neills' high (three million) estimate was due to their assumption of imperfect shifting. Remove this assumption, and their estimates of job losses fall, but estimates of wage losses rise.

Implications

From the viewpoint of policy, are high medical benefits costs for *voluntary* coverage a matter of concern for employment? The answer from the preceding analysis is largely negative. The minimum wage workers who might be affected in terms of employment often are not provided employer-paid coverage, for reasons having to do with low income and the absence of tax subsidies. Some teenager and young adult unemployment could result in those firms paying minimum wages and offering benefits, but it is likely that the lost jobs could be re-created as jobs that do not have as large an employer payment for insurance.

With mandated benefits it is quite another story. Job loss based on static considerations is likely to be small, but the hit on profits is fairly substantial, even with Clinton-type subsidies. Firms (often small) with minimum wage workers that opposed the Clinton plan even with subsidies were behaving in a rational manner. Over time, more jobs would be lost as the escalation of the payment obligation continues to pressure minimum wage employment. Although discharging workers cushions the blow on profits somewhat, if the expectation of rapidly growing mandated benefits costs turns out to be true, the fall in profits will continue.

The messages for management are important. If one takes the economic view, one message is that there is no need to respond to benefit cost increases by reducing the workforce for non–minimum wage workers; managerial effort is better devoted to constraining money wages. In contrast, the cost like any other cost view would point toward discharge of expensive workers as a reasonable response across wage levels.

The other message is that minimum wage workers may have to be let go. There are other adjustments possible, since money wages cannot be touched. Other benefits (vacation pay, etc.) could be eliminated or steps taken to increase productivity (faster pace of work, less time off, more overtime, or employment at less preferred hours). Note that employers would do this not because they want to harm workers but because they want to avoid the worse harm of cutting insurance benefits or firing workers. Moreover, if the benefits are of additional value to workers, employers can increase the "desirability" of minimum wage work and still expect to find good workers.

Portability and Job Lock

Most employment-based insurance is tied to a job with a specific firm. If the worker switches firms, he or she will lose whatever coverage accompanied the initial job and obtain whatever coverage goes with the new job. There are three threats to continuous insurance coverage that can arise in this process. First, the worker may not be able to find any new job, at least for a time. Federal legislation requires that many of those who were insured be permitted to continue that coverage for 18 months at group rates while unemployed or self employed. Of course, if the employer formerly paid some compensation as insurance premiums, it will appear to the unemployed person that the cost of the insurance went up, since now he or she will have to pay the entire premium. But it is more correct to say that, when the worker lost the job, both the money wage and the employer premium contribution were lost—but he or she pays the same amount for insurance out of reduced total income as before.

The second threat is that the new job may not come with health insurance, or with as generous an insurance policy as the old job. If the rate of job switching is no higher for firms that offer insurance than for those that do not, this influence cannot contribute to a higher net rate of uninsurance: for every person who loses a job with insurance and gains one without insurance, there will be someone who leaves a job without insurance and takes one with insurance.

The third threat is that coverage will be provided but it will exclude, for a time, coverage of preexisting conditions. It would appear that people who move quickly between jobs that carry insurance benefits would lose nothing. However, it is fairly common for the new insurer to refuse to cover conditions that began under the old insurer, at least for a period of time. This means that those persons in the midst of an episode of illness lose coverage for preexisting conditions.

The collapse of efforts for large-scale health reform led to renewed interest in incremental efforts to achieve the goals of cost containment and improved access to medical services and medical insurance, culminating in the passage of the Kassebaum-Kennedy bill in the summer of 1996. This bill uses federal regulation of private insurance offerings (as an alternative to direct government subsidies); it limits to no more than 12 months the period of time during which an insurer or employer (in the case of self-insured plans) can refuse to pay medical claims for conditions or illnesses whose onset occurred before the effective date of coverage purchased from that insurer. It reduces the waiting period depending on the length of prior coverage. Such regulations have obvious populist appeal, since they appear to force the insurer to pay benefits to people who need them and had made some previous attempts to have them covered. As long as the new insurer is also an employment-based group, it should be relatively easy to enforce such an open enrollment rule. However, if the new coverage were to be an individual insurance policy, insurers have much more concern about the requirements in the bill. From the experience in Washington State, requiring open enrollment for individual coverage with no requirement for prior coverage can cause substantial increases in premiums (Richards 1995).

A more realistic view will note, however, that these are governmental regulations in the pure sense of the term; if they constrain sellers, they also constrain buyers. In particular, they forbid employees from purchasing insurance that insures everything but does not cover preexisting conditions. In the group insurance context, they forbid workers from taking or keeping jobs at firms that do not cover preexisting conditions. Such a restriction on choice would not be harmful except for another virtually certain feature: requiring coverage of preexisting conditions will, in competitive insurance markets, cause the premiums for coverage to be higher than would be the case if exclusions remained. How much the premiums will increase depends, of course, on the magnitude of the problem of pre-existing condition exclusions. Premiums will rise by small amounts only if denial of benefits was an insurer problem. If it was a serious problem, increases will be substantial.

However much benefit forbidding exclusion provides to that small minority of new insurance purchasers with preexisting conditions, this regulation raises the price of insurance. Who will bear the cost of this increase? The answer, in line with the earlier analysis, is all current workers and all new workers without such conditions. Such buyers may reasonably wonder why they are the subjects of transfers to others—if "society" wants to make it cheaper for persons with such conditions to buy coverage, why doesn't society (rather than just people employed at firms that offer coverage) pay for the additional benefits? The equity of this type of mandate, when there is no overall obligation to buy coverage, might be questioned. These buyers will seek out insurers and employers that try to avoid complying with the regulations. If they cannot find such alternatives, at least some of them may choose not to purchase coverage for themselves.

These observations do not mean that the regulation should not be imposed. They do mean that the costs and benefits of the regulation should have been documented before it is enacted. There are two ways of describing such a cost-benefit trade-off. One way is to measure costs and benefits, a task that is both laborious and almost always imprecise. The other approach is to investigate the functioning, in theory and in practice, of competitive markets, to see whether one can identify reasons why or whether the market fails in its usual function of offering all those products and product characteristics whose benefit to consumers exceeds their cost.

This approach will be followed here. I will examine whether we can conclude that market-determined preexisting condition exclusions are inefficient and whether regulations can be counted on to improve efficiency.

To understand what effects the link to employment causes, I first describe the type of insurance coverage one would expect to emerge in competitive markets without such a link. Imagine that people bought insurance individually, from insurers who are highly competitive. What conditions would an insurer selling insurance to new customers impose on payments for health conditions that had begun before the insurance purchase?

The answer to this question depends in part on the information the insurer can reasonably have at the time of purchase. If the insurer knows the conditions each buyer has, premiums will reflect the presence of conditions associated with higher than average expected costs (but if the level or event of high cost is still uncertain, insurance at those premiums will still be purchased).

In the more realistic case in which the insurance purchaser knows more about preexisting conditions than does the insurer, adverse selection becomes a possibility. Buyers will go without coverage when they expect low expenses and only seek coverage when they expect to use it. This is adverse selection of the most adverse kind, and sellers of insurance would be expected to take steps to inhibit it. The most obvious step to take is for sellers of insurance to refuse to cover expenses associated with illnesses that purchasers already knew about. The evidence for prior knowledge usually is some prior treatment or indicator of the onset of the condition. The advantage of excluding coverage (rather than ascertaining the risk of each buyer) is that exclusion only comes into play for a small number of buyers: those who both have a condition and choose to make a claim related to that condition during the exclusion period.

Such provisions will reduce (though not prevent entirely) adverse selection. But they potentially expose insurance purchasers to a new risk. If, for some reason unrelated to the existence of a condition, a person wishes to change insurers, he or she will pay a penalty for doing so if a condition happens to be present. Moving from one area of the country to another, or just changing one's preferred source of insurance, are things that can and do happen to people, but the presence of preexisting condition clauses means that they expose people to new risks.

Those changes in health status that can be identified as definitely *not* due to adverse selection sometimes are given special treatment. Moving into an area, or the desire to change insurance on the part of someone who maintained continuous coverage up to that point, would not signify adverse selection. We would therefore expect that competitive insurers would waive the preexisting conditions exclusion in such cases. The insurer might, however, choose to charge higher premiums in the first period for all others with preexisting conditions, since otherwise an insurer that did exclude coverage could pick off those customers for new insurance not in the middle of an episode of illness. Such premium variation would presumably apply to repeat customers as well as to new ones, however.

The real problem with preexisting conditions exclusion then is that of maintaining a guarantee against premium jumps and at the same time avoiding being locked into one insurer, that is, of preserving the option to switch insurers. Moreover, as noted, the higher premium itself will discourage some good risks from maintaining coverage.

There is a trade-off here in social policy. The increase in premium for good risks can be kept to small levels only by limiting the guaranteed renewability privilege strictly—for example, by limiting it to those with continuous coverage. While this may represent an improvement over a situation in which even such persons would be subject to exclusions, it would hardly seem to need to be required by law and, more importantly, it still is not ideal. Low risk persons who experience unexpected drops in income when they lose their jobs may still drop coverage because there is no option to buy coverage at reasonable (or fair) premiums.

In the debate over group-to-individual coverage in the Kassebaum-Kennedy bill, the intrinsic inefficiency of requiring employers to guarantee coverage while at the same time permitting low risks to drop coverage has been ignored. There have been dueling estimates of the amount by which individual premiums would rise. Given some population of high risks who would take up new individual coverage under the law, we know that the aggregate amount added to other persons' premiums will be the same. Whether the increase will be 2 percent or 20 percent depends on the number of buyers in the other group. If the premium increase is smaller in percentage terms, it must affect a larger number of people. This implies that, if demand elasticity is constant, the number of low risks who will react to a premium increase by dropping coverage will be the same regardless of the size of the group over which losses are spread. The problem is that the regulations amount to the levy of a specific excise tax on insurance purchases by low risks; efficiency can only be assured by breaking the link between the subsidy to high risks and the premiums paid by low risks.

There is a way to preserve the option of group-to-individual portability and still keep low risk premiums and coverage constant: build in "runout coverage." Formally, this would mean that if I buy coverage from insurer X in time period t, and then I begin an illness in period t that does not end by the close of the period, insurer X agrees to continue to cover the expected expenses of that episode of illness. Of course, if I buy my coverage in period $t + 1$ from insurer X, there is no need to distinguish between continuing illnesses and new illnesses; the runout coverage only becomes effective if I wish to change insurers. Then the ideal arrangement would be one in which my new insurer charges me the same premium as charged to all insureds but in which coverage for my preexisting conditions is excluded. Instead, payment for expenses associated with those conditions remains the responsibility of my former insurer (although payments might be administered by a transfer of funds rather than direct payment).

This conclusion brings us to the counterintuitive heart of what would be needed for competitive markets to offer coverage of preexisting conditions at a new insurer in an efficient fashion: insurers would offer contracts that would continue to pay benefits to people who switched their profitable business to competitors. Making it easy for your customers to switch runs against the grain for most red-blooded managers, but the reason why such devices ought to emerge is not because managers want them, but because customers ought to want them, and ought to be willing to pay enough to make them profitable.

Do such contracts ever emerge? The federal COBRA law requires employers to continue to offer coverage to departed workers, but it does not require them to cover specific illnesses when the worker obtains additional coverage.

The parallel with employment-based insurance should be obvious by now. Employers offer employment-based coverage to attract and retain good workers at low money wages and low total compensation costs. Covering departed workers in their new jobs makes it much more difficult for coverage to perform the "job lock" function for which it was created, and one would not be surprised if employers were unenthusiastic about making it easy for their workers—even those in the midst of an episode of illness—to leave. Job lock is, after all, not bad from an employer's perspective and not necessarily bad from a social perspective if there are generic job training costs to employers.

These observations suggest several conclusions. First, if people are risk averse, they will prefer insurance that provides them with continuous coverage at no jumps in premiums. Despite their regulatory character, rules to forbid denial of coverage for preexisting conditions for those who were continuously insured with equal or greater coverage probably lead to efficient levels of coverage. However, the question of whether the cost of such coverage should be imposed on the original or the new insurer is not so easily answered. Should the cost be paid beforehand by the worker who will get the benefit, or should it be paid after a job change by the other workers in the new group (and, to the extent that a group has a higher than average proportion of high risks, by the employer)? Second, denial of coverage for preexisting conditions to those who dropped coverage, or those who had less generous coverage, is essential to prevent adverse selection. If information that this rule exists is made generally available, fewer rational buyers will engage in adverse selection by dropping coverage. Those who drop coverage for other reasons and then attempt to restart it are more difficult to discuss. The difficulty here is one shared with all "get tough" policies intended to promote responsible behavior. They harm further those who behave irresponsibly, but to abolish them is to offer incentives for irresponsible behavior. For those whose loss of insurance coverage is not to be punished, a public subsidy to first-time insurers would be most efficient and equitable. There is certainly no reason to charge the cost of helping the uninsured to become insured to those insureds who happen to buy from the same insurer they choose.

This leaves the issue of whether it is easier to enforce payment on the first or the second insurer. The problem with requiring the second insurer to pay is that doing so offers that insurer an incentive to avoid offering insurance to a high risk person, an incentive that may cause costs or distortions. If coverage by the first insurer could be continued for some fixed period of time (with the coverage for preexisting conditions set at the level that prevailed under the old insurance), the outcome could be efficient. Of course, efficiency would require insurers, employers, and other workers to stifle their anger at paying insurance benefits for someone who quit.

The fundamental message is that enacting regulations that require employers to cover preexisting conditions for newly hired workers has some desirable aspects, precisely because no rational consumer would want to drop insurance coverage in the midst of an episode of illness just because of a change in employment. The cost of producing this benefit will, however, not generally be borne by employers. Instead, it will fall on workers in the form of (modestly) lower money wages than would have been the case if new workers could have been denied benefits.

There are, nevertheless, three dangers for employers and regulators to watch out for. First, if forced to cover a costly condition for a new worker, an employer will either be reluctant to hire or likely to offer lower money wages. There is no way of avoiding the incentive that employers (and all the other workers currently at the firm) would have to avoid picking up the cost of an event that has already happened. The key policy question is whether the trouble of enforcing rules about hiring and wages is worth the effort to spread risk.

The second problem is that some firms may, by chance alone, have the bad luck of attracting a larger than expected number of new workers with preexisting conditions. In the short run this cost, special to this firm and not shared across the market, will fall on the employer. Unless there is some intrinsic reason why some firm attracts sicker workers—something that seems implausible—one can say that this is just temporary bad luck and that the employer should "tough it out"; over time, these things will even out. If the variation in costs across firms from abiding by a ban on exclusions is large, thought might be given to some sort of high risk pool. Here again, however, the question is whether the problem, despite its certain existence, is bad enough to require intervention.

The third potential problem would arise if employees would make choices about jobs and continuation of employment based on comparisons of insurance coverage and their expected expenses. That is, preexisting conditions exclusions do serve to reduce adverse selection, which could be a problem if the exclusions are banned or limited. The Kassebaum-Kennedy rules permitting exclusions for new employees who move from jobs with no coverage into jobs with coverage would help but still would not solve the problem of variations in coverage levels.

For persons with coverage in the old job, if the level of coverage could be defined precisely, one could require that preexisting conditions be covered, but with the old coverage (e.g., high deductibles) for a period of time, or one could require that kind of "insurance premium insurance" described in the preceding. Here again, the question is whether this theoretically possible behavioral change is all that likely or that large. There will surely be some employees who will engage in adverse selection behavior, and there will surely be some new employees who show up with preexisting conditions and no prior insurance. But the real question is whether rules banning exclusions will really make this behavior that much worse—relative to the number of continuously insured people who might lose coverage in the absence of a ban.

From the viewpoint of an employer, one threat to profitability from a ban is in the case of the firm that gets more than its expected share of new workers with preexisting conditions. The other threat comes to the firm that wishes to offer a very attractive insurance policy as a way of recruiting high quality workers but finds itself unable to reject large masses of average quality workers with preexisting conditions who might apply. Public policy should determine whether rules to enforce portability of this sort really will do enough good to be worth the harm of the bureaucratic and regulatory consternation they are bound to engender.

It is interesting that not all jobs carry preexisting condition exclusions. The KPMG survey of firms with more than 200 employees found that, in early 1995, 44 percent of employers offering conventional insurance coverage or PPO coverage had no preexisting condition limitations. Only about 30 percent of firms had limitations longer than 12 months. Since the respondents to the survey are primarily (89 percent) self insured, the ERISA preemption of state laws means that the decision to cover preexisting conditions was voluntary. Very large firms (more than 5,000 workers) are somewhat less likely to have preexisting condition clauses, and, in general, firm policy in this regard appears to depend on the competitive conditions in the labor markets in which it hires and its own vulnerability to adverse selection.

Empirical Evidence on the Incidence of Employer-Paid Premiums

The economic theory describing the incidence of employer payment for health insurance is so strong and so durable that it may be unnecessary to search for empirical evidence to confirm the theory. Only if the responsiveness of labor supply were found to be much greater than expected could the economy-wide conclusion be upset, and only if the cost of insurance varied greatly among firms could there be intermediate run effects on profits.

Moreover, finding empirical evidence for incidence on wages is itself fraught with difficulty. The simplest approach—seeing whether those firms that offer coverage, other things equal, pay lower wages than those that do not—is bedeviled by the virtual certainty that other things will not be equal. The reason is that, if some firms chose to offer coverage and other apparently similar ones did not, there must have been—appearances to the contrary notwithstanding—some difference between the firms to explain why some chose to offer and others did not. For instance, if firms in tight labor markets were more likely to offer coverage in order to attract and retain good workers, they probably would offer higher money wages too—and so it would look like generous benefits accompanied higher wages. If we could somehow measure the tightness of the market, we could avoid these biased results, but then we would have no additional or experimental variation in benefits offering to test the theory. If all firms do the rational thing, we will have no observations on fringe benefit offerings that cost more than the wages they save.

The most effective way to find the trade-off postulated by the theory is to find some situations in which the coverage offered or the cost of coverage varies for reasons *not* related to the need to attract and retain good workers. From the viewpoint of research, the ideal setting for this kind of experiment is one in which some outside influence requires some employers to pay for coverage but does not require others to do so, for reasons that have nothing to do with the relative value of coverage. As we shall see, the most closely that researchers have been able to approximate this ideal experiment is in situations in which some states have mandated certain types of coverage while other states have not done so. If we are willing to assume that such political decisions are made for political reasons or reasons other than the value of coverage, we can use that variation to approximate a real experiment. The other strategy pursued, but with less success, is to find a reason why insurance will cost more for one firm than for another firm with which it competes in the local labor market. The only easily identifiable source of differences in the price of insurance is firm size—since we know that providing a given insurance policy with a given level of customer service costs more per insured for small firms than for larger ones. In practice, as we shall see, implementing this approach has proved difficult for two reasons—it is difficult to find policies with exact matches, and larger firms often differ in other ways, perhaps intrinsically related to labor productivity, from smaller firms.

Rather than look at the tempting but misleading natural variation across firms or groups in insurance provision and money wages, the most definitive empirical work has taken a different approach. It searches for circumstances in which one can be sure that firms are not all voluntarily choosing whether or not to offer coverage. That is, it looks at situations in which specific coverage is politically mandated and compares them to situations in which it is not. The assumption here, probably true but not absolutely guaranteed, is that the political process chooses mandates or their absence without regard to the value workers or firms in different jurisdictions place on coverage but rather primarily based on external political influences.

The two best known studies of this type looked at the effects of two employer mandates: for workers' compensation benefits and for pregnancy benefits added to conventional insurance. In both cases, there was variation across states. Different states require workers' compensation insurance of different degrees of costliness, and some states at various times have required maternity benefits while others did not. In both cases, the message was roughly the same: workers in those states with more costly workers' compensation insurance received less in money wages, and the wages of women of childbearing age and their spouses fell in states that instituted mandated maternity benefits relative to those in states that did not (Gruber and Krueger 1990; Gruber 1994). There was also no evidence of less demand for labor in states with more costly workers' compensation benefits.

The point estimate of the amount of money wage offset for an additional dollar in benefits cost was virtually equal to a dollar in the maternity benefits case and about 83 cents on the dollar in the workers' compensation case (but not significantly different from unity). This finding is consistent, as Gruber (1994) and Gruber and Krueger (1990) have noted, with either of two models: the supply of labor may be almost completely inelastic, or the supply may be somewhat more responsive but the mandated benefits of value just equal to their cost. In any case, these studies have convinced most economists that wage offsets exist and that they are nearly complete. The maternity benefit study did not directly address the question of how long it takes wages to adjust—how long it takes to get to the long run—but did analyze relatively recent mandates and found a result consistent with long run equilibrium.

In many ways, the results of these studies are striking. Despite the relatively modest cost of workers' compensation or maternity coverage, wage offsets can still be detected. Moreover, in the mandated maternity coverage case, the wage offsets are surprisingly discriminatory: they hit wages of women of childbearing age and their spouses but not others.

· More recent work on incidence tends to confirm both of the patterns already set. Louise Sheiner (1995), in looking for differential impacts on the wages of older workers, was able to discover an offset of approximately dollar for dollar. She discovered that, in cities where health insurance costs were unusually high, the wages of older workers (relative to the younger workers) were not as high as in cities with lower medical care costs. Indeed, the implied reduction in wage for an additional dollar of health care or health insurance cost is generally estimated to be a dollar or more.

But we still have not seen a direct test of impacts of general cost or benefit changes on all workers. For example, as the rate of growth in employer contributions to health insurance slowed almost to a stop beginning in 1994, for more than a year there was little evidence of an offset in money wages. Perhaps this was because there was a slowdown in premium growth primarily in larger firms, for which there was an apparent excess supply of labor. However, beginning in 1996, we are at long last seeing increased growth in real money wages. As always, however, there are too many other things also changing to draw definitive conclusions for time series data.

The indirect tests do definitely add to our confidence in the theoretical model and do show that relatively modest mandated benefits may have nearly complete wage offsets. The evidence on offsets is circumstantial, but it is strong and, most importantly, consistent. However, studies of this type leave three important questions still unanswered. For one thing, they do not tell us about changes in premiums or coverage that are both voluntary in some sense and affect some employers and not others, and they do not tell us about the effects of exogenous changes in premiums associated with market-determined changes in medical benefits costs on wages and profits and employment. They also do not tell us about the effects of mandated benefits on workers whose money wages are close enough to the minimum wage that they cannot plausibly absorb the cost of going from no coverage whatever to a generous insurance policy.

Efforts to look at the impact of voluntarily chosen health insurance on wages have not been as successful. The simple relationship between higher spending on health insurance across firms and money wages, observable worker characteristics held constant, is almost always strongly positive. This result is probably due to the endogenous nature of benefit spending: when a firm wishes to hire and retain highly skilled workers, or when it is hiring in a tight labor market, it will offer *both* high money wages and generous benefits. Danzon (1989) attempted to control for the endogeneity of offering insurance by using firm size as an instrument, but continued to find a positive (though somewhat smaller) relationship; this may well be occurring because small firms also appear to offer lower wages and poorer benefits. One thing that ought to serve as a good instrument would be cross-market variation in the real and quality adjusted price of medical services, if only we had a good version of such a measure. An attempt by Brailer and Van Horn (1993) to use a proxy measure failed to find any consistent relationship, either positive or negative, between the costliness of health benefits and either wages or prices. But this study was across industries or over time but not across geographically separated labor markets. If firms differ in unobservable ways in their skill in managing health (and other) benefits, we may never be able to see wage offsets across firms.

U.S. Motor Vehicle Manufacturers' Health Benefits Costs: An Example

We can illustrate the difference between the economic way of analyzing benefits costs and changes or variations in benefits costs and the way corporate managers perform these analyses by looking in more detail at a prominent and controversial example: the health benefits costs of U.S. automobile and motor vehicle manufacturers. During the initial phases of the political debate on the Clinton reform plan, senior executives of the Big Three auto firms were prominent supporters of reform proposals intended to get health costs under (governmental) control and to compel all employers to pay for benefits for their workers. The comparison of the health benefits cost per car with either the cost of steel or the health costs estimated to be included in the cost of a Japanese car (manufactured in Japan, rather than in a U.S. factory owned by a Japanese company) figured prominently in the Clinton team's advocacy of the plan. (Figure 2 shows an example of a graphic used by administration advocates to argue for their plan.) Was this argument, which seemed to originate from benefits managers and was warmly embraced by administration supporters, economically correct? Would it even have been in the interests of stockholders in the motor vehicle manufacturing firms to have the universal employer mandate and the cost-containment features of the Clinton plan passed?

To answer these questions, we first need to make some simplifying assumptions. We will ignore automakers' liability for postretirement benefits to workers who have already retired; lower medical care costs would add to profits in the case of retirees, since the possibility of reducing

United States   # Japan

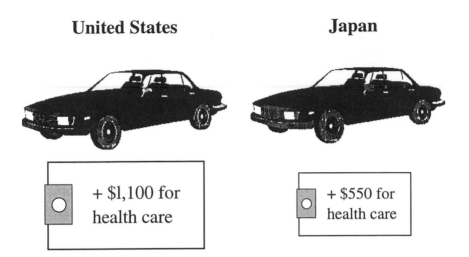

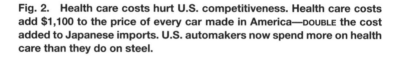

Fig. 2. Health care costs hurt U.S. competitiveness. Health care costs add $1,100 to the price of every car made in America—DOUBLE the cost added to Japanese imports. U.S. automakers now spend more on health care than they do on steel.

their wages no longer exists. We will assume that automakers hire from a pool of skilled workers, largely in the Midwest, who are unlikely to migrate to other parts of the country or to Japan in search of more attractive jobs; the labor market is geographically separate. Finally, we will assume that compensation for autoworkers is set through collective bargaining with unions (constrained by the necessity that the compensation package at those firms is at least as attractive as is available to workers of similar skills in the nonunion portion of the labor market).

With these assumptions, we can say that the level of total compensation for autoworkers is determined either by their productivity and the price of the products they produce (as in any competitive labor market) or is determined by union bargaining that raises the cost of total compensation above the competitive level. We do not know whether unionization actually increases labor income, and so we will analyze both the case in which it does and the case in which it does not. Likewise, we will analyze cases in which the division of compensation into health benefits and other compensation either is determined competitively or is affected by the union.

One possibility is that, despite the presence of collective bargaining, the total cost and the mix of compensation for current workers are at or near the competitive level. This is the classic economic model already presented. It implies that, if health benefits costs for autoworkers are higher than they are in Japan, or in other parts of the United States, those higher costs are offset by lower money wages to workers in the Midwest. Should benefits costs fall, all that would happen is that money wages would have to be increased to keep automakers competitive in the market for skilled labor; no change would be expected in the price of automobiles or the ability of U.S. automakers to sell in the domestic or world markets. Lower health benefits costs in Detroit would not allow Chrysler to sell more cars in Kyoto.

In this story, the relatively higher health benefits costs and the higher total compensation costs for Midwest automakers are attributable to market parameters: workers desire more costly benefits both because they value health benefits highly and because they seek to be protected against the higher medical costs they face; compensation is more generous because workers are more productive and because there is a strong demand for their services.

Now let us consider the other extreme case, in which unions are able to compel firms to pay higher levels of total compensation than would have prevailed in a competitive labor market for skilled Midwestern assembly line workers in the absence of unionization. As far as management is concerned, the key determinant of profitability obviously is total compensation cost; its division between benefits and money wages is immaterial. Despite the rhetoric sometimes heard, from management's point of view, "giving" benefits of a given cost is no more harmful (and no more likely to be resisted) than agreeing to a money wage increase of equal expected costliness. (I will deal with issues of uncertainty subsequently.) There is also no reason to assume that the costliness of the final compensation package that union and management agree on will depend upon the mix between wages and benefits. Management presumably has some amount it will pay, depending on union strike threats and the like, and a skillful union presumably pushes for the package with the maximum value to workers and cost to management.

It therefore follows, in an even more obvious way than with competitive labor markets, that the more costly the health benefits part of the package, the less workers will receive in money wages. That is, from the union's point of view, the trade-off between a dollar of benefits cost and a dollar of wages is one for one, in the immediate run as well as in the long run. If therefore automakers agree to a compensation package that contains generous health benefits and also has a higher total cost than competitive compensation offers, the reason for the higher total cost is the relative bargaining strength and skill of management and union, not the cost of health benefits. If the health benefits package were reduced in value (for instance, by having employees pay more of the premium explicitly with payroll deductions), the bargained level of the money wage payout would be that much greater.

As in the competitive case, tax considerations may affect the division of the package into tax-free benefits and taxable wages, but there is no sense in which lower benefits costs, could they be achieved, would save money for the company. The only way this could happen is if, somehow, lower benefits costs would cause the union to settle for less. This might conceivably happen if the union could be co-opted to settle for a reasonable package to help the market for the company's product, but this would be highly unlikely in the history of U.S. labor bargaining. (Some type of "reasonable real income" standard does sometimes seem to be evident in wage policies in continental European countries with more cooperative and more docile labor unions limited by government-influenced wage policies.)

There is evidence that unions do cause compensation packages of a given total cost to shift in the direction of higher health benefits (Goldstein and Pauly 1976). This may have the effect of causing a package of a given cost to be, in a sense, less efficient than if the health benefits were closer to what the average worker wanted. This "union effect," attributable either to dominance by middle aged workers who get greater benefits from insurance or to union ideology, probably results in a small amount of redistribution among workers but has little effect on company profits.

These are the simple theories. They all say that auto industry health benefits costs per se—even if influenced by cost shifting—do not affect firm profits; they only displace money wages. Automobile industry advocates have therefore invoked some more complicated ideas to explain why higher health care costs hurt them. One argument is that higher health costs in the Midwest disadvantage firms with plants located there compared to firms (predominantly, though not entirely, foreign owned) with plants in the South, where health care costs are lower. This argument has in effect already been addressed; it may be advantageous to locate plants in lower compensation cost areas of the country (if productivity and other costs are similar), but this advantage has nothing directly to do with health benefits costs. The other argument assumes that health benefits are more generous to workers who work in industries whose products compete in international markets; the retailing and food service industries (though not the agricultural sector) in which benefits are lower do not have to compete with Japanese firms with lower health benefits costs. (Interestingly, the cost of employment-related health benefits as a percentage of payroll is nearly 50 percent greater in Germany than in the United States, but little is heard about this.) So, it is argued, the *relative* costs of these products are increased by higher health costs (even if international competition prevents accommodating increases in their relative prices). As already suggested, however, this is an incorrect argument as well. To the extent that workers in retail stores or restaurants do not compete in the same labor market as autoworkers, their compensation is irrelevant. To the extent that they do compete in the same labor market, higher health care costs require employers who wish to retain those workers without offering health benefits to pay *higher* money wages and higher compensation costs; higher health benefits costs actually advantage the larger firms, who can insure workers at lower cost than smaller retail and food service firms.

What evidence is there that bears on this question? There has been no definitive study of the impact of health benefits costs in the automobile industry alone. The Brailer and Van Horn (1993) study of the impact of costs on international competitiveness and wage growth, already cited, failed to support the auto industry view. Moreover, the less sophisticated but probably equally valid analysis of the change over time in total compensation cost per worker in manufacturing between the United States and other countries failed to show an effect in the late 1980s and early 1990s of more rapidly growing U.S. medical benefits costs. There are some stories yet to be examined that may be valid. For example, agreeing to a long term contract with preset money wage increases and a generous health benefits package and then discovering that health costs rise more rapidly than expected will undoubtedly lead to lower profits than expected; employers will have lost the gamble. But this phenomenon cannot explain repetition of bad bets and offers no reason to feel sympathy for those who mismanage.

CHAPTER 5

Using a Total Compensation Approach for Wage and Benefits Planning

One of the most exciting topics in benefit planning is the use by firms of the "total compensation" (or "total remuneration") approach to evaluating and selecting wage and benefit levels. In its simplest form, the total compensation approach is defined as "looking at the cost and value of all elements in the employment package together: salary, bonus, long-term incentives, benefits, perquisites, discounts, work/family programs, and other tangible and intangible rewards of working" (Mercer Consulting 1993).

This is an important and challenging idea, since it obviously implies that firms ought to think about their wage and benefits policies as part of an integrated whole, with common costs and common benefits, rather than viewing them as separate components to be looked at or determined separately. Especially when the growth trend in benefits costs has diverged so dramatically from the growth trend in money wages, and as benefits costs have become such an important part of total compensation costs, an assumption that ideal management could involve setting each component separately, or in separate departments, is not tenable.

However, there is relatively little information available on how firms ought to use the information on total compensation that they are advised to collect. After they look at the information, what should they do? Some firms may reasonably decide that the ideal total compensation approach, however desirable in theory, may not be practical in their situations. Where wages and benefits are collectively bargained, management may not have much discretion in setting levels, and so these situations will not be considered here. Given the many informational complexities and ambiguities in benefits evaluation, it is not surprising that it is rare to find firms executing a total compensation approach on a tactical level. Other firms may be surprised to discover that they have been practicing some aspects

---

This chapter is based on Mark Pauly and Jerry Rosenbloom, "Using a Total Compensation Approach for Wage and Benefits Planning," *Benefits Quarterly* 12 (second quarter): 47–55.

of the total compensation approach all along, without knowing the label for their practices. In either case, deciding whether to move to a full total compensation approach requires a clear understanding of what that approach would require. In this chapter we offer suggestions on several different useful forms that a total compensation approach might take: what information it requires, how that information might be used, and the benefits from doing so.

Our goal is to remove some of the mystery and imprecision surrounding the total compensation approach by suggesting in more detail than is presently available what information should be obtained and how it should be used.

Choosing Compensation Packages: Three Strategies

As background for the discussion of how information should actually be collected and used, we need to develop some alternative general ways that firms view the process of setting their compensation.

One strategy might be called "meet the market." The basic idea is simple: given the number and type of employees that a firm wishes to hire, it chooses its compensation package for each type of employee so that current and potential employees view its offer as equal in value to what they could receive from other employers hiring in the same market. In the simplified (but unrealistic) world where money wages are the only source of compensation, this "meet the market" approach only says that the firm should pay the same wage rates as its competitors do. But in the more complex (but more realistic) world in which different competitors offer different cash wages/benefits combinations, and different actual or potential employees value those benefits differently, it is less obvious what meeting the market means. One version of a total compensation approach tries to spell out that meaning.

A second philosophy might be called "please employees on a budget." This philosophy determines compensation in two steps. First, the employer decides how much total compensation expense per employee is to be incurred. Then (in the more interesting part) the firm must decide how to divide that total amount among money wages and various benefits categories. The concept underlying this philosophy is that the firm ought to "spend" compensation on benefits as long as the value of an additional dollar's worth of benefits to employees exceeds a dollar. For instance, tax advantages for some types of benefits can make spending on untaxed benefits more valuable to employees than paying compensation in the form of cash wages. If employees attach different values to a given benefit, this task becomes more difficult.

The third philosophy is "minimize compensation costs." This approach views the firm's objective as that of choosing the mix of wages and benefits that allows the firm to attract and retain a given type of workforce at the lowest total cost to the firm. This means that the employer worries about the value of various components of the compensation package to each current employee and to all potential employees and considers which benefits will attract employees to work for the firm at the lowest cost. Such an objective implies that the firm will offer a benefit if doing so reduces the cash wages the firm must offer (to attract the workers it wishes) by more than the cost to the firm of the benefit.

These three philosophies are not mutually exclusive; they all overlap somewhat. But how one might interpret total compensation information can be explained differently under each philosophy.

Total Compensation: Some Definitions and Some Observations

The first part of a total compensation approach is to determine the total amount a firm currently spends on compensating its employees—the total compensation *cost*—in the form of cash wages, and in the form of all other items of value, which we will term *benefits*. Although this division is obvious, actually measuring total compensation costs can raise some challenging questions. For instance, should expenditures the firm makes to improve working conditions be included as part of compensation costs? And should deferred wages of various types be labeled cash wages or benefits?

Another key decision or practice is whether the firm attempts to deal with its benefits by means of a flexible benefits program. Tax considerations aside, a flexible benefits program that took the extreme form of allowing employees to choose to spend their benefit dollars on almost any item of value, or to take cash wages, would make implementing a total compensation approach apparently easy. One would simply add together the money value of the benefits contribution provided by the firm (after adjusting for tax advantages) with the value of cash wages and call the total "total compensation." Even this simplicity may be deceptive, however, since such a firm will still be challenged to compare its offering with the offerings of its competitors, which may not be so convenient to analyze, especially if the competitors' benefits are not in a fully flexible form. Moreover, few firms go this far with flexible benefits in any case. In what follows, however, we will not be dealing directly with the more complicated situation of flexible benefits; instead, we will consider firms that offer some of their major benefits in a preselected "inflexible" form.

Once benefits are identified, they need to be measured in money terms. There are three alternative measures of the money "value" or "equivalent" of a benefit that might be used.

The first, and the easiest to determine, is the net cost to the firm of offering the benefit. If the benefit is purchased by the firm from an outside source (e.g., buying dental insurance), the cost is what the firm pays. Even this can be tricky if purchasing a benefit allows the firm to reduce its taxes or obligations: such changes in other expense categories that can be attributed to the purchase of a benefit should be netted out of the explicit cost of the benefit to get the net cost. Calculating the net cost can also be difficult if the firm provides or produces the benefit itself: what do free meals cost, what do self-insured health benefits cost, what will postretirement medical benefits, promised today but provided in the future, actually cost?

The other two measures deal with the *value* of the benefit to employees. One measure is the price or cost to the employee of obtaining the same benefit outside of the work setting. Employees could purchase their own health insurance, their own retirement annuity, and so forth. Of course, oftentimes what is available outside does not quite match what can be provided in connection with employment. For instance, individual insurance is frequently medically underwritten on an individual basis and is subject to cancellation under different terms than would be expected to prevail for employment-related coverage. This value is sometimes called the "economic value" of the benefit.

A complication in calculating the economic value of the benefit is that of deciding the population whose values should be measured. Sometimes consultants advise calculating the value for a "standard population" (Hewitt Associates 1991, 128), in order to determine the cost "based on plan design alone." But if the firm's workforce does not duplicate the standard population, this attempt to make consultants' and actuaries' lives easier may not give the right answer. In addition, it may be plausible to assume that the composition of the workforce will change if some benefits are changed, so that it is unclear whether one ought to use the current or the future population to calculate the value.

The third measure is the "subjective value" of the benefit to the employee. This measures the maximum amount the employee would be willing to pay out of, or sacrifice from, cash wages, in order to obtain the benefit rather than go without. That is, it is the answer to one of two logically equivalent questions: (1) "What is the largest amount of your take-home pay that you would sacrifice to obtain (or retain) this benefit?" (2) What is the largest amount you would pay in the market to obtain (or retain) this benefit?" Ordinarily the answer to the first question will be an amount that is no greater than the economic value, since no one would be willing to sacrifice more for a work-related benefit than the amount he or she would have to pay to get the benefit individually, but it can be a low number, zero, or even negative (if workers hate the food in the cafeteria).

A useful classification of benefits themselves may be to divide them into three categories: mandatory, basic, and competitive advantage. These categories represent, respectively, benefits required by law (e.g., Social Security), benefits provided (at least in some amount) by virtually all of the firm's competitors in the labor markets in which it hires (e.g., health benefits or pensions), and less common benefits it provides to make its jobs more attractive in competitive labor markets (e.g., vision coverage, educational benefits).

In one sense, it is hardly necessary to value mandatory benefits, since there is no managerial discretion about whether or not to offer them and their cost is determined by fairly rigid rules that apply identically to all the firm's competitors. However, even though there is little discretion about the benefits themselves, the firm still must decide how or whether to vary its cash wages when the costs of mandated benefits vary. Workers' compensation and unemployment insurance costs can vary both by state and sometimes (because of experience rating or funding method) by firm. For the two types of optional benefits, the most obvious distinction is that offering special benefits presents more of a managerial challenge (and opportunity) than offering the same basic benefits everyone else does. The interpretation of the total compensation approach we will discuss here does help managers to understand these "atypical" benefits—as well as additions and deletions to the components of the basic benefits.

Some Simple Rules and Some More Complicated Questions

These definitions can help us to specify some easy rules and to refine some more difficult questions. First, it is obvious that, under any of the three philosophies, it will not make sense to provide a benefit whose cost to the firm exceeds its economic value. In such a case, the firm could make employees better off, or reduce its cost, by substituting cash compensation for the benefit.

The more difficult and challenging case is one in which the cost to the firm to provide the benefit is less than the economic value but in which the subjective value, at least for some employees, is less than the economic value. This is the case in which some employees would not be willing to buy the benefit on their own but might value it at more than its cost if the employer obtained it for them. The questions then are—which benefits of this type should be provided by the firm, and how (if at all) should cash wages and other benefits be changed when some particular benefit is provided or its cost to the firm changes? How to answer these questions is what we will discuss in the rest of this chapter.

Some Simplifying Assumptions

We will outline possible strategies for a hypothetical medium-sized firm in a metropolitan area that hires workers in a competitive, nonunionized labor market. By "competitive" here we mean only that this firm seeks to hire just a small portion of the workers at any skill level who work in the metropolitan area and that the firm does not seek workers with any rare skills or with skills or experience specific to the firm.

The firm's overall compensation objective is to "match" competitors in the labor market (rather than to lead or lag). It wishes to be similar to the competition (Milkovich and Newman 1993, 212), both in terms of its current offerings and in terms of what it will offer in all future periods; it wishes to avoid falling behind the competition, either intentionally or inadvertently. A more careful way of defining its philosophy is to say that it wishes to attract employees of average quality in numbers just adequate to its demand; it does not wish to lead the labor market in order to create a surplus of higher than average–quality applicants, and it does not wish to risk lagging the market, which could lead to the possibility of a shortage of employees or lower than average–quality hires.

The firm prices its products to maximize profits, and its product market is sufficiently competitive that it cannot increase prices to offset compensation cost increases.

Strategy 1: Meet the Competition

With these constraints and objectives, how might the firm think about its total compensation if its strategy was one of meeting the competition? Our argument here will be that, despite its apparent appeal of simplicity and tangibility, this strategy is incomplete as a way of defining a feasible plan for compensation.

Let us first consider an obvious case in which this strategy can (and does) work—a world with no nonwage compensation. If the only form of compensation is current wages, then the task of meeting the competition only requires that the firm know the wage offers of other employers in its market, its competitors' future wage offers, and whether or not its competitors are willing to hire employees at the wages they pay currently or will pay in the future. (Gathering of information on competitors' hiring plans as well as their wage rates is not usually included in descriptions of how to design pay structures, but we think it is logically required. After all, the firm will lose employees to other firms only if those firms pay higher wages *and* are hiring employees at those wage rates.) The firm then sets its current money wages at approximately the midpoint of the offerings in its market. (Exactly *which* measure of central tendency—mean, median, or mode—is appropriate will not concern us here.)

How does the firm plan future wages and the raises that adjust pay from current to future levels? This approach implies that the firm needs to forecast the future distribution of cash wages in its market and set its raises at the percentage increase in the statistical measure of central tendency it is using.

How might this approach be modified in the more realistic case in which firms also compensate employees with employee benefits? There is a version of the meet the market approach when benefits are present that is logically consistent. It would say that the firm would make an offer that was at the midpoint not only of current cash compensation but also for *each and every one* of the employee benefit items. That is, it would seek to copy its competitors' decisions not only on wages but also on each type of benefit viewed separately. This approach is logical, but is it sensible or possible? We think there are a number of serious difficulties in implementing this approach.

The most obvious difficulty is the sheer informational burden associated with documenting the details of the variety of employee benefit offerings of competitors. It is difficult enough to gather sensitive information from competitors on wages and hiring plans; obtaining reliable information on the details of complicated employee benefit plans increases the cost and the complexity of the task many times over.

A second difficulty is logical: the more items there are in the benefit package, the more likely it is that a combination of the median or mean values of each item will itself have a value or cost different from the median or mean (Milkovich and Newman 1993, 236–37). The fundamental problem is that there may be no such thing as an average or typical combination of wages and employee benefits.

Third, for benefits that are either provided or not provided, there is no obvious measure of the average or typical offering. For example, if 51 percent of competitors offer dental benefits and 49 percent do not, the only correct statement would be the meaningless one that the firm should offer .51 of a dental benefit.

Fourth, however difficult it is to measure and compare current benefit packages, it is even more difficult to forecast how they will change in the future. Prophecy is difficult, especially when the competitive firms may all be watching each other to decide what to do.

These observations suggest that as soon as the number of discretionary items in the benefits package gets very large, the strategy of meeting the competition item by item becomes unfeasible. The alternative approach that is sometimes suggested is one that reduces all elements in the package to a common measure, money. In this approach, benefit items are converted to a "value," which is summed to get a "total compensation value" for a job (Domat-Connell and Cardinal 1992).

Applying this approach to the meet the competition strategy requires choosing some basis to value the benefits. It is clear that using the cost to the employer is wrong, since a firm that offered a large part of its compensation as expensive but nearly useless benefits could not compete in the labor market. We would argue, for reasons to be explained in more detail subsequently, that the right approach would be to use the worker's subjective value *or* the economic value, whichever is less.

But even this advice is incomplete. If workers differ in the value they attach to benefits, *which* value should one use? To value a competitor's offerings, should you use its employees' values, your employees' values, or some average of the two?

There is another, related question that is left unanswered by the meet the competition approach. Does it matter which benefits you have in your package, if your package has the same total compensation value as your competitors' offerings? The advice to meet the competition would seem to imply that the mix does not matter, which would greatly simplify human resource managers' jobs if true, but which may not be right.

Strategy 2: Please Employees on a Budget

The other two compensation strategies avoid this indeterminacy. One strategy is based on the view that, once the firm decides the total dollar amount to be spent on compensation of an employee, its allocation of that amount among cash wages and different employee benefits should be based on what employees would want. In effect, the firm's benefits department becomes a proxy shopper for employees. Consumers in ordinary markets decide to spend money on something when they feel that the value of the purchase is greater than the value to them of keeping the money for other purposes. The analogue in benefits is that the firms should take money away from cash compensation and "spend" it on a benefit whenever the benefit is of greater value than the cash. Following this policy will make employees as well off (and as happy) as they can be; doing so will yield benefits to the employer as well. Either morale and productivity will be improved in the firms following this policy (compared to others still bumbling along), or the firm that follows this policy can actually reduce money wages by a little more until its employees are equally happy working for it or for its labor market competitors.

This approach then implies that, to decide where to set benefits or to decide how to set money wages, the firm needs to find measures, in dollars, of what benefits are worth. Here we have two large literatures to draw on: the literature in economics that measures willingness to pay for goods not directly offered on the market (usually developed for use by governments) and the literature on marketing that determines how consumers trade off the prices charged for products against (costly) product characteristics, in the form of "conjoint analysis" (usually developed for use by for-profit sellers). Since the process of offering employee benefits casts the firm in a role intermediate between a kind of government and a kind of profit maximizer, either approach could be used. The only difficult parts of the procedure are deciding how to phrase questions so that people give valid answers to the hypothetical questions of what they might be willing to pay and how to aggregate or average answers when different people give different answers.

Firms do sometimes survey their employees about the value of benefits, but those surveys are not usually cast in terms of the money wages that an employee would be willing to sacrifice. Instead, questions are usually less formal and more imprecise. For instance, workers might be asked which benefit they think is the most "important." Not surprisingly, they usually rate the most costly nonmandatory benefit—health insurance—as most important. But such information is of little value in deciding how to alter the benefit mix, especially when the decision (among the basic benefits) is not whether to eliminate a health benefit or a pension benefit completely but instead is one of moderate expansion or contraction. For these choices, the relevant information is the value (in money) employees place on a marginal change in benefits. One might ask what an expansion in pension benefits would be worth if accompanied by a reduction in health benefits of equal cost. If increasing the pension benefit is worth more than the reduction in health insurance premium payments, the message for management is obvious.

In terms of a total compensation approach, this strategy would say that benefits should be valued at the lower of (1) employees' maximum willingness to pay (WTP) to get or keep them or (2) what an equivalent benefit would cost if purchased in the individual market. We will call this value the WTP value. Once one values benefits in this fashion, two uses can be made of the WTP measure. First, to calculate how total compensation at some firm compares with the market, benefits should be valued by the WTP measure and added to (net) cash compensation. Second, a benefit should be offered if its WTP value exceeds the (net of taxes) cost to the firm and should be dropped if its value falls short. In the first case, cash compensation should be reduced by some amount between the WTP value and the cost of the benefit, and in the second case cash compensation should be increased by some amount greater than the WTP value but less than the cost saved. (An alternative, if the firm charges employees for some part of the cost of some benefit, is to alter the amount charged.) Note that, at least in theory, offering a more attractive vacation benefit could be off-set by increasing the employee's contribution to health insurance premiums.

This strategy also offers some advice on what the firm should do if a benefit increases in cost to the firm. Suppose, for example, that the premium cost of the firm's health insurance offering increases because of market-wide increases in medical care costs. The key questions are as follows: (1) does this change affect the WTP value to this firm's employees? and (2) does this change affect the value of competitors' compensation packages?

With regard to health insurance cost increases caused by increases in medical care costs, the answer to the first question is likely to be affirmative. After all, the alternative to not buying insurance is usually to pay the higher medical care costs out of pocket. In contrast, if benefits costs increase because the administrative costs (loading) for group insurance increase, this change will not usually raise the value of the benefit to employees. If the increase in cost pushes the cost to the firm from below the WTP value to above the WTP value, the firm should drop the benefit.

Strategy 3: Minimize Total Compensation Cost

This approach represents a "marginal" method to determine the total compensation package. It is really only a more explicit version of the benefit mix determination process discussed at the end of the last paragraph, which takes into account the possibility that different employees may place different values on the same benefit.

This approach advises employers to evaluate their compensation packages in the following way. Think of adding (or adding to) a particular benefit. Calculate what the addition will cost. Then estimate what effect it will have on the cash wages the firm must pay to continue to attract the same number and the same quality of workers who are currently employed (but these employees do not have to be the *same individuals* as those who are currently hired).

Given some compensation package, some set of employees currently hired, and some total compensation cost, the firm asks the following types of questions. Suppose we added some additional benefit. What would that cost us? And what would that do to the money wages we would have to pay to attract the kind of workers we now attract? The answer to the first question ought to be fairly easy to obtain. The answer to the second question is more complex. The firm could begin to answer it by querying current employees about their WTP values attached to the benefit. If the firm must pay all workers the same cash compensation, and it finds that all current workers have WTPs that exceed the cost of the compensation, it should cut money wages by the lowest (or marginal) WTP. This would allow the firm to retain its current workforce and would reduce its compensation costs per worker by the difference between the lowest WTP and the cost of the benefit per worker.

What if there are some current employees whose WTPs are less than the cost of the benefit? All is not lost; the firm should survey the WTP values of potential replacement workers (job applicants or workers at other firms in its labor market). If it finds enough outside workers with WTPs greater than the per-worker cost who would replace its current employees with WTPs less than the per-worker cost, it should still offer the benefit. Suppose it wishes to hire 100 employees. To calculate where to set the money wage, it should array all respondents—current employees and potential employees—by WTP values, from highest to lowest. Then it should work down the rank ordering from the top and set the money wage reduction at the WTP of the 100th employee in the ordering.

If it sets the cash wage at that level, it will be able to hire 100 qualified workers and will minimize its total compensation costs for doing so. Of course, if this is a new and valuable benefit, offering it and thereby lowering the compensation cost per worker may cause the firm to seek to hire more workers. At lower compensation costs per worker, it will pay for the firm to expand output. So in theory there will need to be some iteration back and forth between design of the compensation package and the number of employees hired. The firm will know that it has done as well as it can when there is no new benefit it could offer for which there are 100 employees with WTPs greater than cost and when there is no benefit it currently offers for which any worker has a WTP less than its current per-employee cost.

This approach also helps with mandated benefits. Obviously if a firm finds that its employees' value of some newly mandated benefit is less than the cost to the firm of that benefit, the firm cannot eliminate or cut back the benefit. However, it can use the information on value as an estimate of the minimum amount by which it should be reducing cash wages because of the addition of the benefit. The estimate is only a minimum, however, because the operation of competitive labor markets may well cause wages to fall by the full cost of the benefit, even if the benefit is not worth its cost.

This last method is the best way to squeeze every last cent out of total compensation costs, but it would obviously be exceedingly difficult to implement fully, since its information demands are enormous. An alternative is for the firm to "feel out" its demand curve by proposing or offering alternative levels of compensation and determining how many workers would wish to obtain a job. Another alternative would be to survey a sample of current and potential employees and use that data to estimate what is, in economic terms, a demand curve for benefits.

What Happens Next?

The fundamental messages so far are as follows: (1) the value of total compensation, the sum of cash wages, and the WTP value of benefits must equal or exceed the value of total compensation offered by other firms; and (2) profit-increasing compensation policy involves adding benefits whose WTP value is more than their cost and deleting benefits whose WTP value is less than their cost.

If a firm follows these strategies, what can it forecast about the impact of a change in its benefits offerings? The answer turns out to depend on whether the change the firm implements is unique, or at least difficult to copy, or whether the same change is or could be implemented by its competitors in the labor market.

Suppose, for instance, that one firm among many similar-sized firms in a labor market develops and introduces a unique new employee benefit whose WTP value is greater than its cost. Then it will be able to reduce its total compensation cost, other things equal, by the difference between the WTP value and the cost—since it can reduce its cash wages by the value of the benefit and still offer the same total compensation as prevails in the market. The firm may be expected to respond to this lower cost by increasing its employment, but that increase will not affect wages and benefits in the market to any appreciable extent.

Now change the example and suppose that other employers can copy this innovation. They would also be expected both to offer the new benefit and to seek to expand hiring somewhat. If they do so, there will be upward pressure on cash wages, and even the initial firm will find its total compensation cost rising. In some (not implausible) circumstances, market cash wage levels may increase enough to erase the initial reduction in total compensation costs for the innovator. The main message here is that the ability to turn an employee benefits improvement into long run reductions in compensation costs and increases in profitability depends on the ease with which it can be imitated; things that are easy to copy produce temporary improvements for those who try them first, while things hard to copy lead to longer term gains—much the same message as for any product innovation.

However, no firm should fail to copy an innovation, because then it would find itself unable to compete for employees unless it raises its cash wages by the value of the benefit. Far better to provide the benefit and incur the lower cost of doing so.

These messages also hold for innovative ways of (or lucky breaks in) reducing the costs of existing benefits. If such things are available to only one or a few employers, they will add to those firms' profits. If they are available to or experienced by all, they will eventually lead to the same profits (but higher cash wages and worker well-being). Even in the latter case, as in the prior example, firms have incentives to adopt the innovation, since the alternative of standing pat will lead to lower profits (and higher total compensation cost) than before the innovation, because of the market-wide increase in cash compensation.

What Others Say

The approach we have taken here differs from some alternatives. An extensive treatment of total compensation by the Hewitt Associates group in the United Kingdom (1991) defines what we have called "economic value" as "actual value" and what we have defined as "subjective value" as "perceived value," the latter calculated "by using perceptual indices." They then argue that a measure of compensation efficiency is whether the ratio of actual value to cost is high. A secondary ratio is the ratio of perceived to actual value.

They are not explicit on how these ratios should be used, but presumably the firm should try to maximize the ratio of actual value to cost and then maximize the ratio of perceived value to actual value. However, if perceived values are known and fixed (that is, if they cannot be affected by further changes in how the firm explains its benefits to its workers), no advantage is obtained by calculating "actual value" or its ratio to cost, since the only thing that matters in terms of benefits-wage trade-offs is the perceived value. Our approach would give prominence to perceived or subjective value and view actual or economic value as a secondary category, of use only as a first-cut estimate of subjective value.

Another approach is the "risk-return" approach recently proposed by Rabin (1995). Rabin's article is primarily directed at valuation of benefits packages that impose some risk on the employee, such as stock options. The notion is that such components should be valued at what they are worth to the worker—and in the case of risk averse workers, there will generally be a risk premium discount.

This is quite consistent with the subjective value approach we have advocated, but it does raise an additional question. If such benefits are worth less than their cost because of the risk premium, why should a firm offer them? The obvious answer is to offer incentives to employees for better performance. But then those incentives, and their value *and* cost to the employee ("I will have to work harder and worry more to get this bonus"), ought to be incorporated. A subjective value WTP approach will incorporate such considerations, while the finance-theory–based approach in this chapter will not.

Conclusion

The key piece of information for a proper total compensation approach, according to the arguments presented here, is the WTP measure. Estimating the cost of benefits helps the employer to know what benefits to offer, but judging whether a compensation package is adequate for the competitive labor market also requires information on what benefits are worth to potential employees. The price charged for a similar benefit outside the work setting sets an upper bound to employee value, but, for many employee benefits, the crucial issue is the subjective value to employees— not only its average level but also its distribution over workers. Techniques to measure this value with perfect precision do not now exist, but there are ways to generate estimates or approximations that firms may find useful in planning their total compensation strategies.

CHAPTER 6

The Macroeconomics of
Medical Benefits

The preceding chapters have dealt with the impact of high or growing medical spending on the decisions of individual firms. But the overall value of firms in the United States is also affected by overall economic conditions. If medical care spending has something to do with those conditions, high levels of such spending may still properly be of concern to business leaders. What impact does higher or more rapidly growing medical care spending have on the economy? Is lower spending beneficial?

In this case, in contrast to the previous ones, we can find bipartisan agreement among noneconomists. As already noted, some business leaders, especially in the domestic motor vehicle industry, expressed concern that the level of spending in the United States was so much higher (relative to gross domestic product) than in any other country and indicated that the nation could not afford high levels of medical care spending. These expressions persuaded President-elect Clinton that he would have their support for federal spending controls on private health expenditures or premiums. Both Haley Barbour, for the Republican National Committee, and Clinton administration spokespersons expressed the same types of concerns—though their solutions were quite different. All politicians were as concerned as they thought business leaders were about the ruinously high levels of medical care costs in the United States, relative to our international competitors. Are medical care spending levels that are higher than in other countries and growing more rapidly than real GDP (something still true in the late 1990s, even after the decline in the rate of private sector medical spending growth) reasons to worry? And, if they are, exactly what *are* the reasons that businesses should worry?

In this chapter I want to argue that much of the worry is unnecessary but that the amount that remains is important from the viewpoint of overall national well-being. Nevertheless, I will argue that even this amount is

The material in this chapter is largely based on Mark Pauly, "When Does Curbing Health Costs Help the Economy?" *Health Affairs* 14, no. 2 (summer 1995): 68–82. Copyright © 1995, "The People-to-People Health Foundation, Inc., Project HOPE, http://www.projhope.org/HA/."

not primarily a concern of business as such. Rather, the concern arises from attention to the welfare of American families, primarily as affected by government taxes, public services, and private consumption spending.

Some Stylized Facts and Theories

Before I turn to the question of the role of medical care spending in national economic growth and international competitiveness, it will be useful to review some simple economic theories and facts about what does affect these matters.

With regard to economic growth, the most important concept to note is that the level of real income in an economy at any point in time is determined by the amount of resources the economy has available and the productivity of those resources. For industrialized nations whose output is not dominated by production of commodities or raw materials, the two main resources are labor and capital. The amount of labor is largely determined by population demographics and, to a lesser extent, by labor force participation. The level of physical capital at any point in time depends on the net investment that has been made up to that point; such investment can either be financed by domestic savings (for which the returns become income for the country's citizens) or by foreign investment (whose returns flow to citizens of other countries).

For a country with a given population of a given demographic composition, economic well-being and economic growth then largely depend on three things: productivity of labor, productivity of capital, and capital investment. Economic growth historically has been explained by rates of capital investment and by growth in labor productivity; the latter factor has to a considerable extent been due to education as a kind of investment in human capital, as well as the positive influence of higher levels of capital on labor productivity.

These inputs then determine a country's potential real output. Of course, a country can fail to realize that potential if it wastes resources or (what is the same thing) produces output that is useless or of low value. (It was production of these kinds of nearly useless goods that explained the coexistence of a low standard of living with a fairly high level of GDP per capita, as officially measured, in the waning days of the Soviet Union.)

The message then is that if medical care spending is to affect a country's overall level of economic well-being and its rate of growth over time, it must do so by affecting one of these four influences: the productivity of labor, the productivity of capital, the investment rate, or the extent of inefficiency. If medical care spending rises primarily because of higher prices or incomes received by suppliers of medical inputs, that change in and of itself need not affect any of the four influences and therefore will not affect (one way or another) the overall economy. That is, changes in medical spending are not necessarily the same as changes in real medical costs.

Spending and Costs

One of the problems that bedevils attempts to understand how health costs affect the economy is that we do not really have accurate measures of health costs. I do not mean to criticize the efforts governments make to tabulate medical care spending; while those efforts can be faulted, I believe that in the United States and most high income developed countries, spending is measured reasonably accurately. (In low income countries there is often much under-the-table payment for medical services out of pocket and payments to nontraditional providers that are not well accounted.) The fundamental problem is that spending is not the same as cost.

The reason for potential divergence between spending and cost is that medical services are not sold in markets we know to be perfectly competitive. In fact, many critics would argue that the bulk of medical markets are examples par excellence of uncompetitive markets where the usual forces of competition do not operate to discipline producers of services. Poorly informed consumers, cartels of suppliers, government licensure rules, and the presence of insurance can all operate to create market settings in which providers of services have the potential to set prices above cost for extended periods of time. Conversely, in countries with heavy government dominance in their health care systems, government officials, not markets, set the prices that the great bulk of the population may pay for medical services, and they may well set these prices below the competitive level, again potentially for long periods of time. But since spending is simply the product of prices and quantities, it follows that spending may substantially (and unsystematically) differ from cost because prices received by suppliers of medical services or key inputs into medical services may differ from cost.

To be more concrete: if spending rises because prices rise, and prices rise because profit margins rise or because wages/incomes exceed competitive levels by larger amounts, that increase in spending does not necessarily imply that real costs of medical services to the economy have risen. If real costs have not risen, harm is not necessarily done. Also, if U.S. health spending exceeds spending (relative to GDP) in some other country because returns to people providing specialized health inputs are greater here, costs could be the same here as elsewhere. If so, high spending per se has much different meaning for the economy as a whole than if spending is higher because a larger number of productive resources are drawn into the production of health services.

In what follows I first investigate the consequences of rising medical care spending in terms of its direct impact on the economy through "inefficiency." Then I turn to the question of potential indirect effects on productivity or investment.

Spending and Well-Being

Real costs obviously can rise when more inputs (of a given real cost) are drawn into producing medical costs and services. They can also rise even if employment stays constant if the cost per input rises. As we shall see, such increases in the real cost of medical care as have occurred in the United States largely have occurred because of increases in employment of inputs, not because of increases in the cost per input. So I will discuss the employment-growth version of real cost increases first.

When is it undesirable for the United States to incur more real cost for medical services? Recall that real cost here means, not an accounting entry, but rather what *other* outputs could have been produced with the inputs being used in health care. In virtually a literal sense, the growth in the cost of health care in the United States means that other outputs were lost to consumers because smart young people want to become part of the medical sector rather than taking jobs in other industries; the cost is the lost output they could have produced.

This economically correct way of looking at medical care cost growth has an immediate and important implication: rising medical care costs will be undesirable if and only if the value of the additional medical care they represent is less than the value of the other goods and services that would otherwise have been produced. That is, a judgment that health care cost inflation is undesirable is, at base, a judgment about *values,* not about money. More than that, it is a judgment about the value of other outputs. No one can legitimately claim to know that medical cost growth is harmful, and ought to be contained, unless that person is in a position to know the value of medical services produced by a given set of resources *and* the value of the alternative outputs these resources could produce. Very few of the experts in health policy who have commented on the need to contain health care inflation, and the desirability of our current partial success in doing so, have any expertise or knowledge of the value of other outputs in the economy.

These pedantic but important points do shed a somewhat different light on how one interprets some components of medical cost growth.

They suggest that medical spending growth associated with increasing numbers of persons employed in the health professions and in the administrative and housekeeping services in medical facilities will *not* be harmful to the economy if those inputs would not otherwise be employed or would be employed in low value activities. While this may not be true of educated health professionals, it may well be that many other health workers, especially less skilled nursing assistants and housekeeping workers in urban hospitals, would have few alternatives. Even health professionals may not have alternatives producing services of as high a value to consumers as health services; this judgment depends to a considerable extent on whether one thinks markets (both in medical services and in other products) allocate resources to their highest valued use.

In contrast, in the case in which prices increase but marginal cost does not, there is no harm to the economy regardless of the values of different kinds of outputs. The only effect on the economy is one of redistribution, from consumers to producers of medical services. (This is not the only reason why price may increase; marginal cost [per unit] may increase, because inputs experience higher productivity elsewhere in the economy. I will deal with this case in more detail subsequently, but, for the moment, assume that the opportunity cost per unit of input *and* the productivity of inputs remain constant.) Of course, if quantity demanded responds to prices, there will be a change in employment and a change in opportunity cost. The demand for medical care appears to be fairly unresponsive to price (at least at the individual patient level; managed care firms may be more responsive). But the main point is that "pure inflation" in medical care spending, when prices increase but nothing else changes, does not reduce the total amount of consumption or well-being in the economy.

If demand for medical care is roughly fixed, consumers of medical care will use smaller quantities of goods and services other than medical care. But these reductions will be exactly offset (at least in terms of total monetary value) by higher consumption by producers of medical care. If the savings rate of medical producers is the same as that of medical care buyers, national consumption per capita does not fall; it is only shifted. Since nurses, hospital dietary staff, doctors, and most stockholders in drug companies or for-profit hospitals are Americans too, Americans, on average, neither gain nor lose. If health workers or medical firm stockholders are regarded as less deserving of consumption opportunities than medical service buyers, this redistribution might be judged to be undesirable (though it could not be said to harm the economy in the sense of GDP or consumption per capita). However, I am not sure that such a distributional judgment has been made for the full set of health workers. Some claim that there is a consensus that physicians do not deserve any more income (Ginsburg 1995), but I do not think that this judgment extends to other health workers, who still receive slightly lower wages per year (after controlling for education and experience) than the average worker. Even in the case of physicians, whatever "we" say, actions have not been taken to freeze incomes, even in the public Medicare and Medicaid programs. In fact, if doctors (and other medical workers) save more out of their additional incomes than do consumers on average, the transfer will either increase investment or reduce foreign capital inflows—either way causing a higher rate of economic growth for Americans.

The interesting in-between case occurs when the opportunity cost per worker rises. This will occur, and will matter, if productivity elsewhere in the economy increases at a rate higher than that in medical services. For instance, if the alternative to being a technician at a hospital is a technical job in the computer industry, and the productivity of computer technicians increases, two things will happen. First, the pay of technically adept workers will be bid up by employers in the industry (computers) in which their productivity increases. But second, even if the productivity of similar workers does not increase in hospitals, those hospitals will also have to pay higher wages in order to stay competitive. So the effect of productivity increases in one sector spills over into higher wages in sectors that compete for labor, even if productivity in those sectors is not increasing.

If this phenomenon occurs, as economist William Baumol (1992) has pointed out, there will be an increase in the relative price of those products (such as hospital services or live music performances) for which productivity has not increased. If demand for those products is not very responsive, total spending (and total opportunity cost) will increase as well.

Is this sort of change, which Baumol has labeled the "service disease," harmful to the economy? The answer is—probably not. It is obviously good for an economy for productivity to increase, and if the rate of productivity increases were not uniform—which is the most likely outcome—at least it is better than no increase at all. If productivity in U.S. manufacturing and agriculture had not increased, the share of manufacturing and agriculture in GDP would probably be larger, and the share of medical services smaller, but the overall welfare of Americans would not be higher. Paradoxically, the United States might have been able to keep its share of GDP for medical services down closer to that of the United Kingdom if it had experienced the slower rate of growth in manufacturing productivity the United Kingdom has, but no one would regard that as a desirable outcome.

Roughly speaking, real productivity of U.S. labor has increased at a real rate of about 1 percent per year, although the year-to-year pattern fluctuates considerably. If the demand for medical services were perfectly price inelastic, this would imply that real health worker wages, medical care unit prices, total medical spending, and the total real opportunity cost of medical care would all increase by 1 percent per year. If productivity in the medical sector had also increased by 1 percent per year, and demand was indeed perfectly inelastic, then total spending would not increase (since prices would fall by 1 percent). But if there is no increase in productivity in the medical services sector, and if demand is fixed, then real spending will increase at the rate of growth of productivity in the other sectors. As with increases that are caused by rising output prices associated with higher profits or rents, this increase in cost is not per se harmful to the economy. The failure of quantity to decline means that demanders view the benefit from medical service as unchanging and high. In and of itself, a rise in the share of medical spending caused by an increase in the opportunity cost per medical worker is neither harmful nor helpful to the economy. To be sure, if medical worker productivity could be increased as well, that would be even more beneficial.

What of the potential effect of rising medical spending on productivity or investment? We can at least say that higher medical spending is unlikely to lower productivity—and so it could not be viewed as harmful on this score. A case can be made, though not an especially strong one, that some forms of higher medical spending may actually increase worker productivity. Effective treatment for alcoholism or drug abuse may reduce absenteeism, vaccinating workers' children against chicken pox may reduce days lost from work, and medications to prevent migraine headaches that drive workers from the job may increase productivity. The model of the competitive labor market implies that the benefit from these improvements in productivity and work time will ultimately go to workers in the form of higher wages—and so employers should not expect to gain in the long run from reduced sick leave benefits and the like—but they would be of benefit to the economy. However, while there is some medical care spending that does seem to be able to have this effect, much medical spending is on services for populations and conditions for which work productivity is unlikely to be affected. Treatment for the elderly, care that palliates rather than cures, and care that prevents illnesses that harm people but do not affect their ability to work do consume a large share of medical resources. On balance, it would be difficult to argue that in the past or in the future higher medical care spending will pay for itself through an increase in worker-generated additions to gross domestic product.

The effect of higher medical care spending on private sector investment, which (along with worker productivity) is the primary driver of economic growth, is unlikely to be large. Most directly, the rate of investment in the United States must depend on the expected returns from investment and the worldwide cost of capital, and neither of these will be affected by the level of medical care spending relative to GDP. Indeed, there is some reason to believe that the attractiveness of investments in medical technology and pharmaceuticals in the United States has been enhanced (relative to other countries) by our more permissive structure toward pricing and profits in the medical care sector. One cannot reasonably expect to cut the amounts people spend on drugs and devices and then still expect investment in those industries to be attractive—there may be an export market, but it cannot make up all of a cut.

While medical care spending is therefore unlikely to have a negative effect on aggregate national investment rates, it *might* affect the national savings rate. The conceptual argument is sound: if people spend more on a consumption good like medical care, they will have less left to devote to other purposes, including saving. Lower saving does not mean lower investment, since the global capital market efficiently searches out profitable investment opportunities. It does, however, mean a higher proportion of foreign investment in the short run and a reduction in returns to aggregate domestic investment over time. So if higher spending does displace some domestic savings, it surely does not help the economy and may harm it a little.

Whether higher medical spending necessarily will have this effect is harder to say. To the extent that spending rises because incomes paid to health workers or owners of health-related businesses rise, the impact on savings will depend on whether these persons save at a higher rate than would consumers of medical services. The effect could even be positive, though it is likely to be small. To the extent that medical spending represents higher employment in the medical care sector, but the level of investment remains the same, then the output of investment goods will not decrease—but the investment goods will be owned by investors in other countries, not by Americans.

Tax-Financed Medical Care

The discussion to this point has assumed that higher medical care spending simply displaces an equal amount of other spending. If the medical spending represents higher private out of pocket or premium payments (including those employees "pay" through lower wages), this assumption is plausible. But about 40 percent of medical spending is made by government, and almost all of that is financed through taxes rather than premium payments. This difference in financing can make a difference in outcome.

Consider the effects of increasing tax rates to pay for higher levels of government expenditures for medical care. Higher tax rates are believed to cause distortion of private sector economic behavior. For example, if the taxes are on income or payroll, they may discourage work effort. If they are on earnings from capital, they may discourage investment. While there is considerable difference of opinion among economists and politicians about how large these distortions are, there is general agreement that they are large enough to matter. Economists call this distortion the "excess burden" of taxation; typical (though by no means definitive) estimates of its magnitude are in the range of 20 to 30 percent of the amount collected (Browning 1987; Snow and Warren 1996). If these estimates are correct, the implication is that higher government medical spending funded by higher taxes costs the economy about 20 percent more than the amount of money raised. (These calculations assume that additional spending on health care does not affect the supply of labor when income from wages is the primary tax base.)

An alternative to increasing taxes is to borrow. Deficit finance only postpones, but does not avoid, the excess burden cost. Moreover, a higher federal deficit will increase interest rates, which is usually thought to reduce the level of economic activity, especially if money wages are not free to adjust. Some analysts attribute high negative impacts on GDP to such spending–borrowing–interest rate effects of rising health care costs (Monaco and Phelps 1995).

Rather than raise revenues by taxing or borrowing, an alternative available to government (as to private citizens) is to cut other types of spending. Just as for private sector spending, whether or not cutting other government spending to accommodate higher medical spending is harmful to the economy depends on the relative values of the two types of spending. If the higher medical spending represents more or better services (roughly proxied by higher employment), the question is whether the displaced alternative spending is worth more or less than the additional medical spending. If one thinks that other government spending is excessive (pork barrel, frivolous activities), then rising medical spending may actually do good. If, in contrast, one thinks that other spending produces large benefits (public education, repair of the social infrastructure), then cutting this spending will be harmful. Much the same argument applies if the medical spending growth is caused by higher wages for medical workers. In the limit, if the government is choosing its other spending to be at the efficient level at which an additional dollar of spending just equals in value an additional dollar of private spending, higher medical wages, which transfer money from government spending to the private wages and then private spending of medical workers, do neither good nor harm to the economy as a whole but rather, as before, only redistribute well-being.

The Composition of Spending Growth

The consequences of spending growth depend on whether that growth is fueled by price or wage increases, on the one hand, or an increased use of productive inputs, on the other. What has been the relative importance of these components in recent medical spending growth? In principle the answer to this question is straightforward—divide total spending growth into the part attributable to growth in inputs and the part attributable to growth in income to inputs. Unfortunately, we have direct measures of neither of these factors. Instead, we have measures of *output* or *input* prices, and we also have measures of labor inputs. What empirical strategies could we pursue, and what would they mean? There are two possible price indexes to use for measuring output prices for medical care—the medical care component of the Consumer Price Index (CPI) and the medical care component of the Producer Price Index (PPI). Both indexes suffer from the problem that the items whose prices they measure change in quality or type and mix over time. Failure to adjust the indexes for increases in quality means that they overstate the extent of price change. The CPI also suffers because the mix of services it is based on is the mix of out of pocket payments by consumers, not the mix of services covered by both out of pocket and third party payments. The PPI is not subject to this criticism, but it is available only for recent years.

One way of partially eliminating quality change from the price measure is to use an index of input prices rather than an index of output prices. Suppose that profit margins do not grow over time, wages increase 10 percent, and the level of inputs per unit of output associated with higher quality increases by 5 percent. Then the output price for that unit will increase by 15 percent, rather than by the correct amount of 10 percent indicated by the wage index. However, if profits—the "wages" paid to equity capital— do indeed grow, the input price measure will miss this effect.

Regardless of which measure is used, the estimate of input quantity is the residual—roughly speaking, what is left over after we take out of the total growth in medical spending the portion attributable to higher prices. This residual is an indirect measure of the more intensive use of inputs caused by growing population, by more services per capita, and by more inputs per service.

The other broad strategy is to use a measure or index of input quantities to deflate the total spending data; this approach in effect makes prices the residual. The most frequently measured component of health inputs is the rate of growth in private health services employment. If this measure is correlated with the other inputs it leaves out—employment in public health care, employment in the production of medical products (drugs and devices), and nonlabor inputs—it can proxy the share of the growth due to inputs.

Tables 1 and 2 show a decomposition of recent growth in personal health expenditures based on these numbers. Table 1 shows a decomposition based on the use of the medical CPI and one based on an index of hospital input prices developed by the American Hospital Association. Table 2 shows the results of a decomposition based on the growth in private health employment. In both cases, the message is clear: a substantial proportion of medical spending growth in the 1980s and the first half of the 1990s is attributable to rising prices or wages rather than to a diversion of resources into medical care. This is in contrast to the experience of the

TABLE 1. Alternative Partitions of Growth in Real Personal Health Care Expenditures, Using Various Price Indexes, 1965–93

		Percentage of Growth Attributable to Excess Medical Inflation	
Year	Real Growth Rate[a] %	Percentage from Medical Care CPI (output price)	Percentage from Alternate (uses AHA market basket for all outputs)
1965–70	8.4	—	—[b]
1970–80	4.8	—	—[b]
1980–90	6.1	54	51
1990–93	5.2	80	42

Source: Health Care Financing Review, various years; Levit et al., "National Spending Trends, 1960–1993," *Health Affairs* (winter 1994): 19; and data from American Hospital Association (AHA), *Economic Trends,* various years.

[a]Deflated by CPI less medical care.
[b]Not available.

TABLE 2. Alternative Partitions of Growth in Real Personal Health Expenditures, Using Employment Measures, 1965–93

Year	(Private) Health Services Employment, Growth Rate	Percentage of Growth Attributable to Excess Medical Inflation
1965–71	6.6	—[a]
1971–81	5.8	—[a]
1981–85	3.4	42
1985–90	4.5	25
1991	4.7	13
1992	3.8	36
1993	3.3	23

Source: Calculated from data in *Health Care Financing Review,* various years.

[a]No excess medical inflation in time period.

1970s, during which price growth was small. The divergence between medical input prices and prices in general appears to have greatly diminished in 1994, but is forecasted by some experts to widen in the late 1990s.

The implication then is that much of recent cost growth has been of the economically neutral type, not of the harmful type associated with the diversion of resources into wasteful medical care employment rather than into employment more valuable in other uses. We really do not know the relative values of employment either, but even this "harm" to the economy, should it occur, falls on consumers in terms of achieving a lower level of well-being out of a given level of resources available. It does not fall on business, and it does not even reduce the level of measured GDP. Overall, based on this analysis, it is difficult to see much basis for business concern about the effect of medical spending on the economy. Short of a massive outbreak of waste—something that seems unlikely in the current climate of growing managed care—the rate of growth of medical spending, whatever it turns out to be, is unlikely to do the economy harm. In contrast, financing a large chunk of that growth through the public sector in the form of Medicaid and (especially) Medicare can do some harm to the economy, and it is this prospect that in part has motivated the current proposals for Medicare and Medicaid reform. Even here, however, the harm will primarily fall on citizens as taxpayers, not on businesses or their owners.

International Competition and Health Care Costs

One of the other macroeconomic issues raised in the health reform debate by some large corporations was the possibility that high health care costs, translated into high health benefits costs, caused U.S. firms that provided benefits to be less able to compete in international markets. The most straightforward way of addressing this question is to turn to the simple economic theory discussed earlier: if the incidence of benefits costs is almost entirely on money wages, total compensation costs will not be affected by the level of health benefits. If U.S. firms' production costs are unaffected, their international competitiveness can hardly be reduced. American workers will have lower take-home pay than would otherwise have been the case, and, if the higher medical costs are not accompanied by matching benefits, workers will have lower real incomes. But the ability of U.S. firms to sell in international markets, to compete with foreign firms in the U.S. market, or to earn profits, will be unaffected.

There have been some attempts to go beyond the simple theory (and the specific empirical studies that show that its predictions about incidence are correct) to examine the question of international competitiveness more directly. One relatively unsophisticated but powerful analysis examines the relationship between total compensation cost per worker in the United States and total compensation cost per worker in other countries, adjusted for productivity. This comparison shows that labor costs are not high in the United States relative to other countries. More importantly, it shows that in the 1980s, when U.S. health care costs and U.S. firms' health benefits costs were substantially outpacing those in other countries, compensation costs for American workers actually *fell* relative to those of many other countries (Cromwell 1993).

The other attempt was a multidisciplinary econometric study by Brailer and Van Horn (1993), which tried a large number of tests intended to see whether higher or rising U.S. benefits costs could be related to indicators of international competitiveness, such as the balance of trade or relative international price levels. While it turned out to be difficult to develop models that explained variation well in any case, there was no evidence that health benefits costs had anything to do with what was happening.

Conclusion

The overall message, based on theory and empirical studies, is that the level or rate of growth in medical spending does not appreciably affect the economy as a whole. Rising spending is not harmful, and falling spending is not beneficial. Individual groups within the economy may be affected (primarily consumers or medical producers), but, in aggregate, such effects only represent transfers. Consumer welfare can be altered if medical spending is wasteful. However, even in this case, the well-being of businesses (or capital owners) is independent of what is happening in the medical care sector.

CHAPTER 7

How Business Looks at Health Benefits Incidence and Reform

In this chapter I report on the reactions of business decision makers or policymakers to the economic view of incidence. When asked whether and why they treat health benefits costs as paid out of profits rather than paid out of wages, what do they say? I report on the results of two sets of interviews and questionnaires—one set conducted in 1994 by Sharon Silow-Carroll and Jack Meyer of the Economic and Social Research Institute (Silow-Carroll et al. 1995) and another smaller but more focused set of interviews and case study exercises that I undertook in spring and summer 1995. The Silow-Carroll/Meyer study was specifically focused on business's views of health reform and especially on the Clinton proposal; I have already made reference to the relevant parts of that proposal in chapter 2. In this chapter I will deal with their more general inquiries into how businesses think about benefits costs. In both cases, I will relate the results of the in-depth probing of attitudes to the larger-sampled but less focused insights that can be gained from polls of business owners.

How to Get at the Truth

One of the main messages from the economic approach to looking at health benefits is that decisions on benefits ought to be part of a larger system of compensation and employment planning, because such decisions are bound to have repercussions beyond their immediate impact on benefits costs. In particular, the impact of benefits decisions on money wages is critical, but that impact in turn potentially affects the numbers and types of persons employed at a given firm, what other employers will do, and the overall level of output and prices in the economy. The necessary link between one decision and another means that not all outcomes people would like are necessarily attainable. For instance, an owner of a business would presumably like benefits costs to fall if that could guarantee higher profits, but the economic models of competitive labor markets suggest that such a result is neither guaranteed nor expected. The necessary interconnection between actions and outcomes means that simple surveys of what owners like (or fear) are not especially helpful, since it is necessary in such surveys to keep questions simple and therefore it is quite difficult to force the subject to recognize that one answer necessarily implies another or that there are trade-offs (Tanaka 1996). Most business owners, like people in general, would like low health costs, high health quality, high access, and free choice of providers—but they cannot have all of these good things simultaneously. Trade-offs are the essential feature of health reform, and yet it is very difficult to question people about trade-offs.

The interviews or structured questionnaires that I will discuss in the following do try to focus on these trade-offs, at least in part, but keeping the respondent constrained by trade-offs is difficult at best and probably impossible to do with any degree of validity or reliability in simple surveys. Accordingly the in-depth character of the information collected, while itself requiring a trade-off in sample size or randomness of selection, is probably unavoidable.

How Businesses Should Think about Changes in Health Benefits Costs

Imagine that a benefits manager notices a 15 percent increase in health benefits costs. What should he or she do? The correct answer, of course, is "It all depends." In this case, the answer depends on three kinds of information (ranged in roughly increasing difficulty of obtaining). First, is this increase occurring only in my firm or is it occurring in others in my *labor* market? (What is happening in my product market is irrelevant.) Second, was the increase unexpected, by me and by my competitors? Third, is the increase accompanied by improvements in quality of care or not?

If the answer to these three questions is "Everyone is experiencing an anticipated increase in cost that is not at all associated with higher quality," the answer is the economic one—cut cash wages by the amount of the increase in cost and do not worry any further. Moreover, we can also ask the public policy question—should the firm spend money to influence the political process so as to reduce the size of the cost increase? The answer here is "No."

What of the mirror image question of whether the firm should do something (costly) through internal management to reduce the size of the increase it will experience. If the cost of the action is less than the cost of the saving, as the previous chapter showed, the answer is always, "Do it!" If you cut your net costs and your competitors do not, you gain financial advantage. If you cut your costs and your competitors do likewise, at least you do not have financial disadvantage.

So the most troublesome question is not how to manage a new cost increase as much as how much (or whether) to adjust wages and whether to take political action. Benefits specialists always think about the first; they sometimes think about the last; and they least often think about the second. So it is the last two strategies I will focus on.

There were, as we shall see in more detail subsequently, very few circumstances in which managers completely rejected the economic view that the cost of health benefits largely falls on worker wages. A common view was that, in some ultimate sense, this conclusion must be true. But an equally common follow-up was that this conclusion was not especially relevant to the actual decisions managers had to make—either decisions involving political positions or decisions involving benefits management. I first summarize and comment on these "Yes, but" views in general terms, before turning to managers' responses to more specific decisions or trade-offs.

A. It's Not My Job

It seems most natural to pose questions about the valuation of benefits and about public policy toward benefits to managers in the benefits departments of firms. However, the decentralized structure of large corporations, while highly useful for many purposes, makes it hard for such persons to answer theoretical questions about wage-benefit trade-offs or to make those trade-offs in practice. As noted in chapter 5, those with the responsibilities of managing benefits and monitoring spending for benefits are frequently in organizationally distinct departments or divisions from those who set cash wages and also from those who manage the total compensation costs of the firm. The head of the benefits department, the director of compensation, and the chief financial officer often operate independently. The direct and immediate consequence of such a division of authority is that no one of these individuals has the responsibility (or the power) to make decisions that reflect the economic concept of trading wages for benefits.

The biases that this arrangement yields are in the direction of excessive restriction on the level of benefit spending. If the CFO evaluates each of the "nonrevenue" departments on the level or rate of growth of cost they incur, the manager of benefits has an incentive to choose plans that lower costs, as long as this can be done without too much outcry. If the manager of compensation then finds that money wages must be increased or worker quality will fall, that's his or her problem. More to the point of this discussion, if the benefits manager is invited to draft the company's position on employer mandates, government cost controls, cooperative efforts with other firms to hold down benefits costs, or similar issues—as would seem natural—the trade-off question and the long run equilibrium questions get ignored or underestimated.

Little purpose would have been served by asking respondents why their firms were organized in a way that inhibited profit-increasing coordination. But are there any more general explanations of why firms seem to have chosen dysfunctional structures? The most obvious explanation is that the firm has more important objectives than rationalizing the benefits part of its compensation structure; decentralization of decision making and incentives, whatever its flaws when it comes to benefits, serves other firm objectives. The most obvious objective is the vague but true one—no large organization can have one or a small number of people making all decisions, down to the most detailed; you *have* to have some division of power and responsibility. If the compensation people are to focus on their main challenge—how to structure cash compensation within the firm so that it attracts the right employees, motivates them properly, and maintains morale (and a sense of within-firm equity), they cannot be distracted by worrying about health benefits (which are after all less than 10 percent of total compensation costs). Likewise the benefits people who are supposed to worry about the cesarean section rate in the firm's current HMOs can hardly be bothered with thinking about the raises workers get.

There is no way to solve this dilemma in theory. It could be that the wasted motion, the errors, and the confusion that come from that lack of coordination are just unavoidable, like ants at a picnic. A safe but not meaningless comment is that firms should look at their organizational structure and division of responsibilities to determine that this hopeless state is really ideal (unable to be improved). They should look to see whether messages can somehow be carried from one task to another and whether a decentralized structure that made sense when benefits were cheap still makes sense when they are expensive. At least they should make sure that the lack of coordination is acknowledged and excused (with a good excuse), rather than just the result of oversight or obtuseness.

B. Let's Do It Together

Some businesses have formed coalitions and purchasing groups in order to reduce their health benefits costs. In Memphis, in Cleveland, and in the entire state of Florida, money has been or is being spent and people are being hired to staff these organizations, and the money largely comes from businesses. Based on the economic view of fringe benefits costs, is this money well spent?

Part of the answer depends on the nature of coalition activities. One set of activities we may call "civic planning." These activities affect providers' outputs, costs, and prices charged to *all* buyers of their services. The other activity we may call "price negotiation," which involves seeking lower prices for health insurance and health benefits, either from health care providers or from health insurance plans, only for the specific set of buyers in the coalition and, most emphatically, not for others.

Civic planning activities usually refer to some type of oversight, commentary, and pressure applied to spending decisions of large health care providers in a market area. For instance, a business coalition may review (and object to) a hospital's proposal to build new facilities, or to add new programs, or to contract at a high price for some services. Businesspersons have always served on hospital boards and engaged in this activity to some extent, but often those decisions were made with an eye to the financial health of the particular hospital rather than to that of the trustees' businesses. The kind of decision a coalition may review and attempt to discourage is the addition of some facility or service a hospital may be able to cover with higher charges (perhaps because they believe that the hospital occupies a prominent market position), because the charge will ultimately have to be paid by businesses.

The economic view says that, if applied to a hospital used by employees of all employers in a market area, such group or civic planning efforts are a waste of time and money. The high hospital prices, in this view, will simply reduce market-wide money wages but will not raise total compensation costs at any firm. The negative morale effects already discussed might still cause firms to oppose an unnecessary or duplicative expenditure, but the impacts are surely small. The basic message, regrettably, is that saving health care costs for everyone in town will not add to the bottom line. Preventing a market area from *becoming* a high health cost area will not raise profits either, unless potential employees are likely to migrate in large numbers to other areas for more attractive jobs.

Negotiating lower insurance rates may be to the advantage of the firms involved if it allows them to achieve lower prices than other firms with which they compete in the employment market. From the viewpoint of a single firm, the best coalition is one that excludes other employers who hire the same kinds of workers you do but that includes enough employers who hire in other labor markets to have some influence on providers. There is obviously a trade-off here—the more inclusive the coalition, the more effective it will be in lowering premiums and prices but the less advantage those lower prices will offer to any one member. However, if a highly inclusive coalition is formed, by the same token no one firm would want to be left out, paying higher prices. As usual, there is not a great deal of advantage in joining a club that is too eager to have you as a member— but you wouldn't want to be excluded either.

Often the reason for forming a coalition is to allow members of the coalition, usually medium-sized or small employers, to have access to the same allegedly lower health care costs as large employers with bargaining power. Achieving lower costs will undoubtedly help firm employees if there is no reduction in quality. But will it help their employers? The answer depends on whether these firms are competing with the larger firms in hiring of labor. If they are, then any lower costs will fall largely to the bottom line. But often they may be hiring in labor markets differentiated by skill or type of occupation. In such cases, there is no gain from achieving low costs if almost all other small employers are in the coalition.

This analysis may help to explain both the confusion and the results that surrounded a set of efforts to help businesses to organize to reduce health care (especially hospital) costs. In the late 1980s the Robert Wood Johnson Foundation funded a number of multimillion dollar grants to groups and coalitions in 17 cities. The purpose of these groups was to organize "Community Programs for Affordable Health Care" (CPAHC) that would unite the entire business community to combine with hospitals to reduce overcapacity, duplication, and unnecessary use of services.

The evaluation of these projects, by Brown and McLaughlin (1990), indicated two things. First, it was possible to form coalitions to apply for the grants; businesses were willing to agree to participate, and did indeed participate, in coalition activities. But second, the activities appeared to have no consistent and appreciable impact on hospital costs and use. The reason the evaluators give for this absence of success was that, when it really became necessary for business to make the effort to exert pressure on hospitals, businesses were unwilling to make that effort. There were some logical excuses—business leaders sometimes served on hospital boards and were unwilling to pressure their friends on the board, out of loyalty or because they were co-opted; hospital managers came to dominate the coalitions; there were free rider problems. But the fundamental message was that the businesses did not see that controlling hospital costs in their town really mattered to them. The judgment was that "most communities cannot summon the collective *will* (emphasis in original) that cost containment demanded . . . Business leaders knew that health care costs too much, but their willingness to act on the problem usually ends at the benefit manager's door . . . But if not business, who?" This lack of enthusiasm for controlling a "skyrocketing" cost puzzled the evaluators. They pessimistically (if less than prophetically) concluded that this was "the last best shot to see if anyone in the voluntary sector would take on the cost issue. CPAHC's record suggests that the answer is unambiguously 'no'."

One possible interpretation is suggested by the economic view of health benefits cost: a reduction in the level or rate of growth of hospital costs that was shared by virtually all employer-paid benefit plans in the area would not benefit employers; it would not be expected to increase profits. It would benefit employees, if the forgone hospital benefits were truly wasteful (in the sense of being worthless or worth less than the costs saved), but those benefits would show up as higher raises for the workers, not higher net incomes for their employers. What happened in this experiment is consistent with the hypothesis that, when push comes to shove, employers do have an intuitive understanding of the economic view, that they really do realize which side of the bread has the butter.

It is equally clear, however, that both businesses and the noneconomist analysts of this project did not really understand this intuition (although, to their credit, the analysts did hold a slim hope that voluntary business-*only* coalitions might work). They submitted a report expressing puzzlement and confusion to the foundation, unable to explain why businesses did not even seem to recognize their own self-interest. They concluded that "misguided thinking among private purchasers is the single most formidable obstacle to a sensible cost containment debate." The "misguided thinking" they had in mind was not confusion about incidence, however; rather, it was the misguided belief by businesses that government intervention was unnecessary and harmful when it came to controlling costs. The analysts suggested strongly that, if businesses were going to continue to be so obtuse, governmental action would be necessary for their own good. The eventual Clinton proposal for government-imposed limits on private spending and government-mandated market-wide business purchasing coalitions was consistent with the evaluators' erroneous conclusions.

The Robert Wood Johnson Foundation experiments investigated one kind of community effort: one in which all or most health providers were supposed to cooperate with all or most employers to hold down health care costs. The failure of this experiment can be contrasted with the apparent success of a different kind of community effort: buying coalitions. Early results from efforts of groups of employer-buyers to obtain lower prices for medical service and medical insurance suggest that they can be successful—although no definitive evaluation has yet been performed. Why might such coalitions succeed where the Johnson Foundation coalitions failed?

One obvious answer is that buyer coalitions exclude producers; they dispense with the polite fiction that sellers of health care might prefer their revenues to grow less rapidly if this was judged to be in the community's interest. Defining sellers as outside the coalition probably helped to avoid the co-opting that sometimes occurred in the Robert Wood Johnson Foundation experiments, but it leaves open the question of why buyers did not resist the co-opting when sellers sat at the same table. An answer to that question is provided by the economic model. It proceeds from another difference; in the buyer coalition approach, the lower prices that the coalition negotiates are only available to members of the coalition, not to other employers in town—in contrast to the Johnson Foundation model, in which costs were to be contained to the benefit of all buyers (including Medicaid).

The difference, of course, is that having lower costs than other competitors can lead to profits. Buyer coalitions' strong advantage is that they *exclude* some buyers. One implication is that the more inclusive the buyer coalition, the more effective it may be at negotiating lower prices and premiums, but the *less* effective those lower prices will be in adding to firm profits. This implication seems not yet to have dawned on advocates of buyer groups, who often still operate under the assumption that bigger is better. But I believe that it will soon become apparent.

C. In the Long Run, I've Retired

Another common argument is that, while wages *eventually* fall when benefits costs rise, it can take a long time before wages can adjust, and, in the meantime, higher benefits costs do erode profits. An alleged premium in U.S. firms on short term financial results, and penalties imposed on managers when they are not forthcoming, is also mentioned. When asked whether this argument is valid when the benefits cost increases should have been anticipated, the answer is no—but the counterargument is that almost all benefits cost increases (in nonmandatory benefits) are unanticipated.

There is a mirror image of this argument—what happens to wages when benefits costs fall? Recent slight declines in the premiums some large employers have had to pay have turned this pipe dream into a reality—but will it lead to higher money wages? The short term circumstantial evidence is not convincing—the benefits cost growth rate fell from about 50 percent higher than for wages in the late 1980s and early 1990s to a rate equal to that of wages in 1994–95—and yet the growth in both wages and total compensation has been flat since mid-1992, in the face of rising productivity, only increasing slightly in 1996. Most of the arguments about why it would take a while for wages to adjust downward—union contracts, minimum wage limits, possible effects on employee morale—do not hold for benefit cost declines. It is always possible, on any given day, to give workers raises; minimum wages set no ceiling, and more take-home pay should raise morale. I will comment in more detail in the following on what managers said about benefits costs declines, but for the present we should note that it poses a problem.

D. We'd Rather Do It Ourselves

One very common and very important answer goes a long way toward explaining why many larger businesses that initially supported the Clinton plan bailed out when its details became known. "Large employers, all of whom provide comprehensive health plans, regard the mandate as a 'camel's nose under the tent' that would further increase government interference with the internal operations of private business" (Silow-Carroll et al. 1995, 62). The plan envisioned that firms up to a fairly large size would have to purchase their insurance through a purchasing cooperative (a health alliance). The cooperative, not the benefits department of the individual firm, would make all the important decisions: which plans to contract with, what premiums to accept, what benefits and plan characteristics to require. And all employees of every employer would be able to choose from the same set of plans, at the same prices.

Even if the health alliance was as well managed as it could be, it is easy to see why some employers would lose from this arrangement. It takes away their power to earn profits by managing their health benefits more effectively than other employers in the local labor market. That is, it would have eliminated the possibility of obtaining sustainable competitive advantage through benefits management.

This observation alone might explain why about half of employers offering health insurance—those who are able to manage better than average—would oppose losing their edge. However, one might have expected those other firms in the bottom half of the distribution of managerial skill—and they have to be there—to favor the Clinton plan. In truth, there were some employers, a minority, who did tell the Economic and Social Research Institute (ESRI) that they preferred the Clinton plan because it allowed them to wash their hands of employee benefits, something they were happy to do. Even many of the potential gainers felt, however, that they as employers would still be blamed by their workers if the local health alliance was incompetent—since they would be required to pay most of the higher premiums and therefore would have to cut wages. Moreover, some employers felt that the community rating that was also built into health alliances, a community rating that encompassed the very high cost Medicaid population, would mean that their costs would rise anyway. But it was the defection of those employers who felt capable of controlling benefits costs themselves that sank business support for the Clinton plan. In the short term, it appears that these employers were right.

E. Polls and Opinions

While the debate over health reform provided a substantial stimulus to the public opinion survey industry, most of the polling did not explicitly tap the opinions of employers, even though they would be paying 80 percent of the bill. There were a number of polls of small business owners, all saying little more than the same thing: most of them hated a mandate because they felt they could not "afford" it. However, there were more targeted polls of employers of all types sponsored by the Robert Wood Johnson and Kaiser Family Foundations that are of some interest. The Johnson Foundation poll (Cantor et al. 1995) was most remarkable for documenting the virtual absence of employer belief that individual employees were or should be "responsible for their coverage"— despite the economic conclusion that workers pay for everything. Only 34 percent of surveyed employers thought that individuals should be responsible for basic hospitalization coverage, in contrast to 84 percent of employers willing to assume full responsibility. But even for insurance for catastrophic illnesses, such as cancer or AIDS, for which more than 60 percent of employers would reject responsibility, only 1.6 percent felt that individual employees should pay.

The Kaiser Family Foundation survey (Smith et al. 1992) was one of the few that asked about wage–benefit costs trade-offs. It surveyed a random sample of consumers and found that only 31 percent of them were concerned that employer health care costs would limit wage increases. In both cases then there was little appreciation for the economic viewpoint.

Specific Choices and Trade-offs

In what follows I describe the results of an informal experiment with a small but representative sample of benefits managers in which the managers were confronted with a set of scenarios intended to spotlight the trade-off between wages and benefits in a number of settings and were then asked what decisions they would make. I report here both the answers the managers gave in response to the set of teaching cases described in the appendix to this chapter and the resulting class discussion of the answers to these cases.

The ISCEBS Experiment

This experiment presented a sample of 16 benefits professionals from large organizations with a set of "minicases" and asked them how they would change their compensation policy in response to changes in benefits costs or regulations. These professionals had been selected to attend an executive education course held at the Wharton School in June 1995, organized by the International Society of Certified Employee Benefits Specialists (ISCEBS). The reported responses were given before the sessions at which the minicases were discussed.

The description of the cases used to solicit information is included as an appendix at the end of the chapter. I will identify each question discussed by its section and roman numeral.

I first inquired about overall compensation strategies. The great majority (eleven) of the participants, responding to question A-I, followed a "meet the market, item-by-item" strategy (answer 1). No one followed the total compensation approach, but only two respondents indicated that affordability dictated their decisions.

I then posed three different scenarios, or minicases, and asked the participants what they would do. Case A (question B-I) described a benefits cost increase that was affecting all employers in the labor market. The "correct" economic answers would be "cut the raise, and cut it by about $50." The respondents evenly split (eight to eight) between "cut" and "do not cut"; however, of those who would make a cut, nearly all (seven out of eight) would cut by less than the $50 amount of the benefit cost increase. Subsequent discussion of the consistency of these answers with the economic model emphasized the separation of wages and benefits as the primary reason for the "no cut" answer, as well as a combination of uncertainty, anticipated lags in market response, and possible adverse morale effects if all of the cost increase were to be taken out of raises immediately.

Case B (question B-II) is virtually identical to case A but asked about a *decrease* (rather than an increase) in benefits cost. Here the proportions changed; only a quarter (four) of the participants would give back the money in raises, and those participants were evenly split between giving back some or all of the savings. Subsequent discussion of this case emphasized again the disconnection between setting wage rates and benefits costs and also took the view that many of these firms were having no difficulty attracting high quality workers now, so they saw no need to share savings in benefits costs with workers.

Case C (question B-IV) dealt with a benefits cost decline that could only be produced by moving the employees to an unattractive HMO.

Results here were perfectly consistent with Case A—a 50-50 split between giving back some savings and not giving back any. The economically correct answer—that we might have to return more than the cost savings if employees hate this new option—was not given by any of the participants. Subsequent discussion of the case raised the themes of an oversupply of qualified workers and the difficulty of communication. Whether or not firms would go ahead with this strategy, as far as benefits specialists were concerned, appeared to depend more on worker "hue and cry" than on wage or labor market responses.

Finally, Case D (question C-IV) tried to deal explicitly with the question of trade-offs. Would specifically allowing wage reductions (which generally are not legally forbidden in any case, except when the minimum wage binds) make a mandate to add benefits more palatable? No participant took the economic view (answer [1]) that the incidence would be on workers. Instead, most respondents either opposed the change because of morale effects (answer [2]) or because of opposition to government interference (answer [4]). Some participants (presumably those with decentralized compensation management) felt that they could not cut wages even if they were allowed to do so.

The Silow-Carroll/Meyer Interviews

This study interviewed representatives of 40 businesses, about half of whom were human resources executives for Fortune 500 firms and about half of whom were owners of small business. Almost all the interviewed firms were already providing benefits.

While this study was intended to probe "the marriage between employers and health care," it did not specifically address the issue of wage trade-offs in the interviews it administered. However, answers to two of the questions should imply something about how employers view incidence. One question asked about employer preferences with regard to the fraction of the premium for mandated coverage an employer should be required to pay; recall that the economic model says that this obligation makes no difference to employer profits. Another question raised the issue of an individual mandate (to reduce alleged cost shifting from the uninsured); again, economics would imply that employers should have the same attitude toward a mandate regardless of whether the funds were paid by the employer or the individual employee.

The answers to the question of optimal employer share spanned a "wide range." "Small employers were more likely to choose 50 percent, while larger companies gave answers that evenly spanned the range from 50 to 80 percent. Most employers believe, however, that the level should be set low enough to make employees more cost-conscious consumers, and to avoid creating undue hardship for marginally successful businesses. Many also thought it would be more equitable to establish a sliding scale for contribution levels, based on the size and profitability of each company." A more recent survey by the same group found that 42 percent of surveyed employers thought that they should pay half or less of workers' insurance premiums (Dentzer 1996).

These answers do not seem to be consistent with the economic view; if there is any rationale to them, they seemed designed to minimize the impact of a mandate or regulations on status quo payment levels. Large employers, who usually pay a high share of premiums, did not mind being required to pay a high share; small firms, who often pay nothing (although they appear to pay relatively high shares when they pay anything), think that the mandated employer payment should be kept down to the lowest share and offered as an option, with some cushioning of this obligation on small and low profit firms.

In the interviews, employers were asked a kind of trade-off question: if an employer currently paid a high share of premiums, and a mandate did not require such a high share, would the employer then "consider" lowering its share? The answer to this question was that, if the mandated coverage was no more costly than current coverage, some employers said they would never reduce their contribution, while others would do so only if "the competition" did and only if "it were absolutely necessary." There was no strong sentiment for aggressive wage cuts.

When asked about individual mandate (assuming that it could be enforced) many thought it was a "good idea" but questioned how people without the necessary income could afford it. Measures of the relative proportion of respondents favoring individual or employer mandates were not given, but it is clear that many respondents were confused by questions of the enforceability and administrative issues concerning such a mandate.

In this set of interviews, as in those that I conducted, there was a clear recognition of the value of employer-paid premiums in competing in the labor market. But there was as well the usual obsession with the affordability of premiums for small, low wage firms. Split personalities continue to dominate.

Toward a Resolution. What Can We Expect of Managers?

Managers facing changes in benefits costs confront a difficult problem. *Sometimes* those changes will end up being offset by changes in money wages, so that it makes no sense to be concerned about the changes or to use firm resources to advocate public actions that would affect those changes. *Sometimes* the changes will not be offset by money wage changes, and will fall as directly to the bottom line as any other managerial decision; in such cases public actions will be of no help, but publicly imposed regulations that limit management's freedom of movement will be harmful. The problem is that the busy manager at a minimum may find it difficult and costly to determine, when confronted with a change in benefits cost, which situation is which—and sometimes it may even be impossible to know with reasonable certainty. Rules of thumb will have to be evolved to deal with this kind of problem.

Both my interviews and those of Sharon Silow-Carroll and Jack Meyer suggest that busy businesspersons sometimes tend toward economically correct views. They do realize that cutting benefits will reduce their ability to recruit, and they do understand that they must meet the market. They also understand that benefits costs trade off against wages to some extent. But they do not think the trade-off is close to 100 percent, and there is believed to be an asymmetry between increases in costs (which do cut wages somewhat) and declines in cost (which do not raise wages). The economic insights are there, but they are garbled.

One thing the manager knows for sure: increases in benefits costs can never help the company, and declines in benefits costs can never do it harm—as long as the company makes the right reaction. Resisting cost increases and relaxing during cost decreases would probably turn out to be a better strategy than the reverse but like all rules of thumb will sometimes be wrong.

What about firm attitudes toward public policy that follow from these confused views on managerial policy? There are really two issues here—one is whether firms should support or oppose the regulations requiring more generous benefits that politicians or advocacy groups might propose, and the other is whether there are actions that firms might propose even if others would not. With regard to regulation, a general rule of thumb is that regulation of benefits will probably reduce firm profits if it will do anything at all; conversely, it is difficult to think of a health benefits regulation that would make firms more profitable. Of course, benefits regulations, even when nominally applied to employers (like mandates to pay premiums), primarily affect worker well-being, not company profits. Public subsidies to low wage or high risk workers obviously make them better off, but, beyond this, it is hard to think of a regulation that will improve the welfare of the average worker.

Despite the lure of "working with" politicians and making things happen, firms probably felt better off avoiding doing so. Even the firm able to get some politicians to cater to its special interests will find it hard to capitalize on this asset by lobbying on benefits regulatory policy. And it is likely that firms will find that regulations they thought would help them with some specific problem will become irritating and profit-reducing constraints over a longer period of time. (This could be the future of the Kassebaum-Kennedy law and its sequels.)

Some Important Exceptions

There are two important exceptions to the general economic conclusion that public actions on health benefits do not affect firm profits. One case is when firms have different costs of complying with rules or actions, for instance, in the case of a mandate that affects some firms and not others. As I indicated in chapter 3, such a mandate could be considered as an action that imposes *higher* costs on smaller firms than it imposes on (or are already borne by) larger firms. Raising a firm's costs in ways that cannot be fully offset through wage changes will affect profits.

From this viewpoint, the opposition of small businesses to the Clinton mandate was rational. Distrusting the promise of temporary subsidies, they felt that it would have imposed higher costs on them, which would have reduced the value of capital they had invested and could not recover. Larger firms that did not offer coverage (such as Pizza Hut), in contrast, would not have been harmed by the mandate. They might have even been helped a little, to the extent that they have small firm competitors in the labor market, but fundamentally the mandate would have made no difference. Even though the president of Pizza Hut did not get the economics right in his congressional testimony, as noted in chapter 2, it may be more noteworthy that neither he nor his company volunteered an opinion on the Clinton plan until they were wounded by an attack from a public interest group.

The other issue that may matter is that of within-firm incidence. Different employers will make different decisions about how to spread the cost of group health insurance over group members. Objectives having to do with total compensation, with protection against changes in risk, and with attracting and retaining certain employees are all involved. These delicate and often important matters will be affected when regulations to limit premiums and underwriting are put into place—as the Kassebaum-Kennedy bill does to a modest extent. While there is a role for some minimal regulations that require things that every firm would want anyway *ex ante* (such as guaranteed renewability), more stringent rules will produce certain costs and uncertain benefits.

APPENDIX

HOW BUSINESS LOOKS AT HEALTH BENEFITS INCIDENCE AND REFORM

ISCEBS SURVEY

INTRODUCTION: The purpose of this survey is to determine how benefits specialists like yourself think about the process of setting wages and benefits, and how they think about responding to changes government regulations may make in what they can do. I want to base what I say on what you think, and to discuss the range of different views people have about what government actions will do. All answers will be kept confidential.

SECTION A: GENERAL COMPENSATION STRATEGY

These questions are intended to summarize how your firm views compensation in general, and to explore how your views on the effects of government action are related to your compensation strategy. All of these questions should be assumed to apply to your non-unionized, non-minimum wage workers.

I.   What is your firm's overall philosophy for setting levels of money wages and benefits for non-unionized workers? (Circle on the answer sheet the number of the statement that is closest.)

(1) We set money wages and individual benefit items at approximately the level that prevails among our competitors in the labor market.

(2) We check to make sure that the value of our total compensation package is competitive, but we are not very concerned about individual items.

(3) We choose the total compensation amount we can afford to pay, given our overall profitability targets, and we offer those benefits we think are good for our workers.

(4) We offer our non-unionized workers the same raises and benefits as we have negotiated for our unionized workers.

(5) None of the above are close to our strategy. Our strategy is_____
_____.
(Write in the answer on the answer sheet.)

II.   Circle the number for the statement that is closest to your strategy for hiring decisions.
(1) We decide how many workers to hire, given the compensation cost determined as described above, by comparing an estimate of the total compensation cost for an additional worker with an estimate of the addition to net revenue hiring worker would make possible.

(2) We hire the number of workers we need to produce a predetermined amount of output.

(3) Neither of the above are close to our strategy. Our strategy is_____

SECTION B: REACTIONS TO CHANGES IN BENEFITS COSTS

CIRCLE ANSWERS ON THE ANSWER SHEET

I.   Suppose there is an increase in the cost of the health benefits you offer which you know is also affecting all the other employers with which you compete in hiring workers in the same way. (a) Compared to smaller increases in cost, will this change cause you to offer smaller money wage raises? (Circle yes or no on the answer sheet.) (b) If the increase in benefits cost per worker is $50 per month, will you cut the raise (1) by more than $50, (2) by less than $50, or (3) by just about $50?

II.   Suppose there is a decrease in your health benefits cost which you know is also affecting all other employers in the same way. (a) Compared to a situation of no change in cost, will this cause you to offer a larger money wage raise? (b) If so, and if the decrease in cost per worker is $50, by how much will you increase the raise -- (1) by more than $50, (2) by less than $50, or (3) by just about $50?

III.   Suppose you know that the decrease in your health benefits cost is due to your skillful benefits management, and is not being experienced by your competitors in the labor market, whose costs are not changing. Would your answer to the previous question change?

IV.   Suppose you knew that by enrolling all of your employees in an especially aggressive HMO, you could cut your health benefits costs per employee by $50 per month. However, you also know that many of your employees would not like being switched into this HMO. (a) If you decided to make the switch anyway, would you think it necessary to raise the money compensation of workers? (Yes or no?) (b) If you answered yes to part (a), by how much would you increase wages? (a) More than $50, (b) less than $50, or (c) just about $50.

SECTION C: POLITICAL IMPACTS ON PRIVATE BENEFITS: DO THEY MATTER (MUCH)?

I.   Politicians and regulators often seek to affect what employers must offer in terms of health insurance benefits, and how they must finance those benefits. (For example, required benefits, limits on preexisting condition exclusions.)

II.   If you firm is strongly or moderately concerned, is that because you expect such proposals to have large impacts on....(cirlce all answers that apply):

1)   labor costs
2)   prices we must change

3)   profits
4)   labor relations
5)   Other _____(fill in)

III.   If your firm is unconcerned, is that because .....(circle all answers that apply):

1)   such rules primarily affect workers and the money wages they are paid, but not total labor costs.
2)   such rules raise what we have to pay for labor, but we can always raise prices and see little or no drop in business.
3)   we expect to be able to earn our profit targets regardless of the kinds of rules and laws usually discussed.
4)   Other _____(fill in)

IV.   Suppose a law was passed requiring you and all other employers to offer more generous health benefits than you now do, but the law specifically allowed (but did not require) you to reduce money wages to offset the higher cost of the benefit. Which of the following statements most closely describes your reaction to such a law?

(1)   I would not strongly oppose such a law; it wouldn't matter to my firm because I could keep my labor costs at the same level as before the law since I could offset cost increases through wage reductions.

(2)   I would oppose the law because I dislike reducing my workers' wages for the government's benefit, and because so doing would have serious adverse effects on morale, even if wages were falling at all other employers.

(3)   I would oppose the law because cutting money wages would make if hard for me to hire or retain qualified workers, even if all other employers were cutting wages. But if I do not cut wages, my labor costs would rise.

(4)   I would oppose such a law because careful choice of a unique set of benefits or ways of managing benefits is one of the competitive advantages our firm has, and this law would require me to do the same thing as everyone else.

(5)   Other_____.

SECTION D: SPECIFIC POLITICAL QUESTIONS

For each of the following "reform" proposals, indicate whether you think each proposal would (1) greatly reduce, (2) moderately reduce, (3) leave unaffected, (4) moderately increase or (5) greatly increase profits, labor costs (in the sense of total compensation cost per worker) and average worker well-being in your firm only.

I.   Require employees to include employer health insurance premium payments as part of their taxable income; the employer could continue to deduct the cost.

Profits (1) to (5)
Labor costs (1) to (5)
Worker well-being, on average (1) to (5)

II.   Require every employer who offers insurance to insure all new employees with no more than a three-month preexisting condition exclusion.

Profits (1) to (5)
Labor costs (1) to (5)
Worker well-being, on average (1) to (5)

III.   Require all insures to practice modified community rating, with the requirement not applicable to firms or groups that self insure.

Profits (1) to (5)
Labor costs (1) to (5)
Worker well-being, on average (1) to (5)

IV.   Allow states to receive federal waivers of the ERISA preemption so that they may regulate all firms' health insurance benefits.

Profits (1) to (5)
Labor costs (1) to (5)
Worker well-being, on average (1) to (5)

V.   Allow employers to set up and offer tax-shielded Medical Savings Accounts combined with catastrophic insurance coverage.

Profits (1) to (5)
Labor costs (1) to (5)
Worker well-being, on average (1) to (5)

CHAPTER 8

Conclusion: Toward Optimal Health Benefits Policy, Public and Private

The statements and the analysis of business behavior with regard to health benefits make one thing clear: businesses are unclear on how their interests are affected when things that affect benefits change. They suffer from a kind of schizophrenia. At the conscious and practical level, for the greatest part, they proceed as if benefits costs are like other input costs, and therefore any method to contain them will provide lasting bottom line benefits. This instinctive reaction sometimes spills over to positive attitudes toward politicians who promise to help keep these costs down and into negative attitudes toward analysts who propose to raise costs through things like taxation of employer contributions or mandation of universally desired benefits. The other part of the managerial personality, however, both understands intellectually and knows viscerally that employee benefits are ultimately the employees' business and not really the boss's affair. So when the time comes to pay up, by sacrificing lobbying resources, by spending political chips, or by paying the price of additional regulations, businesses back out of deals with government to contain their benefits costs. They end up preferring to go their own way but (beyond currently popular slogans about inefficient government) not really being able to explain why.

If businesses are somewhat at sea but ultimately find their way to dry land, politicians are still struggling. They want businesses to discharge their "obligation" to provide generous insurance coverage without exclusions or restrictions, and they still respond favorably (even when they are Republicans) when businesses choose to do so. The main differences between parties are in the relative faith put in coercion versus subsidies and perhaps in the importance attached to the final outcome (relative to other social problems). The parties agree on the desirability of an outcome in which employers agree to "give" workers generous health benefits.

Given the presence of this confusion, we are faced with two questions. Would reduction in that confusion change political outcomes, and would those changes constitute an overall improvement? The first question is easier to answer positively than is the second one. At an abstract, intellectual level we know that there is no guarantee that democratic political processes, even with well-informed electorates, will necessarily arrive at desirable outcomes. If the definition of "desirability" is one based on economic efficiency, we know that a majority may ignore a minority, even one with intense preferences. If the definition is based on stability, we know that cyclical majorities are in theory possible. And if the definition is based on what I and people like me prefer, we know that we can be outvoted.

More practically, if perhaps more tautologically, we can endorse informed choice under a constitutionally defined and accepted set of rules as itself defining a desirable process. Absent obvious reasons to the contrary—as in the case in which an informed majority chooses to violate some group's civil rights—we can accept the verdict of a well-informed majoritarian democracy as the best we can expect. Beyond this general observation we need to be more concrete about how specific changes in information and positions might affect the political outcome.

What If?

What would happen if businesses explicitly decided and overtly announced that they would no longer give any employees health benefits? Instead, henceforth, they would buy (or themselves produce) health insurance, which they would then resell to workers in trade for lower money wages? What would happen if there were explicit recognition, announcement, and policy that benefits were the property of, the choice of, and (ultimately) the obligation of workers? Firms may compete for workers by trying to secure the best deal in benefits that they can then resell, but ultimately they are spending the workers' money for the workers' benefit (and benefits). Some firms already are taking tentative steps in this direction, providing workers with statements of total compensation that include not only money wages (before withholding) but also the cost of benefits. What I am suggesting here is a more explicit recognition of the economic view.

Changing governmental policy to regard benefits as part and parcel of total worker compensation—and therefore to be taxed and accounted in the same fashion as money wages—would help businesses to make the transition. So would adoption by more businesses of the total compensation approach. There would still be some ties that would bind the employer to benefits management, primarily the way in which the cost of group insurance would be divided among workers (within-firm incidence) and the extent to which benefits options are managed to avoid adverse selection. Given our woeful ignorance about how these processes work and what is better, it would probably be best policy to let firms manage these actions as part of their overall competitive strategies in the labor market. If a necessarily small minority of workers end up paying what society regards as too much for their health insurance, relating some type of subsidy to risk (or the creation of risk pools to do the same thing) can make this minor problem even less important.

What would this kind of explicit recognition of benefits incidence do? Would such a "declaration of independence" (of benefits from profits) actually work to shape political discourse in a better fashion? It would allow almost everyone to be better off than under the alternative—except for political entrepreneurs and regulators. Employees would be better off because they would get the benefits-wages combination they prefer. Employers would be better off because they could manage these benefits with a free hand.

The biggest obstacle is that this change would require someone to invest time and resources in education—in educating politicians, in educating workers, and even in educating managers to go with their instincts, not with their account books. I do not have an easy answer to the question of where this investment will come from. For help we look to analysts, we look to nonprofit foundations, we even look to politicians who would rather be right on employee benefits than be reelected. Perhaps there is hope.

More General Messages

What lessons does this discussion provide toward a more generalizable understanding of businesses' management of their own commercial and public affairs? On the first count, we seem to have yet another example of a common pattern in public policy issues: business managements honestly misunderstand what is in their own long term interests and then staunchly defend that misunderstanding. Part of the misunderstanding arises from the need to stay close to day to day managerial decisions, which requires the development of rules of thumb and standard operating procedures that usually work fairly well, that can accommodate the cases considered by more analytical models as exceptions to a pragmatic procedure, but that fail to deal with large scale changes or big picture issues.

The old debate over marginal cost pricing by businesses was settled by discovery that businesses generally price at a fixed markup—except when the marginal cost rule dictates that the markup be changed to increase profits. The same situation applies with health benefits. Firms manage their health benefits as a cost like any other cost—except when consideration of the firm's role as proxy purchaser clashes with that rule. Half-hearted efforts, seat-of-the-pants fine tuning, and the rarity of real challenges usually make following a slightly incorrect rule still an apparently reasonable thing to do.

The dangers of following an incorrect theory therefore only arise occasionally, when large changes in the environment have occurred or when large changes in policy are contemplated. Then, in this case as in most others, one of two things appears to happen. Some firms that continue to follow the incorrect rule do themselves harm—and suffer from more disgruntled employees or higher total compensation costs than they need to. It would be overstating the case to say that many firms put themselves into bankruptcy by mismanaged benefits policy—although this seems to have been risked in the case of postretirement benefits. More likely there is some sacrifice of firm value, and some lag until the workforce accommodates to the benefits offered, rather than the other way around. Other firms see eventually the error of treating benefits costs like any other cost and do consider (if only in an informal way) what employees want and what values they place on various benefits and what tradeoffs the firm should offer. Oftentimes this requires bringing in consultants with the full panoply of reengineering, but frequently firms are able to muddle through to a solution on their own.

In contrast to this relatively benign outcome offered by flexible competitive management in the face of market changes, the threats from government actions offered by a misunderstanding of the correct theory of benefits are more substantial and more permanent. Government, after all, is large and universal so that its mistakes affect everyone and are harder to change or to adjust to. As already noted, larger businesses eventually determined that the Clinton plan probably was not in their stockholders' interests, although it would not be very harmful. As a consequence, their position changed from one of strong and noble support to one of mild and disinterested opposition. Combined with the strong opposition (probably stronger than it needed to be) from lobbyists for small businesses, some of which would be harmed, this opposition served to push the already limping proposal to defeat.

What Difference Did Error Make?

What difference would acceptance of the economic view on employer payment for health insurance premiums have made to the outcome of the process? Obviously answering such a counterfactual question is very difficult, since there is no accepted theory of exactly what went wrong. Still, some speculation may be helpful.

The business group most strongly opposed to the Clinton plan was the National Federation of Independent Businesses (NFIB), and a sizable portion of their opposition was driven by their members' belief that they could not afford to pay for regulated health insurance. In some cases, small businesses did not pay for any health insurance, and in other cases either the extent of coverage or the employer's share was below the levels mandated in the bill. This opposition from an economic viewpoint was in the right place, but it was much stronger than it should have been.

The amount of additional compensation cost imposed by a mandate in a small business is, at a maximum, equal to the difference in loading between the firm size just at the margin of current willingness to offer insurance and the loading in the uninsured small firm. That difference surely amounts to less than 20 percent of premiums and probably less than 10 percent. Since employer-paid health insurance usually amounts to less than one-tenth of total compensation costs, the implied addition to those costs for small firms is in the range of 1 to 2 percent at the most. The reduction in profits would generally be less than the increase in compensation costs, because there will be some adjustment of labor and prices.

The total reduction in profits will therefore not be inconsequential, but it will not represent Armageddon for small businesses either. In addition, there were two important features of the Clinton plan that would have substantially cushioned the impact of imposed higher health insurance loading. First, small businesses were to be pooled with much larger businesses in the health alliances, and all were to be charged the same premiums. Second, low wage small businesses were to receive subsidies.

If small businesses believed that the subsidies would be paid, and if they believed that the health alliances would have provided their workers with the kind of health insurance the workers wanted, the Clinton plan would have imposed only small costs on the profitability of small businesses, based on a correct economic analysis. Since we do not know what it cost NFIB to fight the Clinton plan, it is still possible that the fight would have been cost effective even if the anticipated hit on profits (under correct economic reasoning) would have been small. There is, however, little doubt that the belief that all of the mandated cost would be "unaffordable" and would therefore come out of profits was a reason for the strength of this opposition.

Some of the opposition to the mandate from those firms with minimum wage workers would also have remained. The subsidies in the Clinton bill were intended to reduce this opposition but may not have been fully effective in doing so, for two reasons. First, employers were skeptical about the political durability of such subsidies in a deficit budget. The absence of earmarked funding or any other source of reassurance was noted. Second, even in firms with high average wages, there would have been some minimum wage workers whose money wages could not be reduced to offset the cost of the mandated employer payment. That the firm employed other workers whose wages could legally be reduced would not be much help if labor market conditions prevented the firm from cutting the pay of high pay workers.

Those employers who favored the bill because it might cut their benefits costs likewise still might have retained some of that benign attitude even if they accepted the economic model. One reason is that the initial version of the bill promised to pick up the cost of retired employees not yet on Medicare, and there is obviously no way for those persons' wages to be offset. The other reason is that, even if competition forced the firm to raise wages for its workers, it might count improved morale as a benefit. Redistribution from some workers to others primarily affects workers, but it does not harm the employers of the benefited workers.

In all cases, however, correct economic thinking would generally have caused the strength of opinion to erode, which in turn would have been expected to affect the size of lobbying expenditures and effort. Those who attribute the defeat of the bill to lobbying might therefore expect that things could have been different.

There are two other constituencies that we might want to think about. One is the health insurers, at least the commercial insurers represented by Health Insurance Association of America (HIAA) and its "Harry and Louise" television spots. Would HIAA have been less effective if people had taken a correct view of incidence? I think the answer might be affirmative, because of the role of another constituency—workers. In a correct view of incidence, workers pay for their health insurance. Those workers who were currently uninsured but alleged to be the primary "beneficiaries" of the mandate would have known that their incomes were to be cut by thousands of dollars a year as mandates affected wages, and this presumably would have made them even less favorably inclined to the Clinton bill. However, the bill also promised lower premium growth for currently insured workers. Those workers were told by Harry and Louise to expect some restriction or limitation in the health benefits they might receive under the Clinton plan. Despite charges of distortion, there clearly was a possible sequence of events under which this could happen. But, if it did, it would be matched by higher money wages, something Harry and Louise failed to mention. On balance, what might a worker-voter have decided? The answer, ideally, would depend on whether the reduction in insurance quality was more or less than offset by the increase in cash wages. The failure to mention cash wages probably biased things against the Clinton plan—but the fact that the change in benefits would occur immediately but the cost-containment features would only be phased in later probably did not help.

It is quite likely that the Clinton bill would still have been defeated if a correct view had been held. However, if a correct view had been held, the Clinton bill in the form it took would probably never have been proposed. Employer mandates were attractive politically primarily because they seemed to make the boss pay; remove that pretext, and perhaps a more realistic proposal might have been made. For low wage workers in all but small groups, after all, the Clinton plan in effect proposed head taxes, which are usually not politically popular. We will never know, of course, but it still seems plausible that a different view of incidence might have made a difference.

Now we are really outside mapped political waters, but it is possible to imagine that, had a correct view of incidence prevailed, a different bill might have been crafted; citizens might have been persuasively instructed on the incidence of benefits (by such excellent teachers as Secretary Reich or Senator Gramm, both former college professors, for example); and universal coverage might have been passed. At least we might have come close.

The most serious harm from this episode of misunderstanding was the harm done to the advocates of the Clinton proposal. They have a real and legitimate grievance: they were double-crossed. They thought they had devised a plan that offered benefits to businesses complaining about the high cost of health benefits, one that promised to contain that cost with relatively moderate regulation. When the final (and reasonably well crafted) version of a legislative proposal that embodied this objective was presented, business backed out, offering lame excuses about the dangers of government control. Imagine how differently the debate on health reform might have gone if businesses had correctly stated that they had little at stake but their workers had a lot to lose and to gain. (I will return to this issue subsequently.)

Part of what initially happened—the "statesmanlike phase"— appeared to reflect a natural desire of large businesses and trade associations with Washington, DC, public policy presence to want to appear to be players and to appear as public spirited advocates of the public interest. In contrast to competitive markets, in which small mistakes tend to wash out, playing this game in the public sphere can lead to considerable harm all around if businesses mistake either their own interests or the consequences of their actions. I am not suggesting here that businesses have no right or opportunity to influence public policy, but what I am suggesting is that such actions, in contrast to the usual managerial tasks, are much more delicate and dangerous and can do much more harm if they are a little off the mark. The political process, intrinsically and essentially, is much less tolerant of imprecision and small goofs than is a competitive market; it has a much less effective gyroscope to chart a course of benign muddling through.

What if businesses large and small had accepted the economic view during the Clinton health reform debate? Endorsement of the president-elect's views that getting health care costs under control was important would not have been forthcoming. Big business might have thanked the president-elect for helping to bail them out of their postretirement benefits promises but would have advised him to concentrate his cost-containment efforts on the public programs, Medicare and Medicaid, where there was need for the government to get its own house in order, and not to be concerned about limiting spending or restructuring health insurance purchasing for employers. An individual mandate would have been accepted all around as the vehicle of choice for attaining universal coverage.

Small businesses would have been much less vehement in their opposition to a mandate for coverage if they had understood the incidence of the cost, if the mandate had taken the form of an individual mandate, and if they had trusted the administration's proposal to use subsidies and buying groups to even out the cost of insurance for small business.

The generalizable message from this episode is obvious: in matters of public policy, when their own stockholders' interests are not crystal clear, businesses should be careful. They should not take positions based on journalistic analysis of the consequences of complicated economic problems; they should not be players unless they really understand the game. It appears that in the future big businesses will be more timid in approaching the government for help in managing health benefits; and small business was on record as wanting it to stay out—but has been tempted to let it back in. The most serious cost of this lesson was a missed opportunity for universal or at least substantially increased insurance coverage, an opportunity that will not resurface for many years.

Post-Clinton Developments

Since the end of any serious political interest in large scale health reforms, is there evidence that businesses are changing the way they view benefits? To answer this, we first need to review what seems to be happening. Among larger firms, the most striking fact is that, after many years, the growth in both employer payments and total premiums has slowed dramatically, with one well known study of a nonrandom sample of larger firms showing a decline of about 1 percent in average employer payments in 1994—both because the rate of growth of premiums slowed and because employees moved to lower premium managed care plans

(A. Foster Higgins 1994). The evidence for 1994 does suggest that the growth of private insurance premiums slowed to a rate of about 3 percent per year, still higher than the long term growth of real GDP but a much smaller multiple than has historically prevailed. Results for 1995 show only a slight uptick. It is fair to say that the private sector has experienced rates of increase in health costs lower than those seen for years and at levels which fail to upset corporate benefits managers (Levit, Lazenby, and Sivarajan 1996).

The passage of the Kassebaum-Kennedy bill does not much alter this analysis. Even though the cost of extended protection against preexisting condition exclusions in group health insurance will fall on workers, those cost increases are tiny because the number of people who will receive additional benefits is tiny. Businesses did not fight this bill—but we do not know whether that was because they thought they would bear a cost too small to argue about, because they thought workers would bear the cost, or because they thought that the improvement in employee relations from a minimum-cost adjustment was a good trade.

What does seem clear is that, for the present, the growth in health benefits costs has fallen to a level most firms find tolerable and a level that extinguished any remaining embers of desire for government intervention for cost containment. At the moment, most firms profess to be much more concerned about possible cost shifting from cutbacks in the public Medicare and Medicaid programs than from any developments in their own benefits areas.

Matching the apparent attainment of control over costs has been a broader effort, advocated by the Jackson Hole Group, to measure and improve the quality of the benefits offered. At the same time, many firms have moved toward offering multiple managed care plans, with the employer contribution taking the form of a fixed dollar amount. Both the achievements in terms of cost containment and the prospect for quality improvement are alleged to come from harder bargaining by individual employers and groups of employers and from employer efforts to force health plans to provide more measures of quality.

At one level, this type of policy seems both internally inconsistent and schizophrenic. If firms are pulling back in terms of using their funds to direct employees to one health plan, they should hardly expect to have much success in bargaining with those plans. Benefits specialists are torn between wanting to use their newly discovered bargaining power to get what they regard as better deals in benefits for their firms and ceding the ultimate power of choice to individual employees. The model that seems to be emerging, if there is a coherent story, is one in which the employer acts as a screener and bargainer with plans who wish to be on a list of employee options but then permits employees to choose as they wish among those plans.

Which model of benefits policy is consistent with this story? In some important parts, the policy seems to have moved away from the incorrect cost-like-any-other cost view, both in terms of the movement toward fixed employer contributions and in terms of the emphasis on quality as well as cost. In other parts, however, it seems that benefits managers are still having trouble; this trouble shows up in the difficulty they have in explaining exactly *why* it should be in their interest to improve quality. There is a strong tendency to emphasize alleged benefits in terms of reduced sick leave pay, rather than turning to the more economically obvious point that better outcomes, if perceived by workers, will cause them to be willing to sacrifice more money wages. The thought that a higher quality program for dealing with employee heart attacks will have a cost offset in terms of reduced disability or sick leave payments seems so much more obvious— even though, in a competitive labor market, workers should be able to capture higher productivity in higher wages for themselves as well.

The message seems to be that there is some progress in groping toward an economically correct view of benefits policy but still in only a oblique and confused fashion. The decline of efforts to enlist government help seems part of a (probably temporary) belief that government knows less than private consultants about what to do—rather than a rejection in principle of a government role. Even here, there are some calls for government to certify some single method of measuring quality or outcomes and to require insurers to "give" certain benefits.

The most immediate problem employers will face will not be skyrocketing health care costs. It will be intensifying employee resentment whenever health care under managed care does not turn out as well as people expect. The fact that employees benefit from higher money wages even as they are required to accept managed care restrictions is not known to employees and may not be believed by benefits managers. For private sector coverage, the future struggle will probably not be explicitly political, nor will it deal directly with the existence of coverage and its financing. I believe that this new debate over quality could also be much better informed by a correct view on incidence. The effort to provide that information should start now.

References

Acknowledgments

Goldstein, G. S., and M. V. Pauly. 1976. Group Health Insurance as a Local Public Good. In *The Role of Health Insurance in the Health Services Sector,* ed. R. Rosett. New York: National Bureau of Economic Research.

Pauly, M. V. 1988. The Incidence of Health Insurance Costs: Is Everyone out of Step but Economists? Proceedings of the 41st Annual Meeting of the Industrial Relations Research Association. New York City, NY, December 29, 387–410.

Chapter 1

Lewin-VHI. 1993. *The Financial Impact of the Health Security Act.* Fairfax, VA: Lewin-VHI.

Pauly, M. V. 1994. Making a Case for Employer-Enforced Individual Mandates. *Health Affairs* 13 (spring): 21–33.

Chapter 2

Barbour, H. 1994. "Memo for Republican Leaders: The Clintons' Health Care Mandate," June 21.

Becker, M. 1994. "Employer Mandate and Related Provisions in the Administration's Health Security Act." Congressional testimony before the House Ways and Means Committee. 103 Cong., 2 sess., February 3.

Bollier, D. 1994. Do Business? Do Good? No. Do Both. *New York Times,* September 18, 11.

Brown, L. 1993. Dogmatic Slumbers: American Business and Health Policy. *Journal of Health Politics, Policy and Law* 18: 339–57.

Bullock, R. 1993. "Small Business Community's Recommendations for National Health Care Reform." Congressional Testimony before the House Senate Committee on Small Business. 103 Cong., 1 sess., August 4.

Chollet, D. 1994. Employer-Based Health Insurance in a Changing Work Force. *Health Affairs* 13 (spring): 315–26.

Connolly, C. 1993. "Business Mandate at Center of Health Care Debate." *Congressional Quarterly,* November 13, 3120–25.

CONSAD Research Corporation. 1993. The Employment Impact of Proposed

Health Care Reform on Small Business. May 6. Report prepared by CON-SAD, Pittsburgh.

Cooper, Rep. Jim. 1994. "The Managed Competition Act of 1993." Testimony before the House Committee on Education and Labor. 103 Cong., 2 sess., March 3.

Cromwell, J. 1993. *The Nation's Health Care Bill: Who Bears the Burden?* Chestnut Hill, MA: Center for Health Economics Research.

EBRI/ERF Policy Forum. 1994. The Changing Health Care Delivery System. Special Report 21, 81. April. EBRI, Washington, DC.

EBRI. 1994. Sources of Health Insurance and Characteristics of the Uninsured. EBRI Brief No. 145. January. EBRI, Washington, DC.

Families USA Foundation. 1994. 411,000 Businesses with 10,436,000 Workers at Risk Today: The Crushing Burden of Health Insurance. June. Report prepared by Families USA Foundation, Washington, DC.

Gillilland, D. 1993. *Congressional Quarterly,* November 13, 3121.

Goldwasser, T. 1990. Two Health Tales. *Independent Business* 1 (March/April), 40.

Huston, A. S. 1994. "Dual Standard: Health Insurance for American and Foreign Employees of Multinational Companies." Testimony before the Senate Labor and Human Resources Committee. 103 Cong., 2 sess. July 22.

Iglehart, J. C. 1991. Health Care and American Business: One CEO's View. *Health Affairs* 10 (spring): 76–86.

Johnson, H., and D. Broder. 1996. *The System.* Boston: Little, Brown and Co.

Kaslow, A. 1992. Health Care Tops Clinton Meeting Agenda. *Christian Science Monitor,* 15 December, 1.

Kehrer, D. 1990. Health Horrors: Coping with Soaring Costs. *Independent Business* 1 (March/April): 28–29.

Kimble, C. 1990. Questions and Answers. *Independent Business* 1 (March/April): 30–31.

Kosterlitz, J. 1994. Unmanaged Care? *National Journal* 26 (December): 2903–7.

Kronick, R. 1991. Health Insurance, 1979–1989: The Frayed Connection between Employment and Insurance. *Inquiry* 28 (winter): 318–32.

Lewin, J. 1994. "Small Business and Health Care Reform." Testimony before the Committee on Small Business. 103 Cong., 2 sess., March 16.

Lewin-VHI. 1993. *The Financial Impact of the Health Security Act.* Fairfax, VA: Lewin-VHI.

Martin, C. J. 1993. Together again: Business, Government, and the Quest for Cost Control. *Journal of Health Politics Policy and Law* 18 (summer): 359–93.

Morrisey, M. A. 1994. *Cost Shifting in Health Care: Separating Evidence from Rhetoric.* Washington, DC: AEI Press.

Morrisey, M. A., G. Jensen, and R. Morlock. 1994. Small Employers and the Health Insurance Market. *Health Affairs* 13 (winter): 149–61.

O'Neill, J. E., and D. M. O'Neill. 1994. *The Employment and Distributional Effects of Mandated Benefits.* Washington, DC: AEI Press.

Pauly, M. V. 1994. Universal Health Insurance in the Clinton Plan. *Journal of Economic Perspectives* 8 (summer): 43–53.

Reuters. 1992. The Transition: Excerpts from Clinton's Conference on the State of the Economy. *New York Times,* December 15, sec. B, p. 10.

Service Employers International Union. 1994. Hammering the Middle Class: The Impact of Taxing Health Benefits. Report prepared by Service Employers International Union, Washington, DC.

Simmons, H. 1993. Statement at National Press Club Meeting, Washington, DC, December 15.

Sinai, A. 1992. A Memo for the New President. *New York Times,* December 27, sec. 3, p. 11.

Skocpol, T. 1996. *Boomerang: Clinton's Health Security Act and the Turn against Government in U.S. Politics.* New York: W. W. Norton and Co.

USA Today. 1993. Text of Republican Response to Clinton's Health Proposal. September 23.

White, A. 1995. *Christian Science Monitor,* December 15.

Yates, R. E. 1993. Big Employer: Plan Stacks Deck against Innovation. *Chicago Tribune,* September 24, Business section, p. 1.

Zall, M. 1990. Fighting Back. *Independent Business* 1 (March/April): 34–35.

Zelman, W. 1994. The Rationale behind the Clinton Health Reform Plan. *Health Affairs* 13 (spring): 9–29.

Chapter 3

Bowen, D., and C. Wadley. 1989. Designing a Strategic Benefits Program. *Compensation and Benefits Review* 21 (September/October): 44–56.

Clymer, A. 1994. The Health Care Debate: Bipartisan Group in Senate Offers New Health Plan. *New York Times,* August 20, sec. 1, col. 6, p. 1.

Danzon, P. M. 1989. Mandated Employment-Based Health Insurance: Incidence and Efficiency Effects. Leonard Davis Institute management discussion paper no. 66. Leonard Davis Institute of Health Economics, University of Pennsylvania, Philadelphia, PA.

Feldman, R. 1993. Who Pays for Mandated Health Insurance Benefits? *Journal of Health Economics* 12, no. 3: 341–48.

Gephardt, R. 1994. "A Debate on Health Care Reform" (with Senator Phil Gramm). American Enterprise Institute, August 5.

Gruber, J. 1994. The Incidence of Mandated Maternity Benefits. *American Economic Review* 84 (June): 622–41.

Reinhardt, U. E., and A. B. Krueger. 1994. The Economics of Employer versus Individual Mandates. *Health Affairs* 13 (spring): 34–53.

Sheiner, L. 1995. Health Costs, Aging, and Wages. Report prepared for Federal Reserve Board, Washington, DC.

Stein, H. 1994. The Tangled Web of Health Care Reform. *Wall Street Journal,* August 18, sec. A, p. 2.

Summers, L. 1989. Some Simple Economics of Mandated Benefits. *American Economic Review* 79 (May): 177–83.

Uchitelle, L. 1994. The Health Care Debate: The Employer Mandate, Big Companies Use Little-Company Arguments to Resist Insuring Workers. *New York Times,* August 20, sec. 1, col. 1, p. 9.

Viscusi, W. K., and M. J. Moore. 1989. Promoting Safety through Workers' Compensation: The Efficiency and Net Wage Costs of Injury Insurance. *RAND Journal of Economics* 20 (winter): 499–515.

Chapter 4

Acs, G. 1995. Explaining Trends in Health Insurance Coverage between 1988 and 1991. *Inquiry* 32 (spring): 102–10.

Bandian, S., and L. Lewin. 1995. Overview of Insurance Market Reforms: Theory and Practice. March 22. Report prepared for Lewin-VHI, Fairfax, VA.

Brailer, D., and R. L. Van Horn. 1993. Health and the Welfare of U.S. Business. *Harvard Business Review* 71 (March/April): 125–32.

CONSAD Research Corporation. 1993. The Employment Impact of Proposed Health Care Reform on Small Business. May 6. Report prepared by CONSAD, Pittsburgh.

Cutler, D. 1994. Market Failure in Small Group Insurance. NBER working paper series no. 4879. October. NBER, New York.

Cutler, D., and J. Gruber. 1995. Does Public Insurance Crowd out Private Insurance? National Bureau of Economic Research working paper series no. 5082. April. NBER, New York.

Danzon, P. M. 1989. Mandated Employment-Based Health Insurance: Incidence and Efficiency Effects. Leonard Davis Institute management discussion paper no. 66. Leonard Davis Institute of Health Economics, University of Pennsylvania, Philadelphia, PA.

Goldstein, G. S., and M. V. Pauly. 1976. Group Health Insurance as a Local Public Good. In *The Role of Health Insurance in the Health Services Sector,* ed. R. Rosett. New York: National Bureau of Economic Research.

Gruber, J. 1994. State-Mandated Maternity Benefits and Employer-Provided Health Insurance. *Journal of Public Economics* 55 (November): 433–64.

Gruber, J., and A. B. Krueger. 1990. The Incidence of Mandated Employer-Provided Insurance: Lessons from Workers' Compensation Insurance. In *Tax Policy and the Economy,* ed. D. Bradford, 111–43. Cambridge: National Bureau of Economic Research and MIT Press.

Holahan, J., C. Winterbottom, and S. Rajan. 1995. A Shifting Picture of Health Insurance Coverage. *Health Affairs* 14 (winter): 253–64.

Klerman, J., and D. Goldman. 1994. Job Losses Due to Insurance Mandates. *Journal of the American Medical Association* 272:552–56.

KPMG Peat Marwick. 1995. Health Insurance in 1995. Report prepared by KPMG, Washington DC.

Kronick, R. 1991. Health Insurance, 1979–1989: The Frayed Connection between Employment and Insurance. *Inquiry* 28 (winter): 318–32.

Neumark, D., and W. Wascher. 1992. Employment Effects of Minimum and Subminimum Wages: Panel Data on State Minimum Wage Laws. *Industrial and Labor Relations Review* 46 (October): 55–81.

O'Neill, J. E., and D. M. O'Neill. 1994. *The Employment and Distributional Effects of Mandated Benefits.* Washington, DC: AEI Press.

Richards, B. 1995. Perils of Pioneering: Health Care Reform in State of Washington Riles Nearly Everyone. *Wall Street Journal,* April 15, sec. A, pp. 1, 10.

Shactman, D., and S. Altman. 1995. A Study of the Decline in Employment Based Health Insurance. Working paper, Council on the Economic Impact of Health Care Reform, Washington, DC. May 1.

Sheils, J., and L. Alexcih. 1996. Recent Trends in Employer Health Insurance Coverage and Benefits. Report prepared for the Lewin Group, Inc., Washington, DC. September 3.

Sheiner, L. 1995. Health Costs, Aging, and Wages. Report prepared for Federal Reserve Board, Washington, DC.

Chapter 5

Domat-Connell, J., and A. Cardinal. 1992. Beyond Total Compensation: The Total Cost Perspective. *Compensation and Benefits Review* 24 (January/February): 56–60.

Hewitt Associates. 1991. *Total Compensation Management.* Cambridge: Basil Blackwell Business.

Mercer Consulting. 1993. Total Remuneration: Where the Lines Converge. *Mercer Bulletin,* no. 213.

Milkovich, G. T., and J. M. Newman. 1993. *Compensation,* 4th ed. Homewood, IL: Irwin.

Rabin, B. R. 1995. Total Compensation: A Risk/Return Approach. *Benefits Quarterly* 11:6–17.

Chapter 6

Baumol, W. J. 1992. Private Affluence, Public Squalor. RR 92-15. April. C. V. Starr Center for Applied Economics, New York University, New York.

Brailer, D. J., and R. L. Van Horn. 1993. Health and the Welfare of U.S. Business. *Harvard Business Review* 71 (March/April): 125–32.

Browning, E. K. 1987. On the Marginal Welfare Cost of Taxation. *American Economic Review* 77 (March): 11–23.

Cromwell, J. 1993. *The Nation's Health Care Bill: Who Bears The Burden?* Chestnut Hill, MA: Center for Health Economics Research.

Ginsburg, P. 1995. The Role of Society in Making Distributive Judgments. *Health Affairs* 14 (fall): 283.

Monaco, R., and J. Phelps. 1995. Health Prices, the Federal Budget, and Economic Growth. *Health Affairs* 14 (summer): 248–60.

Pauly, M. V. 1995. When Does Curbing Health Costs Help the Economy? *Health Affairs* (summer): 68–82.

Snow, A., and R. Warren. 1996. The Marginal Welfare Cost of Public Funds: The-
    ory and Estimates. *Journal of Public Economics* 61: 289–305.

Chapter 7

Brown, L., and C. McLaughlin. 1990. Constraining Costs at the Community
    Level. *Health Affairs* 9:5–28.
Cantor J., S. Long, and M. Susan Marquis. 1995. Private Employment-Based
    Health Insurance Coverage in Ten States. *Health Affairs* (summer): 229–40.
Dentzer, S. 1996. For Mercy's Sake, Let's Cover Kids. *U.S. News and World
    Report,* October 14, 69.
Silow-Carroll, S., J. Meyer, M. Regenstein, and N. Bagby. 1995. *In Sickness and in
    Health? The Marriage between Employers and Health Care.* Washington, DC:
    Economic and Social Research Institute (ESRI).
Smith, M., D. E. Altman, R. Leitman, T. W. Moloney, and H. Taylor. 1992. Tak-
    ing the Public's Pulse on Health System Reform. *Health Affairs* 11 (summer):
    125–33.
Tanaka, S. 1996. The Public Can Make Hard Choices. *The Future of the Public
    Sector.* The Urban Institute: Washington, DC.

Chapter 8

A. Foster Higgins, Inc. 1994. National Survey of Employer-Sponsored Health
    Plans. Princeton: A. Foster Higgins.
Levit, K. R., H. C. Lazenby, and L. Sivarajan. 1996. Health Care Spending in
    1994: Slowest in Decades. *Health Affairs* 15 (summer): 130–44.

Index

Acs, G., 78, 82
A. Foster Higgins, 177
Alcoa, 27–28
Alexcih, L., 78, 79, 83
Alpha Center, 31
Altman, S., 78

Bandian, S., 90
Bank of America, 61
Barbour, H., 21, 26, 135
Baumol, W. J., 140
Becker, M., 25, 31
B. F. Goodrich, 29
Bollier, D., 33
Bowen, D., 60
Brailer, D. J., 115, 119, 147
Broder, D., 18, 23, 25, 29
Brown, L., 154
Browning, E. K., 143
Bullock, R., 26–27

Cantor, J., 158
Cardinal, A., 128
Catastrophic policy, 93
Chollet, D., 31
Chronic condition, 60, 70–71, 86,
    88–90, 158
Chrysler Corp., 117
Clinton, Hillary Rodham, 23
Clinton administration, 5, 12, 135
Clinton plan, 1, 3, 5, 11–12, 18, 21,
    25, 27, 32, 53, 58, 62, 65, 79, 102,
    104, 115, 149, 155, 157–58, 163,
    172–77
Clymer, A., 66, 68
COBRA, 108

Community Program for Affordable
    Health Care (CPAHC), 154–55
Community rating, 70, 86–94, 157
Connolly, C., 23, 24, 31, 32
CONSAD, 17, 23, 101
Consumer Price Index, 144–45
Cooper, Rep., 32
Corporate Health Care Coalition, 25
Cromwell, J., 31, 147
Cutler, D., 82

Danzon, P. M., 58, 115
Dental benefits, 124, 127
Dentzer, S., 161
Domat-Connel, J., 128

EBRI/ERF, 16, 24, 33
Economic and Social Research Insti-
    tute (ESRI), 149, 157
Educational benefits, 125
Employer mandate, 4, 7–8, 11–12,
    18–22, 25–26, 31, 37–44, 54, 62,
    75–76, 80, 102, 113, 115, 151, 155,
    157, 158, 160–63, 175–77
Employer-paid health insurance, 1–3,
    7, 9–10, 15–17, 30, 32, 41, 44, 54,
    64, 67–68, 78–80, 83, 95, 99–100,
    111, 155, 161, 173
ERISA, 7, 16, 91, 111

Fallacy of composition, 46
Families USA Foundation, 26
Federal Employees Health Benefit Pro-
    gram, 9
Feldman, R., 76
Ford Motor Company, 28–29

General Motors, 83
Gephardt, R., 66, 68
Germany, 24, 119
Gillilland, D., 23, 24
Ginsburg, P., 140
Goldman, D., 101, 102
Goldstein, G. S., 118
Goldwasser, T., 18
Gramm, Sen., 175
Gruber, J., 41–44, 60, 82, 113

Health Affairs, 1, 135
Health Insurance Association of
    America (HIAA), 174
Hewitt Association, 124, 133
Holahan, J., 79
Huston, A. S., 24

Iglehart, J. C., 28
Insurance
    individual, 41, 55, 65, 72, 78, 85,
        87–88, 105, 106, 108, 124
    large group, 9, 19, 38, 58, 60–62,
        63–64, 78–79, 83, 88, 95, 102, 103,
        111, 146, 151–52, 154, 156, 157,
        158, 160–61, 163, 172–73, 175, 176
    small group, 48, 50, 52, 55, 57–58,
        60, 63, 64, 66, 72, 79, 81, 83, 87,
        88–89, 91, 95, 112–13, 115, 119,
        154, 158, 160, 161, 163, 172, 173,
        176
International Society of Certified
    Employee Benefits Specialists
    (ISCEBS), 159

Jackson Hole Group, 177
Japan, 24, 28, 115–18
Jasenowski, Jerry, 25
Jensen, G., 17
Johnson, H., 18, 23, 25, 29

Kaiser Family Foundation, 158
Kaslow, A., 20
Kassebaum-Kennedy bill, 105, 108,
    111, 163, 177
Kehrer, Daniel, 18

Kennedy, Edward, 24
Kimble, C., 17
Klerman, J., 101, 102
Kosterlitz, J., 31
KPMG, 78, 111
Kronick, R., 22, 78, 82
Krueger, A. B., 37, 46, 113

Lazenby, H. C., 177
Levit, K. R., 177
Lewin-VHI, 6, 30, 32–33, 90
Little Rock, Arkansas, meeting, 28–30
Long, S., 158

Marquis, M. S., 158
Martin, C. J., 27
McDonnell Douglas Corp., 25, 31, 54
McLaughlin, C., 154
Medicaid, 30, 54, 67, 79, 81–82, 140,
    146, 158, 176, 177
Medicare, 30–31, 94, 140, 146, 176,
    177
Mercer Consulting, 121
Milkovich, G. T., 126, 127
Mitchell, Sen., 32
Monaco, R., 143
Moore, R. J., 76
Moral hazard, 81
Morrisey, M. A., 17, 30
Morlock, R., 17

National Association of Manufactur-
    ers, 25, 26
National Federation of Independent
    Business Owners (NFIB), 29, 172,
    173
National Leadership Coalition on
    Health Reform, 25
Neumark, D., 101
Newman, J. M., 126, 127
New York Times, 61, 64

O'Neill, D. M., 23, 101, 102, 103
O'Neill, J. E., 23, 101, 102, 103
O'Neill, Paul, 27–28
Ong, J., 29

Pauly, M. V., 21, 118, 135
Phelps, J., 143
Pizza Hut, 24, 25, 163
Producer Price Index, 144

Rabin, B. R., 133
Reagan, Ronald, 81
Rajan, S., 79
Reich, Sec., 175
Reinhardt, U. E., 31, 37, 46
Reuters, 28–29
Richards, B., 105
Risk aversion, 50, 51, 53–54, 60, 80,
    84, 89, 91, 92, 109, 133
Risk variation, 50, 54, 60, 70–71,
    86–91, 94
Robert Wood Johnson Foundation,
    154, 155–56, 158

Service Employers International
    Union, 23
Shactman, D., 78
Sheils, J., 78, 79, 83
Sheiner, L., 60, 90, 114
Silow-Carroll/Meyer study, 149, 157,
    160–62
Simmons, H., 25–26, 31
Sinai, A., 29
Sivarajan, L., 177
Skocpol, T., 27
Smith, M., 158
Snow, A., 143
Soviet Union, 136
Starbucks Corp., 33
Stein, H., 51
Summers, L., 74–76

Tanaka, S., 150
Tax treatment of health insurance,

21–22, 24, 31, 32–34, 50, 54,
    57–58, 59, 66–67, 70, 71,
    74, 80, 81, 82, 84–86, 88, 91, 92,
    94–99, 108, 118, 122–24, 142–43,
    170, 175
Tilwell, Congr. Harris, 23
Total compensation, 1, 5, 16–17, 34,
    48–49, 51, 52, 53, 60–62, 66, 67,
    69, 74–75, 89, 99, 109, 116–17,
    119, 146, 151–53, 156, 159, 163,
    170, 172–73

Uchitelle, L., 61, 64
Uninsured persons, 11, 22–24, 30–33,
    34, 50, 54, 57, 60–63, 66–69, 73,
    78–79, 80–84, 85, 89, 90, 102, 110,
    160, 173, 174
Unions, 25, 28, 63, 116, 117–18, 157
United Kingdom, 133, 140
Universal mandate, 44–45, 68,
    173–74
U.S. Chamber of Commerce,
    27, 32
USA Today, 22

Van Horn, R. L., 115, 119, 147
Viscusi, W. K., 76

Wadley, C., 60
Warren, R., 143
Wascher, W., 101
Wharton School of Business, 159
White, Alan, 29–30
Winterbottom, C., 79

Yates, R. E., 29

Zall, M., 17
Zelman, W., 21